Response to *The Insanity of God*

The Insanity of God is a book you could read in a single sitting but you won't. You can't. Time and again you will have to stop, go aside, and weep. At times you will weep for our suffering brothers and sisters around the world who experience persecution for King Jesus as normal Christianity. At other times you will weep for joy at how the gospel continues to run wide across the globe in spite of demonic opposition. And, you will also weep as the anemic and tepid "Christianity" of the American Church is exposed for the shameful counterfeit it too often is. I was literally "undone" by this book. I will not be the same for reading it. Be warned: neither will you!
—Daniel L. Akin
President, Southeastern Baptist Theological Seminary

What can I possibly say about this book? It completely and utterly wrecked me. Half the time I found myself sitting in heartbreaking silence on the verge of tears, and the other half I found myself wanting to shout and dance over some of the stories. No one will read this book and be the same person after the last page. If you want a front row seat to the raw, potent, heart transforming power of Jesus, this book is a must read.
—Jeff Bethke
Author, *Why I Hate Religion, But Love Jesus*

This is a book that every well-meaning Christian ought to read. It gives the most comprehensive overview of what life is like for the true followers of Jesus who are willing to pay the whole price for following Him. Extremely touching at times. It makes you cry and it makes

you laugh. But remember they are your brothers and mine. Therefore we have a responsibility of standing with them as part of the body of Christ worldwide.
—Brother Andrew
Founder, Open Doors International
Author, *God's Smuggler* and *Secret Believers*

The Insanity of God is a compelling, convicting and life-changing book. This true story grips you from the introduction and keeps you reading page after page. You will weep as you read about persecution around the world. You will fall under conviction as you read about the commitment of Christians in dark places who risk their own lives to share the good news of Jesus. You will be encouraged as you realize that the power of the gospel supersedes evil and the malevolent intentions of men. In the end you will come away with a renewed sense of faith in God who truly is enough, even in the face of extreme persecution.
—Dr. Mac Brunson
Pastor, First Baptist Church Jacksonville, FL

In his book, *The Insanity of God*, Nik Ripkin takes us on a journey of extreme emotional highs and lows to demonstrate that our limited understanding of events in our lives is only one piece of God's larger puzzle of fulfillment and salvation. This book puts our daily struggles into perspective and leaves us inspired and ready for the next challenge.
—Dr. Ben Carson
Benjamin S. Carson, Sr., M.D. and Dr. Evelyn Spiro, R.N. Professor of Pediatric Neurosurgery, Johns Hopkins School of Medicine
President and Cofounder, The Carson Scholars Fund
Author, *Gifted Hands*

The story is gripping; the crisis is universal.
—John Eldredge
Author, *Wild At Heart* and *Beautiful Outlaw*

We are in danger of rapidly losing what it means to feel compassion for those held in the grip of sin on this broken planet. After glancing at a few fleeting photos and hearing the usual review of "today's tragedies" on each evening's network news, we casually top off the evening with a little "weather and sports" before plodding off to an undisturbed sleep. But for Jesus, the very sight of those crushed beneath the boot of the Adversary was nothing short of gut-wrenching. He was compelled to do something about it! Now Nik Ripken takes you on a personal, real-life journey with Jesus into the dark, back-alleys of human depravity where only Christ's love can overcome. With remarkable clarity, this gifted writer transports you into a world where, through the blood-stained glass of persecution, the light of Christ shines brightly.
—Tom Elliff
Former President, International Mission Board

In *The Insanity of God* we are reminded of the power of the gospel to save using biographical sketches that most of us in the American church will struggle to comprehend. Deeply moving, intensely powerful and challenging describes the stories contained in these pages. I cannot recommend it strongly enough. This book will help you walk closely with Jesus and challenge you to take great risks for the sake of His name.
—Micah Fries
Senior Pastor, Brainerd Baptist Church, Chattanooga, TN

Nik and Ruth Ripken have long been heroes of mine as I have watched and admired them from afar, drawing personal inspiration from their passion, faith, and resilience that comes from the Resurrection Lord they serve. More than once I have been encouraged to keep going, because they kept going, overcoming challenges that would crush lesser souls. In this, I am not alone. Around the world, I have met countless young missionaries who trace their pilgrimage back to the influence of Nik and Ruth.

The Insanity of God merges the Ripkens' story with those of hundreds of other heroes of the faith who did not consider their present sufferings worth comparing to the glory that will one day be revealed in them. These stories bear telling, and hearing, and reproducing. You need to hear these stories that the Ripkins have rescued from this world's prisons, gulags, and shadows. I pray that they will do for you what they have done for me: encourage you to shake off your slumber and press on to the high calling that is ours in Christ Jesus.

—David Garrison
Author, *Church Planting Movements*

A touching, deeply stirring book about the seriousness of the Great Commission. This book rekindled my passion to do all that God is leading me to do for the nations, to expect and attempt great things. I am grateful for the grace that drips off every page of this great work.

—J.D. Greear
President, Southern Baptist Convention
Pastor, The Summit Church

If there's one thing many desire, it's going deeper and knowing the God of the Bible intimately. When one takes the trip of following Jesus to the ends of the earth, having previously counted the cost, died to self, surrendered fully to His call, they may then know the reality of 2 Timothy 3:12, "all who desire to live godly in Christ Jesus will suffer persecution." The *Insanity of God* will stretch you to new places of trusting God for the impossible in reaching the nations, at any cost.

—Johnny Hunt
Pastor, First Baptist Church, Woodstock, GA
Senior Vice President of Evangelism and Leadership,
North American Mission Board

In this life-changing book, Nik Ripken recounts his adventures as one who walked in faith, hoping against hope, obeying God's call regardless of its costs in hardships, pains, and bewilderments. To the list of the heroes of faith in Hebrews 11, we may add our contemporaries who took God's Word seriously, and at any cost! I heartily recommend this epic story as a necessary "vitamin" to help Christians live out their faith in this terribly secular age, demonstrating that we walk by faith, and not by sight.
—Bassam Michael Madany
Middle East Resources

Nik Ripken has told a great story, and in doing so he has made it clear that the question every believer must answer is whether we have the courage to bear the consequences of obediently exercising our freedom to be salt and light to all peoples, wherever they live. Perhaps Nik has put it best when he says, "Perhaps the question should not be, 'Why are others persecuted?' Perhaps the better question is, 'Why are we not?'"
—John Maxwell
New York Times Best-selling Author

This is not a book. It's a soul earthquake. You don't read it as much as you experience it, and when it's done with you, you'll never be the same. Ripken's story is one of those that shows up once in a generation, and everyone I know needs to read it. *The Insanity of God* may very well be the book of the century.
—Johnnie Moore
The KAIROS Company
Author, *Dirty God: Jesus in the Trenches*

Once I picked up *The Insanity of God* I literally could not put it down! After multiple occasions of participating in the Ripken's persecution workshops with our team at East-West Ministries, I thought I was prepared for what I was about to encounter in *The Insanity of God*. I was wrong. Nik Ripken is truly one of the best, most captivating storytellers that I have ever met. In *The Insanity of God*, these stories literally come to life, carrying the reader on a dramatic, life-changing missionary journey with Nik and Ruth—across Africa and eventually around the world. But these are not simply their stories, these are God's stories. Reading *The Insanity of God* led me to a wonderful, fresh encounter with Jesus—and with His calling upon my life to "go and make disciples of ALL nations," especially those in greatest spiritual darkness where persecution of witness for Jesus is most intense. As I read these compelling stories of resurrected faith, I laughed out loud and I wept aloud as well. I felt as though I was right there—literally witnessing each miraculous story unfold right before my eyes. These are God's stories, powerful stories, like those recorded in the book of Acts, played out in the lives of real, every day men and women all around the world. Men and women whose extraordinary faith in the resurrected Jesus enabled them to endure unspeakable persecution and yet not lose heart. Most of all, these faithful believers did not allow their tormentors to silence their witness for Jesus and for His gospel. *The Insanity of God* ushers one into a fresh encounter with Jesus and with the power of His resurrection, with the joy of being called to suffer for His Name, and with a compelling call to "Find Jesus! Find the gospel"—and then to follow Him and serve Him with resurrection faith and resurrection obedience anywhere He leads.

—Kurt Nelson
President and CEO
East-West Ministries International

If you think being a God-follower will make life safe and secure, buckle your seat belt. *The Insanity of God* will jolt you into a new reality and change your life—for the better. Discover the thrill and adventure of following Jesus like you never have before! This book

will awaken a new boldness in your spirit. Don't miss out on this amazing message!
—Drs. Les Parrott and Leslie Parrott
Authors, *Saving Your Marriage Before It Starts*

The Insanity of God tells an incredible story of faith lived out in the most difficult of circumstances. It showcases the power and glory of God no matter the context, challenge, or opposition. The Ripkens haven't just lived this story, they have been students at each step of the way, learning from those who have suffered most and sharing those lessons with all of us. As a result, you will not be the same person on the last page of this book as you were on the first. You will be struck anew with the unquenchable power of a great God to build His kingdom and bring glory to His name. May we read, may we learn, and may we go forward in the power of Him who brings light to the darkest of places!
—Thom S. Rainer
Former President, LifeWay Christian Resources

Priorities: Survive or thrive? Peace or freedom? Death or life? Where can one find that Jesus is really enough? Read *The Insanity of God* and you'll be surprised how your worldview might change. You might even pray for the persecution of the church by praying that believers in persecution will never stop loving and sharing Jesus. Insane . . .
—Steve Ridgway
CEO, Open Doors USA

A captivating spiritual diary! Join a journey of discovery how God is spreading his kingdom in the midst of adversity, suffering and even the most atrocious persecution. It shares the experiences made in gathering the wisdom of 700 followers of Christ in 72 countries who

are walking with Jesus in hard places. A challenge to radical discipleship! And a helpful source on how to cope with persecution.
—Prof. Dr. Christof Sauer
International Institute for Religious Freedom
Editor, "Suffering, Persecution, and Martyrdom"

It's true. God's thoughts are not our thoughts and His ways are not our ways (Isa. 55:8). *The Insanity of God* is an account of Nik Ripken's life-long and very personal journey of discovery into the ways of God related to persecution and suffering. You've heard that fish are not aware of the water they swim in. Nik chronicles how God has revealed to him the water we all swim in related to persecution in our sojourn in the Kingdom of God on this earth. "All who desire to live godly in Christ Jesus will be persecuted" (2 Tim. 3:12). This book explains why. Just as a pearl is formed from a simple grain of sand with layer upon layer of deposits until it becomes a large and lustrous thing of beauty, God has worked in Nik's life to reveal the beauty of His ways and thoughts which are different from our own. Inspiring. Engaging. Insightful.
—Curtis Sergeant
International Mission Board
Director of Church Planting, Saddleback Church

Jesus' call to discipleship is to come and die. Few Christians take the call literally, but it's not outside the realm of possibility given the current state of the persecuted church. *The Insanity of God* is not for "safe" Christians, or those interested in pursuing comfort over the cross. Be warned, this book is a threat to mediocre, cautious, lukewarm faith.
—Ed Stetzer
Billy Graham Distinguished Chair, Wheaton College
Author, *Subversive Kingdom*

The Insanity of God is one of those rare books you'll want to give to everyone you know. But you may feel the need to apologize to those you give it to, knowing it will shake their world! Give it to them anyway. Its message is one every believer needs to hear, and for those who are looking for evidence that God still loves this world, you'll find it here.
—Jeff Taylor
CEO, Open Doors International

The Ripkens' simple faith and willingness to follow Jesus wherever He said to "Go!" led them to wrestle with and discover some of the deepest truths of the faith. In some of the darkest places on earth, members of the persecuted church experience a fellowship with Christ and life in abundance that few of us have known. As a follower of Christ, a husband, a father, and a missionary, I was alternately encouraged and convicted by what I read. I am humbled to call the people in the pages of this book my brothers and sisters. This is a book I will read again and again and share with others.
—Ryan Williams
Executive Director, Leadership Development, Campus Ministry, CRU

THE INSANITY *of* GOD

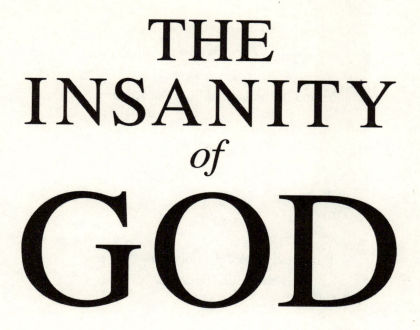

THE INSANITY *of* GOD

A True Story of Faith Resurrected

Nik Ripken
with Gregg Lewis

B&H
PUBLISHING
NASHVILLE, TENNESSEE

Printed in the United States of America

978-1-4336-7308-5

Published by B&H Publishing Group
Nashville, Tennessee

Published in association with
Yates & Yates, www.yates2.com.

Dewey Decimal Classification: 231.1
Subject Heading: GOD \ FAITH \ GOOD AND EVIL

9 10 11 12 13 14 • 23 22 21 20 19

Dedication

I would not trade our sons, our three boys, for any on the planet. They join me; Shane, Tim, and Andrew in dedicating this book to their mom; my wife, mentor, mirror of Jesus, my best friend.

For Ruth

Acknowledgments

There are too many people to thank here for their part in making the book you hold in your hands a reality. Ruth and I dreamed for years about how we could effectively share what Jesus has done in our lives and the lives of all those who have deeply touched ours. We wish we could name every person by name and thank you for the vital part you have each played. It is especially very painful not to be able to share the real names of people whose lives are highlighted throughout this book and to thank them directly for the contributions they each made in our lives and to this book. Yet to do so would, by their words, place them in more danger. Anyway, they would not want us to focus on them. They want our eyes on their Savior. Also there are our colleagues who have lived this book and are still on the frontlines of evil, living each day for Jesus as if this day were their last. You know who you are and you know we owe you a debt we can never repay.

Without the love, encouragement, and very professional help of Yates and Yates, this book would probably not be in your hands. While telling every story, seeing page by page come to life, I could always hear Sealey Yates saying, "It's all about Jesus, Nik. It's all about Jesus."

A special thanks must go to our mission family who sent us out, mentored us, and loved us through some really wonderful and really hard times. And, we want to send our love to that wonderful, invasive, loving, loud herd of college students that were God-sent when we needed them the most. You are world chargers. Aunt Ruth sends her love.

To our great friends at Yates and Yates, B&H Publishing Group, and LifeWay, we extend our deepest gratitude for allowing believers who are in persecution, through this book, to have a broader voice. Your professional help and advice is only exceeded by your joy and faith.

Be faithful, even to the point of death . . .

REVELATION 2:10

Contents

Foreword

David Platt

The completion of the Great Commission will include great suffering, but eternity will prove it is worth the price. This statement assumes three significant truths in Scripture.

First—the Great Commission will one day be complete. One day, disciples will have been made and churches will have been multiplied in every nation and among every people group on the planet. Thousands of these people groups remain unreached today, but one day (hopefully soon), they will be reached. In the words of Jesus, "This gospel of the kingdom will be proclaimed throughout the whole world as a testimony to all nations" (Matt. 24:14). According to the apostle John, one day "a great multitude that no one [can] number, from every nation, from all tribes and peoples and languages" will stand "before the throne and before the Lamb, clothed in white robes, with palm branches in their hands . . . crying out in a loud voice, 'Salvation belongs to our God who sits on the throne, and to the Lamb!'" (Rev. 7:9–10). These words from Jesus and John in Scripture are guarantees. By the power of His Spirit through the testimony of

His church, Christ will be proclaimed as Savior among all the peoples of the world.

Second—this task of proclaiming Christ to all peoples will include great suffering. Jesus assured us of this, as well. Right before his promise in Matthew 24 of the gospel proclaimed to all nations, Jesus told his disciples, "They will deliver you up to tribulation and put you to death" (Matt. 24:9). "If they persecuted me, they will also persecute you," He told them in John 15:20. It is no surprise, then, to see the suffering of God's people on every page of the story of the church in Acts and the history of the church since Acts. Suffering is one of God's ordained means for the growth of His church. He brought salvation to the world through Christ, our suffering Savior, and He now spreads salvation in the world through Christians as suffering saints. In the words of Paul, "All who desire to live a godly life in Christ Jesus will be persecuted" (2 Tim. 3:12). Clearly, there is a sense in which the danger of our lives increases in proportion to the depth of our relationship with Christ.

Third—eternity will prove that such suffering was worth the price. The book of Revelation envisions the day when sin and Satan will ultimately be finally defeated, and followers of Christ who endured suffering in this world will reign with God for all eternity. How will this defeat have come about? Through Christians who "have conquered [Satan] by the blood of the Lamb and by the word of their testimony, for they loved not their lives even unto death" (Rev. 12:11). Men and women who wisely love the gospel and glory of God more than their own lives will enter into and experience eternal life, where God Himself will wipe away every tear from their eyes and dwell with them forever.

The book that you are holding in your hands is dripping with these biblical, global realities. The Ripkens know from time in God's Word and time around the world that this earth is full of sin, sorrow, and suffering. They know that following Jesus, in so many ways, actually increases suffering instead of lessening it. But they also know that

Jesus is better than all the pleasures, possessions, and pursuits of this world put together. I hope and pray that as you read the pages ahead, you will find yourself more cognizant of the needs of the world, more confident in the Word of God, and more committed to making His Word known throughout this world, no matter what it costs you . . . because you realize that God's reward is far greater than anything this world could ever offer you.

Prologue . . . Ready or Not

First, a confession.

My real name is *not* Nik Ripken. My reason for writing under a pseudonym will become apparent soon enough. Rest assured, my story and the people who appear in it are very real. Many of these people are, to this day, in real danger. It is *their* identities that I want to protect. For this story, I have changed my name and I have changed their names too.

This is my own, true account of a long and personal journey. I share this story not as a great heroic adventure; in fact, much of the time this pilgrimage has felt to me like an endless bumbling, stumbling, wandering, feeling-my-way-in-the-dark ordeal. This is a story with a clear beginning—and an uncertain ending. Or maybe it's better to say that this story starts with one beginning—and ends with another one.

When I first encountered God's grace as a young man, I received it eagerly. My trust in God was innocent and childlike. The story that I was told about God's love and about His gift of salvation took hold of my heart. When I read in the Bible that God loved the world, I understood that I was part of that world. When I was told about God's gift of salvation, I knew that I wanted that gift. When I heard about God's desire to reach the entire world with His grace, I quickly saw that I had a personal responsibility to fulfill that mission. And when I opened the book of Acts and encountered God's desire to reach the nations, I concluded quite simply that God intended for me to play a part in that.

Early in my life, it was so matter of fact: *this is what God offers His people; this is what God intends for His people; this is what God expects of His people—and His people, obviously, will respond with obedience and trust.* I am not suggesting that I always got it right, because I did not. But, still, the way to be obedient and trusting seemed so clear. And the need to be obedient was beyond question.

I am not sure if I ever heard it said out loud, but I also picked up the idea that obedience to God's call would result in a life of safety and security. Obedience, it was implied, would lead to effective ministry and measurable results and even success. "The safest place to be," I was told more than once, "is right in the center of God's will." And that sounded both true and reassuring.

I admit, however, my surprise when, many years later, I found myself living a life that was neither safe nor secure. I was stunned when, despite what I considered to be a life of sacrificial obedience, I could point to very little in my ministry that was "effective." There were simply no results to measure. And *success* was a word that I would have never used to describe what I had done.

It might, in fact, be safe to be in the center of God's will—but we would be wise to stop and think about what it means to be safe. I felt that I had lived a life in response to the call of God. Instead of effective ministry, measurable results, and what might pass for success, I felt mostly loss and heartache and failure.

What kind of God would allow this to happen?

That question drove me to a place very close to despair. I was forced to question much of what I believed—much of what I had been taught. The spiritual struggle was intense. Despair was something that I had never known before.

I was familiar with discouragement. In fact, I had been told as a young believer that discouragement would probably surface in my life with Jesus from time to time. But this was something different—something that I had never faced before. And I discovered that I had no tools for dealing with it. Nothing in my background had equipped me to handle despair. I didn't even have a vocabulary to describe it. Like Job in the Old Testament, "I knew that my Redeemer lived"—but I couldn't figure out why He was being so painfully silent. I was desperate for answers, but my questions simply hung in the air.

Does God, in fact, promise His children safety?

Do things always work out for those who are obedient?

Does God really ask us to sacrifice—and to sacrifice everything?

What happens when our best intentions and most creative ideas are not enough?

Is God at work in the hard places? And does He expect us to join Him in those hard places?

Isn't it possible to love God and to pretty much keep living the life I already have?

What does it really mean for God to tell us that His ways are not our ways?

Would He really allow people who love Him dearly to fail? And, if so, is this a God who can use even holy failure for His purposes?

Clearly, I was in a crisis of faith. Eventually, I saw the choice that I held in my hands. Would I choose to trust this God who I could not control? Would I be willing to walk with this God whose ways are so different? Would I, once again, lean on this God who makes impossible demands and promises only His presence?

This is the story of my journey.

Please hear this well: I do not have answers to all of my questions. In fact, I am still not exactly sure where this journey might lead. But

I am certain that the questions are worth asking—and I am certain that God is a patient, though sometimes demanding, teacher.

I am not completely sure about the ending of the story. But the beginning, I believe, was a plane trip to hell . . .

Of course, I was unaware of our destination at the time. No one had written "Hell" on our official flight plan.

In fact, there was an awful lot I didn't know when I walked out onto the tarmac and climbed aboard a twin-engine Red Cross plane at Nairobi's Wilson Airport on a bright February morning in 1992. I had made my "reservations" all of ten minutes before when I had walked up to the Westerner wearing an official-looking Red Cross jumpsuit—(I assumed he was the pilot)—and asked, "Where are you going?"

He told me that he would be delivering medical supplies to Somaliland. I nodded at the small stack of boxes sitting beside the aircraft and asked, "Need some help?"

"Always glad for any assistance," he replied. As we stowed the boxes into the cargo area in the back of the six-seat cabin, I introduced myself and explained why his flights in and out of Somaliland interested me. I told him what I was hoping to do. Finally I asked, "So, could I hitch a ride with you?"

He shrugged and nodded a bit hesitantly: "I can take you in, no problem. I just can't promise when we might be able to get you out." His plans had to be tentative and flexible—dictated by weather conditions and the ongoing conflict in Somaliland. "I might be able to get back in there next week," he told me. "Or it could be two or three weeks, maybe even a month. Things get crazy sometimes. We don't make definite plans."

1

Descent into Hell

Our flight path that day took us away from the fertile green Nairobi hills described so idyllically in the novel *Out of Africa,* across the parched brown terrain of northeast Kenya, and then over the forbidding mountains and desolate desert of southern Ethiopia. We finally dropped out of the sky and descended into hell by way of a bombed-out, single-landing-strip airport on the dusty outskirts of a city called Hargeisa.

This was the regional capital of an area known in colonial days as British Somaliland. Just a few years earlier, the region had declared its independence and attempted to secede from the Somali Democratic Republic. That had prompted the embattled Somali president to order his air force to bomb the second-largest city of his own country into submission.

Within minutes of my arrival there, I was aware that I had never been, or even imagined, any place that felt as oppressed as this. Rough patches on the recently repaired runway covered only the biggest cracks and craters.

Every man I saw working or walking around the airport carried an automatic weapon. Next to a nearby storage shed I saw women and children poking wearily through piles of refuse in search of food.

Inside the shed, which was covered by a bomb-damaged roof and enclosed on only three sides, two Somali guards napped atop stacked cases of hand grenades, AK-47s, rocket grenades, land mines and assorted other ordinance and ammunition. That one cache of weaponry—probably sixty feet wide, fifteen feet deep and piled ten feet high—looked to my untrained eyes to hold enough firepower to overthrow a good-sized developing country. And perhaps it would, one day, do just that.

Once arrangements were made for a private car to "taxi" me into Hargeisa, I thanked the Red Cross crew for the lift. The pilot reminded me that it might be anywhere from a week to a month before he returned. He said that he would try to get word to the airport before he did.

I couldn't begin to comprehend the devastation that I encountered traveling from the airport into the city that day. What should have been a quick, five-kilometer jaunt turned into a long and disturbing drive through utter destruction. If I had ever needed a visual image to illustrate the term *war torn,* that picture popped up everywhere I looked. The few individuals I spotted on the streets seemed to be wandering more than walking. They were people who seemed to be going through the motions of life with little hope, uncertain purpose and no real destination. My driver told me that seventy thousand people still called this tortured city home. I also learned that, in all of Hargeisa, only seven houses still had intact roofs.

The worst of the fighting in this Somaliland region of the country had ended many months earlier. Once the bombing runs had halted, a relentless follow-up mortar and rocket-grenade assault on the city began. With that punishment inflicted, the loyal government troops had turned their attention southward again to continue their battle with the rebel clans' militias for control of Mogadishu and the rest of the country.

The southern clans' insurrection eventually succeeded and the long-time dictator fled into exile. Soon the rebel coalition fell apart and former allies turned their violence against each other to determine which factions might be strong enough to seize ultimate control and govern the country.

The worst of the warfare may have moved elsewhere. But the death and destruction wrought for years on Hargeisa remained.

As my driver carefully picked his way, detouring around rubble from collapsed buildings and dodging bomb-craters in the road, I was told that the local people were still finding as many as fifty land mines a day. Many of the explosives were discovered only when stepped on and triggered accidentally by animals or playing children.

This was Somaliland in early 1992—a land tormented by a deadly and unprecedented drought. Even worse, this horrific natural disaster had come hard on the heels of a brutal civil war as violent and inhumane as any conflict in human history. Yet, tragically, there would still be many more months and countless more deaths before this crippled country's full measure of misery would finally register on the radar screen of world awareness and shock the international community into responding.

I didn't know a soul in Somaliland the day I landed in Hargeisa. An acquaintance who had worked in the country before the civil war somehow made contact on my behalf with a friend of his—a young European man currently working with a German nurse and a Dutch woman who had run an orphanage in Hargeisa for years. Those were the only contacts I had in the entire city. Fortunately, my driver *just happened* to know where to find the westerners who ran the orphanage. They graciously invited me to make their "home" my base of operations for as long as I was in Somaliland.

The three of them lived very simply in the undamaged rooms of an empty shell of a rented house a few blocks from the orphanage that housed about thirty children whom they cared for with the help of a few Somali staff. With no electricity, no running water, and no western furniture in their home, my hosts used a small charcoal stove to prepare a supper consisting of chewy bits of goat simmered in broth and served with potatoes and boiled greens. We sat on the floor to share my first meal in Somaliland, and we remained in that same position for a long after-dinner conversation.

As they told me about their challenges at the orphanage and talked about the children that they worked with, I was moved by their passion and compassion—not just for the girls and boys in their care, but for all the desperate people of Somaliland, old or young, who had suffered so much for so long.

Naturally, my hosts wanted to know about me, especially why I had come to Hargeisa and what I hoped to accomplish. I told them about Ruth and my boys back in Nairobi and then shared some of my personal background: growing up on a farm in middle America, being the second in my family to get a college education, serving as a pastor at a couple of small churches back home, coming to Africa seven years before and working until recently in two different African countries, planting and growing churches.

I saw concern as well as interest on the faces of my listeners. I quickly let them know that I understood that I would never be able to do in Somaliland the kind of work that I had done previously in Malawi and South Africa. Strict regulations had made it extremely difficult for westerners with any kind of religious affiliation to live or even gain entry into the country. Now, in the wake of the recent civil war, it had become virtually impossible.

According to my research, the best estimates indicated that in the entire nation of Somalia (with a population of seven million people) there were only enough followers of Jesus to perhaps fill the pews of one small country church like we had back home in Kentucky. Of course, there was not a single church or enough believers concentrated in one area of Somalia to form even a small house-church congregation.

In light of that, I assured my hosts that Ruth and I were representing several different secular organizations that were interested in providing much-needed relief work in Somalia. Naturally, as believers ourselves, we hoped that our humanitarian relief efforts might demonstrate the love of God as we tried to be obedient to Jesus' teaching that His followers should seek out "the least of these." We wanted to obey His call to give water to the thirsty and food to the hungry, to clothe the naked, to provide shelter for the homeless and lost, to care for the sick, to visit those who had lost their freedom. Like the Good Samaritan in Jesus' parable, we wanted to bind up the wounds and generously provide for the needs of any one of our *neighbors* in need of help.

Even at this early stage, we were well aware that the "forms" of Christianity such as buildings, ordained clergy, and seminaries were not transferable into hostile environments such as Somalia. Words like *church*, *missionary*, and *Christian* were just a few of the words that would harm witness and hinder work within an environment such as this.

If my three dinner partners had written me off as a naïve American, they would have been right. But they listened graciously and assured me that once I began scouting around Hargeisa, I would have no trouble at all finding a multitude of *neighbors* with more needs than I could even imagine.

Later that night, lying on top of a sleeping bag spread out on a concrete floor, I mentally reviewed all that I had seen and heard and learned in just a few hours. I was already experiencing sensory overload. And I was certain that I had only started to scratch the surface.

In that moment, the prayer that I prayed was mostly complaint: *"Lord God, why me? Why here?"* Just in case God had forgotten, I pointed out that nothing in my upbringing, my education, or my professional experience had equipped me to live or work in a place like Somalia. My prayer that night was filled with demands: *"What in the world do you expect me to do here, Lord? There are no churches and hardly any Somali believers. There are no pastors, no deacons, no elders, no Sunday schools, and no Bible studies. There is nothing here that I recognize! There is nothing that I know how to do here! I am hopelessly lost. I am all alone behind enemy lines. Please, Jesus, get me out of here!"*

Forget the months of planning and preparation that had preceded this trip! If there had been a way to contact my Red Cross pilot and persuade him to fly back the next day, I was ready to climb on the plane and never return to Somaliland.

My visit to the orphanage the next day lifted my spirits, despite the fact that getting there was another harrowing adventure. It was difficult and dangerous for anyone to move around Hargeisa. What should have been an eight-block walk that took a few minutes wasn't that simple. And it certainly wasn't safe. I followed my hosts' lead as we trod carefully down deserted alleys and detoured completely around other blocks where they knew the streets had been mined and not yet cleared. By the time we reached our destination, I felt as if I had walked to the end of the world.

The orphanage, however, felt like an oasis of joy and hope in that vast desert of despair. The kids crowded into that little compound were some of the best-fed Somali children I would ever see.

The home itself showed the Arab architectural influence common to many cities in the Horn of Africa—a single-story, flat-roofed structure, its walls constructed of sunbaked bricks covered in plaster and whitewashed inside and out. Sunlight shone in through bar-covered window openings, none of which was screened or glassed. The outer walls of the house were pocked with bullet holes. At night the children slept wall-to-wall on woven mats they rolled out over cement floors. Like the rest of Hargeisa's residents, the residents of the orphanage lived without electricity—except when petrol could be found for a small generator to power a handful of lights.

Without running water, orphanage workers had to search each day for new sources of water that they could afford to purchase. The only toilets consisted of a simple hole in the floor or ground over dug-out latrine pits.

Not one time in my visit that day (nor in any other visit to the orphanage) did I see a child set foot outside the walls of the orphanage. Their entire world had been reduced to that one small compound consisting of the interior of that house and its tiny courtyard. Theirs was a world without toys. There were few books, no modern appliances, and no pieces of furniture. Yet, despite such primitive conditions, the contrast between inside and outside could not have been greater. Beyond those walls I had witnessed the hideous face of evil and its crushing impact on the country. Within the shelter of that home, however, I discovered a surprisingly secure and happy refuge where children smiled and laughed and played.

My first actual attempt at "scouting" came later that day. It was nothing more than a simple trek with the orphanage ladies on their daily walk to the city's open-air market to see what food might be available for the children's supper. I asked if I could tag along. I figured that, if my organization was going to provide the orphanage with food and other relief assistance, I needed to have some firsthand knowledge about what was currently available from local sources.

The short answer to that question was: *Not much!*

The only meat for sale was goat or camel. And there was no sure way to tell whether the meat had been intentionally slaughtered to be sold fresh at market that day, or if a local farmer had simply tried to make the best of a bad situation by carving up the carcass after one of the emaciated animals in his herd had dropped dead of thirst or disease—or maybe wandered accidentally into a minefield.

None of the meat for sale that day would come close to qualifying as "prime." But I had seen my share of animals slaughtered back home on the farm, so I wasn't too squeamish about the skinned and dressed sides and quarters of raw meat hanging from the top of the butchers' stalls. Once the ladies made their choice and pointed to what looked like a whole goat, I did have to wince and swallow hard when the butcher gave the carcass a good whack with the flat side of his machete blade to chase a cloud of flies away before sawing off one scrawny leg-of-goat.

The orphanage children would each get barely one bite of meat from that single goat leg. But there might be enough to flavor a small sack of scrawny potatoes that another vendor had for sale. Along with some onions and two under-sized, shriveled heads of cabbage, those were the *groceries* we bought—simply because that was all anybody had for sale.

Later, I was able to explore some other parts of the city. What struck me most was not what I saw—but what I did not see. For example, nowhere in the city of seventy thousand people did I find a single functioning school. Nor did I find any hospital seeking to provide care for the many people dying of disease and starvation.

Everywhere my friends took me, their tour-guide spiel sounded sadly the same: "A school used to be here, that building over there used to be a hospital, this was where the police station was, a store used to be here, a sports field used to be there."

As I listened to this repeated refrain, I asked myself, *In a place where so many of the things basic to life have to be spoken of in the past tense, is there any hope to turn things around and get to the future tense?*

2

Growing Up Country

Today, looking back on that first trip into Somaliland, I often wonder, *What in the world was I thinking?* In many ways the experience seems just as surreal to me now as it did at the time. There was nothing in my rural Kentucky background that would have hinted at a life of international travel and hair-raising danger.

I was the second oldest of seven children. My family heritage provided me little in the way of privilege. Before I left home at the age of eighteen, I had traveled outside of Kentucky one time. Our family was both poor and proud. My parents instilled in their children a strong sense of family loyalty, a solid foundation of integrity and personal responsibility, a determined self-sufficiency, and a strong work ethic.

Looking back, I don't know whether I would claim to have had a particularly *happy* or *unhappy* childhood. Mostly, I worked hard and kept busy; I didn't have much time to think about whether I was happy or not.

From my parents and my neighbors, I learned that *life is hard work* and that *happiness is being with family and friends.* Those simple lessons have served me well over the years.

No one in my family had ever been to college before my brother and I went. My dad earned his living in the construction business. My mom was a housewife, which meant that she was also a butcher, baker, candlestick maker, and much more. On weeknights and on weekends, our family farmed a nearby piece of land, and there was never an end to the work.

I spent weeks at a time living with and helping out my maternal grandparents who were themselves poor, life-long tenant farmers. They had moved from place to place—working the fields, caring for the livestock, and tending the land for various absentee property-owners.

Typically, I would be up at four o'clock most mornings to help with the daily chores, which often included milking twenty cows by hand. Breakfast would be on the table before six. After breakfast, I caught the bus at the start of its long, meandering two-hour route to school. I would be in class all day, then get back on the bus for the two-hour odyssey back through the countryside to whatever place my grandparents were farming at the time. We would eat supper and head to bed early in hopes of getting enough sleep to rise long before dawn and go through the same routine the next day. There simply wasn't time or opportunity to get into too much trouble with a schedule like that.

We got more than enough exercise working, but for fun and recreation my brothers and I played Little League baseball in the summertime. And, of course, growing up in the Bluegrass State, every kid old enough to dribble or drool followed the exploits of the University of Kentucky Wildcats and their legendary basketball coach Adolph Rupp on the radio all winter. Many people in Kentucky ascribed divine status to Coach Rupp.

Speaking of God, the good people of my community did so often. Many of them seemed to be on a first-name basis with Him. However,

I have to confess that the Lord's name probably came up a lot less frequently, and occasionally less reverently, in my household than it did in the homes of many of our neighbors.

My parents weren't much in the way of churchgoers. The best chance of catching them in a pew would be Christmas Sunday or maybe Easter—and whenever their children had a part in a play or program. To their credit, my mother and father took my siblings and me to church often—getting us up early and dressed in our best clothes to be driven and dropped off for Sunday school and worship.

I suspect that my parents' faithfulness in getting us to church each Sunday may not have been as motivated by their concern for our spiritual nourishment and training as it was by the appeal of free babysitting and the promise of two hours of weekly freedom from their own parental responsibilities. Spiritual instruction at home was limited to an annual reading of the biblical account of the Christmas story, and my dad's occasional verbalized critiques of the sins and shortcomings of the "good church people" he knew—as if he wanted to convince us, and maybe himself, that our family was as good as anyone in town, maybe better, and (without a doubt in his mind) certainly less hypocritical.

I actually liked going to church to see my school friends in Sunday school. I even enjoyed Sunday morning worship. I especially loved the choir music; it prompted my very first sense of awe. Church felt so different from any other part of my life, usually in a good way. *But that also meant that church and real life seemed to have little in common.*

I tried to listen carefully to the sermons, but I usually failed unless the preacher told a good story. My least favorite part of church took place during the closing hymn. At the end of every service, any good preacher worth his salt would give the requisite altar call. Just when a young boy's restless feet were itching to get on with other things, just when I would begin to salivate over thoughts of Sunday dinner, just when everything seemed to be winding down to a merciful and humane conclusion, the service would inevitably grind to an abrupt, albeit predictable, halt. The worst part was not ever knowing how long this pastoral appeal might last. It also felt like a dangerous time, because these appeals could sometimes feel terribly personal.

One Sunday afternoon, after worship, my older brother and I were at home getting changed for an afternoon of Sunday fun. My brother took an unusually serious tone with me to say, "Nik, I think it's time you got saved."

At first I didn't understand what he meant. He saw my puzzled look. He explained, "We were talking about this in my Sunday school class today. And I have been thinking that you're old enough to know what it means to get saved. So next week, at the end of church, when the preacher asks people to go down to the altar, you need to go, Nik. And then just tell the preacher why you're there. Okay?"

I nodded in reply, but I didn't completely understand what my brother meant. I was seven years old. The following Sunday, as the preacher gave the invitation during the closing hymn, my brother nudged me. When I glanced up at him, he motioned toward the front of the church. I wasn't at all sure I was ready for this, whatever *this* was; but I didn't want to disappoint my big brother. So I stepped out of the pew and began walking very slowly down to the front of the sanctuary.

The preacher met me at the altar and bent over to ask me why I had come forward. I said, "My brother told me to!" The pastor got a funny look on his face and told me that we would talk after he dismissed the service. I can't say I remember much about the conversation we had in his office that day—except that he started by asking me a question that I wasn't at all sure how to answer. Then he asked me another question, obviously looking for some different response that I didn't know how to give him. Confused and embarrassed, I quickly dissolved into tears. And that effectively ended our little talk about my spiritual condition.

Some years later, I learned that he had called my mother later that week to tell her what had happened. "I'm not at all sure that Nik really understands the concept of salvation," he said, "or what it means to be saved from our sins. But I'm a little afraid that if we don't go ahead and baptize him, we might set him back in his faith." For that reason, I was baptized the very next Sunday. That service was more memorable because of the coldness of the baptismal water than because of any real meaning or significance the experience held for me at the time.

The first truly significant and personal spiritual experience I ever had in church didn't occur until four years later. It was Easter Sunday. I was eleven. I remember the details vividly.

The church was already packed by the time we got there. Our regular pew was already full. In fact, the church was so full that our family had to split up. I slipped into a single spot in a pew near the front. Perhaps it was the different-from-usual-feel to the experience that made me somehow more attentive to my environment that morning.

I remember it being a sparkling day. The sun shone extra bright outside, making the stained glass windows of the sanctuary glow with a deeper, richer color than I had ever noticed before. The congregation sang with more gusto than normal. And when the choir sang their especially triumphant anthem, I could feel my inner spirit soaring with them.

And the unusual and powerful feeling I was experiencing in church that morning didn't even stop when the pastor stood and began to preach. As he recounted what should have been the familiar story of all that had happened to Jesus at the very end of His life on Earth, I found myself drawn into the story.

I absorbed the pastor's words like background narration, while actually seeing in my mind, and feeling in my heart, all that took place with Jesus and His disciples during that holy Passover week.

I sensed the love and the closeness between Jesus and His disciples at the Last Supper. I felt the sadness, disappointment, grief, and fear in the garden. I felt genuine outrage at the mistreatment of Jesus in the course of His trial and His execution. I desperately wanted to do something, or see God do something, to make it all right.

For the first time, I understood something of the price that Jesus paid for the sins of the world, and for me. I could imagine the deep despair that the disciples must have felt after He died and His body was placed in a tomb. What a dark day that Saturday must have been! When the preacher finally got to the Easter-morning part of the story—the part about the rolled-away stone, the angel, the empty tomb, and the resurrected Jesus—something deep inside of me wanted to shout right out loud: "Hooray!" I felt like breaking into song just like the crowds in Jerusalem on Palm Sunday.

As I tried to imagine what would happen if I actually did that, I quickly glanced around at the people around me. Other children were drawing or writing on their bulletins; some fidgeted, others stared blankly, deep into their private daydreams. The majority of the adults that I could see seemed to be sitting and listening intently enough—looking and acting no different from any other Sunday during any other sermon.

I felt like shouting "Hey everyone! Are you listening to this?" I had sat around some of those same folks at football games where they would yell and scream. *How in the world was it that these people managed to get so much more excited about what happened at a high school football field on Friday nights than they did about the resurrection of Jesus at church on Easter Sunday morning?*

That didn't compute in my eleven-year-old mind. I simply could not fathom how it was that nobody cared enough to be truly celebrating this incredible story about Jesus' death and resurrection that we were hearing.

Unless . . . the very thought quickly and completely squelched the spirit that I had been feeling that morning. *Unless* . . . the reason that the people sitting around me in church that Sunday were not getting excited about the Easter story was because they had heard the story so many times before. Maybe they had heard the story so many times before that, now, they saw it as . . . *just* a story.

I am sure that they believed that it was the truth—but it was truth that had very little to do with real life. Evidently, it was a story that did not demand much excitement or response. Evidently, it was just another good story, maybe even a great story, which I needed to relegate to my "once upon a time" file along with a lot of other entertaining or inspiring tales that I had heard at other times. When I walked out of that Easter Sunday service that morning, that is exactly what I did. I mentally filed the resurrection story away as "interesting."

For the next seven years of my life, I found little about the Bible, church, or the Christian faith that excited my spirit again.

3

The Face of Evil

Many years later I thought about the excitement of that Easter Sunday, and I wondered again if the story of Jesus had anything to do with real life—especially real life in the Horn of Africa. As my exploring of Hargeisa continued, I happened upon a crew from a British company hired to find, disarm, and remove land mines left in and around the city.

For a while, I watched in fascination (from a distance!) as these men operated a machine called a flail—an armor-plated bulldozer-type contraption with a cab set as far back out of blast range as possible. The machine has a long extension in front with a revolving axel that flings lengths of heavy logging chains ahead of the machine to set off unexploded mines. The machine's heavy blade can then scrape up and push the remains off the road. When the crew took a break, I walked up behind the machine to talk to the men.

Their equipment was designed primarily for clearing anti-personnel mines. Those were usually small explosive charges buried so that their tops are level with, or just barely under, the ground. They are typically packed in plastic casings that won't register on a metal detector, and set with a simple pressure plate or button that can be tripped by stepping on it and exerting merely a few pounds of weight. These mines are designed to kill or at least maim human beings; their original purpose had been to decimate, delay, and demoralize enemy forces. One problem with land mines is that long after a war ends and the combatants go home, the explosives remain hidden—armed and dangerous for years, maybe even decades. Worse yet, they are equal opportunity exploders—unable to distinguish friend from foe, enemies from innocents.

Since there were thousands (maybe tens of thousands) of land mines in and around Hargeisa, and because flail machines were incredibly expensive, this mine-removal company also hired and trained local crews to search for mines manually. That dangerous work required searchers to squat close to the ground and move very slowly and methodically along roads and across fields, inch by inch, watching and feeling for tell-tale warning signs while sometimes gingerly probing the ground ahead with a long, stiff wire. The physical and mental demands required of these manual-detection crews were especially exhausting. The margin for error is tiny and the cost of a mistake is huge. One of the workers told about a crew of Somalis who had been tediously working their way through a farmer's field for hours, finding and marking a number of mines for removal as they went. When it came time for a much needed break, the men all sat down cautiously right in their tracks, just as they had been taught to do. Then one fellow decided to stretch his cramped legs out in front of him, and tripped a mine that blew both of his feet off.

Watching that flail machine work, seeing that crew of men risk life and limb (literally) to find and remove yet another *one* of who-knows-how-many-thousand more mines, raised again the questions that I had been asking myself since my first day in Somaliland: *What kind of place is it where you worry about your child getting blown apart every time he goes out to play?*

I know that the Bible doesn't describe hell in great detail. I know that Scripture does not ever pinpoint its precise location. But I recall that many theologians contend that the worst thing to be endured in hell would be eternal separation from God. In 1992, I had only been in Somaliland for a few days. Yet I had already seen enough of evil and its effects to decide that this place felt like total separation from God. It seemed to be a complete disconnect from all that was good in the universe.

Somaliland in February of 1992 was as close to hell as I ever wanted to be.

Lying on the floor in the dark, I felt so oppressed by the manifestation of the evil I had seen that I again told Jesus: *"If I ever get out of this place, I am never coming back!"* Even the familiar old mantra "Just take it one day at a time" seemed too much to ask. For many Somalis, living *one hour at a time* was as much as they could deal with.

Even as a visitor, my senses were bombarded and so overwhelmed that it was impossible to process all that I was seeing. I simply relied on instinct and tried to keep going.

At other times, I found a way to ignore my instincts. A few days later in Hargeisa, walking alone down an alley, I noticed a little boy, about the same size as my five-year-old son Andrew, on the opposite side of the alleyway some distance ahead. He was turned away, his back toward me. He didn't see me coming. He was preoccupied with something that he was holding, so he didn't seem to *hear* me coming either.

I was almost parallel with him, maybe fifteen feet across the alley, when my mind finally registered what my eyes were seeing. Now able to look over his shoulder, I realized what he was so intently focused on. He clutched a classic, saucer-shaped, anti-personnel mine against his chest with one hand, while at the same time, with the index finger of his other hand, he poked at the button on top.

My heart may have actually stopped at that moment. I do know that every instinct and every nerve ending in my body was screaming, *RUN!* Time seemed to stand still—there is no other way to explain how so many thoughts and images flashed through my mind all at once.

I calculated that in less than five seconds, an adrenalin-fueled sprint would probably carry me out of any blast zone. But in that very same instant I realized that, if I turned and ran, I would never be able to live with myself should that little boy depress the button and blow himself to bits.

It took everything inside of me—all my energy, my determination, and my self-control—just to move. I hurried across the alley as quickly and as quietly as possible. I certainly didn't want the boy to hear me coming and panic. At the same time that I was trying to assure myself that *his little finger must not be strong enough to push the button,* in another part of my mind I was carefully plotting how I would grab the deadly explosive before surprise and fear prompted him finally to press hard enough on the button to blow us both up.

I don't think he ever heard my footsteps. Before he even turned his head, I was able to reach past his shoulder and snatch the land mine out of his hands. The moment I did that, however, I realized that the underside of the saucer which had been turned away from me was hollow. The explosive charge was missing. All the boy had been holding was the empty casing tilted toward himself with the pressure plate button on top. That's all that I had been able to see.

I have no idea what that young Somali boy thought was happening when a desperately frightened white man yanked his newfound prize away from him. I wonder, if he survived to adulthood, whether or not he even remembers the incident today.

But I can assure you that I remember it. I can still see the look of sudden surprise and utter fear (of me) in his eyes. For me, that day was unforgettable. In that experience, I glimpsed yet again the face and the handiwork of pure evil in Somaliland.

I saw evil's impact again countless times. One day my young friend, the orphanage staffer, engaged a vehicle to take us out of the city. My plan for this extended scouting trip had been to observe and document the outlying communities' greatest needs, so as to consider potential projects that my non-government organization (NGO) might begin in the countryside around Hargeisa.

It is important to know that most of Africa's potable water supply is dependent on electricity. Even most communities that depend on ancient village wells for basic survival now use submersible electric pumps powered by small portable generators to bring the water to the surface. Such basic "technology" is not only relatively inexpensive and low-maintenance, it is also a reliable and efficient means to tap meager water supplies in areas where traditional methods are unable to access deep water aquifers.

Unfortunately, such simple equipment is easy to steal or sabotage. Once we got out of the city, we discovered that every communal well had been rendered useless. The village generator had been looted, and/or the submersible pump had been pulled out and taken for use elsewhere. Perhaps thieves had been able to sell their plunder. What was even harder to understand was the pointless destruction and cruelty inflicted on those few villages that had still depended on old fashioned hand pumps—until roaming vandals, armed raiders, enemy clans, or perhaps one-side-or-the-other in the ongoing civil war had simply smashed and destroyed the pumps and then permanently sealed off the old wells by filling them with rocks or sand.

Whoever the culprits, whatever their motivation, the results in nearly every village were the same. Entire herds of goats lay dead in fields where grass no longer grew. Dried and rotting camel carcasses littered the roadsides and filled the air with the stench of death.

Many of the homes in these outlying villages were now empty and abandoned. The farm families who had lived there had either died of starvation or had fled to the city in the desperate but uncertain hope that things had to be better there.

The people of these villages really had no other choice. What once had been productive life-giving land had been rendered uninhabitable.

I had flown into Somaliland to assess the needs in and around Hargeisa. Out in the countryside I quickly concluded: There is *nothing* that these people *don't* need!

What needed to be done? *Everything!*

The more pertinent question for me was: What practical things could a relief organization do that could make a difference for these villages and for these people? Where could we start to help when everyone is destitute—where the *least of these* includes everyone?

The word *overwhelmed* doesn't begin to describe my reaction. I may have been a neophyte in the relief business, but I had talked to enough experts and lived in Africa long enough to understand that before it could address basic human needs, a relief agency must address essential needs of its own:

1. Security
2. Reliable transportation that is adequate to the task
3. A commodity or service that is needed
4. Personnel with the expertise to do the job

By the time we headed back into the city, I knew that I had to face the hard, honest truth. I did not yet have enough of any of those fundamental requirements for a functional relief effort even to begin to tackle the staggering needs that I had seen that day. On some level,

I had started to understand the depth of hopelessness that I saw in the eyes of so many Somalis.

The emotional fallout from that countryside expedition may help explain the intensity of my reaction to an incident I witnessed during a subsequent visit to the Hargeisa marketplace. At first, nothing seemed different from any of my earlier visits. The same vendors offered the same meager fare at the same few stalls. With nothing new to see in the way of merchandise, I stood off to the side and watched the people come and go.

Suddenly I heard the sound of heavy vehicles somewhere in the distance. They slowly, steadily drew closer. Eventually I saw the caravan rolling through the streets toward the market. Finally, the caravan came into view: truck after truck, fifteen in all. Each vehicle was bristling with weaponry. Armed men stood in the back of every vehicle. Each soldier was outfitted with an AK-47 over one shoulder and bandoliers full of bullets draped across his chest. Mounted on some trucks were fifty-caliber machine guns. At least one truck was equipped with anti-aircraft artillery.

What struck me more than the firepower were the emotionally void faces of those men—their imperious looks befitted battle-hardened Roman centurions who had seen the world and were now marching proudly back into Rome.

My immediate reaction was, "Thank God! The cavalry has arrived. A caravan of food and supplies has finally reached Hargeisa." The sudden swarm of people flooding into the market seemed to confirm my assessment. I backed up against a building to make room as the clamoring crowd quickly engulfed the trucks. The convoy's armed guards forced them back to make room as they began to unload their precious cargo.

I watched, sharing the excited anticipation of the throng, trying to imagine what new and wondrous things might be served for supper throughout Hargeisa on this joyful day. The multitude surged forward again as the first boxes were opened.

What I saw then so sickened me that I nearly threw up. What came out of those boxes was not packaged food, canned goods, or bottles of juice or water. I had lived in Africa long enough to recognize the contents immediately. Packed in those boxes were canvass-wrapped bundles of *khat,* a plant grown in the Kenyan and Ethiopian highlands, the leaves of which are stripped from the bundled stems and chewed for their narcotic effect. Considered a recreational drug, some say it works much like amphetamines with the intensity of the party drug Ecstasy.

I could not believe what I was seeing. In a place where tens of thousands of people had no shelter, no running water, no food, and no medicine, someone used the resources required for a heavily armed, fifteen-vehicle caravan to import an addictive drug into the country.

What horrified me even more was the reaction of the crowd—many of whom had not had enough money to buy food for their family in who-knows-how-long. But here they came now! Men carried stereo speakers and other electronic equipment on their shoulders and traded those now-useless items for small bundles of khat. I watched other men bring gold chains and jewelry that their wives had worn—items once considered a woman's life insurance. They exchanged the jewelry for a chewable drug that might enable them to forget their misery for one night. It was as if they believed that their only hope of ever escaping the hell of Somaliland was in a drug-induced forgetfulness that would last but a few short hours.

Only minutes passed before all the boxes had been emptied and the remainder of the crowd gradually drifted away. For me, the vivid and troubling memory of that experience has stuck in my mind for twenty years. For a brief time that afternoon in the Hargeisa market, as I watched those caravan guards nearly mobbed by desperate customers, I saw again the mask pulled back and the face of evil briefly exposed.

I realized then that the supply line for evil was better established, and a lot more efficient, than the supply line for good. And I was not at all sure that I could do anything to change that when, and if, I managed to get back to Nairobi.

Fortunately for me, the grapevine still worked very well in Africa—especially among the international community. Somehow, my European friends at the orphanage got word that a Red Cross plane was coming in the next day.

They didn't have to tell me twice.

As thrilled as I was to be leaving Somaliland, what I wanted more than anything was to get back home to Nairobi to see Ruth and my boys. This was before the cell-phone and satellite communication revolution had reached much of Africa. I had heard nothing from my family, and they had not heard any word about me, for over three weeks.

If I had had a parachute during our descent into Nairobi, I might have exited the plane before we landed at Wilson Airport. Since I hadn't been able to let Ruth know I was coming, I took a taxi home to surprise her.

After three weeks in the alien world of Somaliland it was surreal to be back in my world—to walk through the door of my own home, to eat a *normal* supper sitting at an actual table with my own family, to sleep in my own bed, to live my own familiar life again. I felt as if I had gone from hell to heaven in a single day.

What conflicted feelings! On the one hand, I was absolutely ecstatic to be with my family again. Yet I couldn't help feeling guilty taking a bath.

I had taken hundreds of photographs wherever and whenever that had been possible. As these pictures were developed, I shared them with Ruth and the boys. I tried to recount for Ruth the details of my trip. She would ask questions in response. Eventually I remembered and added more details and told more stories. That was how I finally processed what I had experienced, felt, and hopefully learned during my mind-blowing three weeks in Somaliland.

I still wasn't clear about what a relief organization could accomplish there. Or even where we might start. But if you had asked me for my honest assessment, I would have told you that Somaliland just might have been the neediest, most hopeless, most hellish place to be found on this earth.

I was soon to discover that I was wrong about that. Mogadishu, the capital of Somalia, was even worse. And I was heading there next.

4

But I Wanted to Be a Veterinarian

I had continued to attend church after my eleven-year-old Easter epiphany. But after my brief childhood encounter with religion, I devoted the majority of my time, energy, and interest to work and sports. Because I loved life on the farm—making things grow, caring for animals, riding horses—I began thinking and dreaming of veterinary school. I didn't care much for school, though I knew that it would probably be important for my future.

I was a little surprised the afternoon my dad showed up at my high school and pulled me out of class early in the spring of my senior year. I had barely climbed into his pickup when Dad started talking about my going off to college in the fall, and how pleased he and mom were that I had received a scholarship to the University of Kentucky to study veterinary medicine. (This was about as close to my dad saying that he was proud of me as I was probably going to get.)

He knew that, even with the scholarship, I was going to need money of my own for transportation and other educational and incidental expenses. "So," Dad went on, "I found you a job where you can earn a good bit of money before you head off to college."

While Dad was a blue-collar worker and a part-time farmer who didn't have many financial resources of his own, he was known and respected around the community as a hard worker. Even if he couldn't directly help provide for me financially, he could leverage what he did have in the way of friendships, reputation, and personal contacts to provide me with an opportunity to make my own way. I appreciated that.

"You found me a job?" I asked.

"Yeah," he explained. "I talked to some friends who work at the Kraft Foods Cheese Factory. They say that they have a job that is yours if you'll take it."

"Really?" I responded.

The big food conglomerate had a nearby cottage cheese processing plant. A lot of local people earned enough to support their families working there. Dad knew that I planned on finding some kind of summer job to earn money before college started in the fall. He also knew that I hadn't had any success yet in my job search. We both knew that a job opportunity at Kraft would be more promising than anything that I would find on my own.

"It sounds great," I told him. "Thanks."

But he didn't want me to thank him until I had heard the rest of his news. "The thing is," my dad said, "the job starts tonight. The 7:00 p.m. to 3:30 a.m. shift, Monday through Friday, forty hours per week until you leave for college."

Tonight!? I looked at Dad as my mind raced through all the possible ramifications. *I have nine more weeks of school before graduation. Varsity baseball season has already started. And then there's my part in the senior play.*

Thinking out loud I said, "Probably wouldn't leave time for any extra-curricular activities."

Dad agreed, "No, it won't." He knew what I was thinking. "They say that they need you to fill the job tonight. They can't hold the position open until your school year ends."

"I'll be honest with you, Nik," Dad added. "I don't have any doubts that you can do the work. You've always been a hard worker and a fast learner. I know that you'll do a great job for Kraft."

"But what concerns me," my father went on to say, "is your school work. Can you keep up your grades over these last nine weeks of your senior year with that kind of schedule? "

"It would be a big challenge," I had to admit. "I need to think about that." But there wasn't much time to think. At that moment, Dad was pulling into the parking lot of the Kraft factory and telling me that if I wanted the job, I needed to go in and talk to the people in the personnel office right then.

Less than an hour after my father had picked me up at school, I filled out a job application and was hired to begin working at Kraft that very night. The decision had been fast. But that didn't mean it was easy.

I dreaded having to tell my baseball coach that his starting second baseman and number two hitter was quitting the team. It wasn't much easier telling the drama teacher that I would be dropping out of the senior play. I hated letting anyone down. I hoped that my friends, classmates, and especially the other guys on the baseball team would understand. But I didn't have any serious second thoughts about what I had to give up. I knew what was the right and practical thing to do.

My new job was about two miles from home. It required hard work—which had never really bothered me. The all-night schedule, however, was brutal. Starting work after supper wasn't too bad, but by the time I would clock out every morning at 3:30 a.m., all I could do was stumble home exhausted and literally *fall* into bed.

I somehow managed to fall out of bed every morning in time to drive my beat-up pickup the three miles to school—and I wasn't absent once the rest of the school year. I am sure that all of my teachers soon noticed that I regularly dozed off in class—despite my most creative and heroic efforts to resist doing so. When one of them asked what was going on with me, I explained about the job that my dad had found for me to earn the money that I needed to start college the next fall. Evidently, word got around. My teachers were especially gracious that last semester of my senior year.

Life seemed a lot more manageable after graduation when I could sleep in every morning. The weeks rolled by, the paychecks rolled in, and I began to focus on the future. The reality of college loomed larger and larger on my personal horizon.

My job at Kraft wasn't particularly fun or exciting. It was the sort of mindless, physically demanding work that confirmed the wisdom of my decision to pursue a college education. It was the kind of job where the simple work ethic that my parents had instilled in me served me well: *Life is work. Work is hard. Work is what it is. You do what is expected of you—and you do it well.*

I was doing just that one summer night—working all by myself in a back corner of the Kraft Foods Cheese Factory, struggling to clamp lids on five-hundred-pound containers of what we called *stirred curd.* We were preparing our plant's product for shipping to yet another food manufacturing facility to be further processed and then packaged as the final form of cottage cheese sold in grocery stores.

The far recesses of that factory were so quiet that night that I nearly jumped out of my skin at the sudden sound of a voice asking: "Nik! Are you tired of running?" The words were so clear and so close that I whirled around to see who had managed to sneak up on me.

There was no one there. *Odd.* I turned my attention back to my task, thinking that my mind was playing tricks on me. Ten minutes later I heard the same voice: "Nik, are you tired of running?" I looked around again; no one was there. *What in the world is going on?*

Wary now, I kept looking around. There was not another person near when I heard the voice a third time, "Nik, are you ready to stop running and serve me?" I suspected that a co-worker was playing a trick on me. Quickly, though, I sensed in my heart that the voice that was speaking to me belonged to God.

I didn't realize that it was possible to question or even ignore the Holy Spirit. I was so surprised by what was happening that, all by myself in the back of that food factory, I made what seemed like the only possible response under those circumstances: I gave God my life. And because I had never been told anything different, I simply assumed that a person could be *saved* **and** *called to serve God* in the very same moment. That's exactly what I believed was happening to me. I answered God's voice and I put my life in His control.

On the one hand, what happened to me that night was both unsettling and unexpected. For the longest time I had wanted nothing more than to be a vet! The first real step on the road to that life dream was set to begin in less than a month. In my limited experience, "serving God" was what "preachers" did. And the prospect of being the pastor of a little country church in the hills of Kentucky was not of much interest to me.

> But now, it seemed that God wanted me to do that. What does God have in mind? Does He know what He's doing?

On the other hand, what happened that night in the factory was so real that I had to tell someone. I simply couldn't NOT talk about it. So I sat my parents down the very next day and explained how the voice of God had spoken to me. I told them that I had been saved. I explained that I had not only accepted Christ into my heart and given Him my life, but that I now planned to "serve" Him.

My folks' reaction was not so much negative, as it was neutral. Looking back now, I realize that my story must have seemed strange to them; Mom and Dad simply had no reference point in their own personal experience to process what I told them had happened, or to begin to understand the implications. From their perspective, it sounded as if I was suddenly discarding my long-time dream of becoming a veterinarian for what must have sounded like some mystical spiritual experience. I'm sure that they, too, equated "serving God" with preaching.

Disappointed that my parents couldn't understand or accept what I was explaining, I next went to talk with an older pastor who had known our family for some time. He smiled and listened with interest as I told him about "The Voice" that I had heard in the factory and the part about my accepting Christ. When I went on to explain about feeling called to serve God, the minister's response was, shockingly, more negative than that of my parents. He looked me right in the eye and said "You really don't want to become a preacher, Nik. Churches will eat you alive! That kind of work can kill a man."

I was surprised by the vehemence of his reaction, yet I had a pretty good idea what he meant. I had grown up in a small community where most everyone went to one of three churches, yet always seemed to know what was going on in the other two. I had also attended various country churches from time to time with my grandparents and visited a number of others in the area when my brother had sung in a traveling gospel quartet during high school. Based on that exposure, I guess I had such a narrow view of ministry that I had simply assumed that such things were the necessary downside of any decision to serve the Lord. I figured that I would just give in and say, "Okay God, I guess I will have to do this because you are God—but I'm not going to like it."

I had been just weeks away from heading off to college to study veterinary science and find my way in a bigger, more exciting world. I knew that I had said yes to God and that I would follow and serve the Lord. But now, I was suddenly wondering if, in doing so, I had just condemned myself to hard labor and an unexciting life of misery.

This pastor's reaction only served to underscore my questions and doubts at the very beginning of my personal walk of faith.

Fortunately, I received a much more affirming response when I shared my cheese factory conversion with a friend who was the pastor of a small church nearby. When I told him that I felt that God had called me to serve Him, he got excited enough to introduce me to another young preacher friend of his. The two of them prayed with me.

I didn't really know what to do next, but I felt certain that God had called me. I honestly didn't believe that I had any choice except to accept and obey this call. I saw no separation or distinction between accepting Christ and surrendering my whole life to Him to do what He wanted me to do. And I certainly had no clue at the time that my simple faith and obedience would lead me from a small town in Kentucky to the deserts and camels of Somalia.

I gave up my scholarship at the University of Kentucky. The only alternative I could envision was to go to a denominational college and train to become a minister. That fall, I enrolled at a small Christian college less than an hour's drive from my home. My declared majors were history and religion—two subjects in which I had little personal experience.

I felt like I had been thrown into the deep end of the swimming pool without a single swimming lesson. Just weeks after my encounter with God in the cheese factory, here I was attending a church college and telling people that I was preparing to go into the ministry. I couldn't help feeling as if everyone I met on campus had a better sense of what that meant than I did.

I decided to start reading my new Bible. When I did, I found a lot of very interesting stories, most of which I had never heard, or maybe just never listened to before. I knew that the Bible was the basis of everything Christians believed, but there seemed to be so much in it that I simply didn't understand. Even what I did read and understand, I often had no idea how to apply to my own life.

My theology wasn't any deeper than my understanding of Scripture. All I really knew was that the Bible was God's book and that if I really believed that, then I needed to do what it said.

It didn't take me long to get to the twenty-eighth chapter of Matthew. There, Jesus gives His followers their final instructions to go into all the world to share His Good News and make disciples. When I read that, I thought, *Wow! Wouldn't it be really great to do that—to get out of Kentucky, at least for a little while?* The more I looked at what that passage said, the clearer it seemed to me that Jesus gave that command to every one of His followers. It wasn't a separate call or a special call for *some* of His disciples. Rather, it was the last lesson Jesus wanted to get across to every one of His followers.

Go ye into all the world . . .

When I saw that, I considered it a clear command from God for me personally. I knew that I had to go; I knew that He wanted me to go. I knew that I had no choice. Until or unless He stopped me, I would go. I couldn't imagine how such a thing would be possible. But I took God at His word.

I felt completely out of place. Thankfully, a number of professors and fellow students befriended me. During my freshman year some senior guys invited me to travel with them to churches in neighboring states to conduct weekend youth revivals.

Looking back, I can see that they had a genuine desire to encourage and disciple me after they had learned that I felt called to preach. But I soon realized another reason that they included me on their traveling teams. Whenever I made announcements about the youth revival in a weekend or Sunday morning worship service, people showed up for our meeting that night if for no other reason than to hear "that country boy" talk again.

All in all, my first year of college was a positive, yet stretching, experience for me. I enjoyed college more than I had expected to. I moved into my sophomore year feeling comfortable on campus, yet knowing that I still had a lot to learn.

One of my most memorable experiences that second year at college was my first encounter with a real live missionary. A man by the name of Dr. Butcher visited the campus. He gave a thirty-minute devotional in chapel one evening and shared some of his own ministry experience in Thailand. He made a clear and compelling case for more young people to answer the call to serve God overseas. He certainly got my attention. After the service, I waited around until I could privately approach Dr. Butcher. I asked him, "Let me get this straight: you're telling me that I can go anywhere in the world to tell people about Jesus and that I can get paid to do that?"

He looked at me in a funny way, smiled slightly, and then nodded, "I've never been asked the question quite like that before. But, yes, that is what I'm saying."

"Where do I sign up?" I asked. I was thrilled to know that there was some way to make that "Go ye into all the world" commandment doable. I was ready to go right then.

But I had a lot more to learn before that would happen. And I had just become acquainted that fall of my sophomore year with the one person who would do more than any other person to help me learn it. She was the one person without whom I probably would never have made it to Africa at all.

5

Broken by a Smile

By the time we visited the Somali capital in 1992, Mogadishu had long been the violent epicenter of an ongoing civil war involving more than a dozen different clans, all of them in a vicious struggle for survival. The two largest rebel factions were fighting it out in the streets of the capital for dominance and control of the city and, ultimately, the country.

The conflict resulted in devastation of the country's agricultural production and distribution channels; the destruction of Somalia's already inadequate and primitive transportation system, communication and public utilities infrastructure; the end of any national, regional or local government rule or control; and a non-existent economy that lacked viable banks, businesses or industries, and no longer had a recognized and accepted national currency. It was a total societal collapse.

Virtually all Westerners and international groups, including agencies that had been working in the Horn of Africa for years, had pulled up stakes and left the country before the end of 1991.

Perhaps as many as a million displaced people joined a human flood of refugees pouring over the borders of their homeland into Kenya, Ethiopia, Djibouti, and across the gulf to Yemen. (Only the most fortunate refugees found the means to escape to Western Europe and North America.) With them came horror stories of suffering beyond belief.

After my return to Nairobi from that first trip to Somaliland, Ruth and I tried to find a way into other parts of Somalia to assess needs. We used the same basic strategy that we had used to learn about Hargeisa: we wandered around downtown Nairobi, looking for people we could identify as having a Somali heritage. Then we would follow them into coffee shops or to markets where we would strike up conversations and try to begin establishing relationships.

Over time we heard their stories, tried to encourage and help them, and eventually began also to share our desire to provide assistance to their people still suffering in Somalia. Some of these new refugee friends trusted us enough to pass on the names and stories of clan relatives they wanted us to help when we got into their homeland.

A few Somalis even referred us to western relief agency workers and a handful of western believers who had been forced out of Somalia. These believers were now working among the large Somali immigrant community resettling in Nairobi or with the hundreds of thousands of Somalis now inhabiting refugee camps scattered along the Kenya-Somali border and in the desert region of southern Ethiopia.

Our most reliable sources of information warned us that the focus of violence currently centered around Mogadishu. They said that it wouldn't be safe for us to visit the area until the civil war ended, or at least until the fighting moved elsewhere. The prospect of that happening anytime soon, without the intervention of outside forces, seemed unlikely.

Unfortunately, the suffering in Somalia had received little attention from the international community. Finally, the Secretary-General of the United Nations began calling for a cease-fire among the warring clans. The possibility of United Nations involvement offered the potential for better conditions and the promise of needed resources.

When the United Nations announced that it had brokered a temporary cease-fire, Ruth and I saw a window of opportunity to get into the country and assess the needs in Mogadishu. Some western workers who had fled the country indicated that their organizations wanted to reestablish a presence in country, but they believed that it was still too dangerous to return.

At that time, no one knew how many citizens of Mogadishu had been killed or had fled during the years of conflict. In addition, because of devastating drought, the city had been flooded with refugees from other areas. As in Hargeisa, the people in the capital had nothing and needed everything. Yet conditions seemed even more desperate in this area.

Despite the agreed-upon "cease-fire," combatants continued to battle for territory in the city. Most nights and days were punctuated by the sound of gunfire—much of it distant and easily ignored, but some of it extremely close.

One day, I asked a gunman why he was fighting. He squinted at me through cigarette smoke and said, "It's Thursday. We take Friday off to go to the mosque and pray. This is Thursday. We fight on Thursday."

Within a day or two of my arrival in Mogadishu, several Somalis whose names I had been given (and warned not to go looking for too openly) actually showed up at the gate of the United Nations compound where I was staying. They asked for me by name. I never found out how they knew I was there, but I had lived in Africa long enough to chalk it up to the amazing power of the Holy Spirit and the effectiveness of the oral grapevine.

I passed along greetings from their colleagues and I then explained how other agencies had engaged me to investigate the most serious human needs in the city. My new Somali friends proved to be an invaluable fount of knowledge and guidance in the days that followed. They not only confirmed the reports that I had heard about the enormity of the crisis facing their country—ninety percent unemployment, eighty-five percent starvation or severe malnutrition rate, more than three hundred thousand citizens starved to death over the preceding six months, as many as three thousand starvation deaths a day—they also gave me a personal tour of the city.

My Somali contacts gave me the full tour. They showed me what had once been the wealthiest neighborhoods with their security-gated and walled compounds. They also showed me the pathetic patchwork camps (the word "slums" might not suggest their measure of impermanence) where the influx of rural refugees had taken up residence. In those places, refugees huddled under makeshift traditional rounded homes of tattered cloth, in huts constructed of cardboard boxes, or anywhere else that provided the smallest semblance of privacy or shelter from the tropical sun. As in Hargeisa, I saw a lot of old places where normal, everyday things—like schools and hospitals and stores—had once been. What life remained in Mogadishu was so far from "normal" that it bordered on "insane." And the signs of that insanity were visible everywhere.

Emaciated mothers scratched at the dry earth with nothing but bony fingers and broken sticks. I couldn't imagine what they were doing—until I realized that they were gouging out of that hard, unforgiving ground, graves deep enough to gently lay a child's dead body and cover it with rocks.

A constantly shifting battle line (the "Green Line") split the city into territories occupied by the followers of the country's two most powerful warlords, the bitterest of rivals now, despite their shared genealogy as fellow members of the same clan.

Mogadishu at that time reminded me of an Old Testament world that did not know Jesus and had never been exposed to the Son of Man or His message. Baal, Goliath, and Nebuchadnezzar would have been right at home in this world. Jesus must have had this kind of world in mind when he warned his Pharisee critics in the twelfth chapter of Matthew that "every kingdom divided against itself will be ruined, and every city or household divided against itself will not stand."

Later in the same conversation, Jesus used another analogy that sounded like a prophecy about Somalia: "When an evil spirit comes out of a man, it goes through arid places seeking rest and does not find it. Then it says, 'I will return to the house I left.' When it arrives, it finds the house unoccupied, swept clean and put in order. Then it goes and takes with it seven other spirits more wicked than itself, and they go in and live there. And the final condition of that man is worse than the first. That is how it will be with this wicked generation" (Matt. 12:43–45).

To me, that seemed to describe the condition of Mogadishu perfectly.

I encountered one of the most lasting images of depravity when my Somali guides took me to see the compound that the current leaders had seized (after reportedly slaughtering the entire family that had previously lived there) to serve as military headquarters and personal residence. Inside heavily armed gates, the warlord and his minions generated their own electricity, watched satellite television, and ate like kings.

Just outside was a mob of several hundred desperate children, bellies bloated by malnutrition, gathered around the walls of the compound. The children were anxiously awaiting what was a frequent, though not daily, occurrence. When the carcass of whatever animal had been slaughtered for the leaders' supper was heaved over the wall, the starving children descended like locusts, tearing and ripping off chunks of bloody animal hide to chew on and find the little nutritional value that it provided them.

The conditions were horrifying. I was forced to reconsider both my definition of "evil" and my understanding of the fallen nature of humanity itself.

I cried out to heaven: "God, where are you? Do you know what is happening in this place?"

What kind of God would allow this to happen?

Safely back in Nairobi, I described to Ruth what I had seen. I also reported my findings to the other agencies and contacted my own supporters to let them know what I had seen. I wrote e-mails and letters, gave interviews, and published articles advocating an immediate response to the growing crisis in Somalia. Suffering people were dying by the thousands every day. Somebody needed to do something about the insanity ***now!***

No one disagreed. But until there were better, safer means of access to the country, everyone I talked to concluded that there was little they could do. They were happy, however, to have me return to Somalia as often as I could to do whatever I could do. And I did that, hoping to identify good opportunities once safer conditions came.

One of my next trips took me to the interior city of Afgoie, thirty kilometers west of the coastal capital. That third visit confirmed what I had already suspected: the entire country was in desperate shape and in need of life support. And there was one unforgettable experience that drove that conclusion home.

I had heard about a hospital that the Russians had built in Afgoie decades before. Obviously, the civil war had gotten there before me. Part of the roof was gone and some of the outer walls had been damaged during the fighting. Inside I found one middle-aged Somali doctor who told me in excellent English that she had received her medical training in Russia and had worked in Afgoie for years. She told me that she was trying to keep dozens of young patients alive—including many seriously wounded and burned children injured during the most recent fighting in the area. She was doing this in the shell of a hospital without electricity, running water, or any other professionally-trained staff.

I spent the first part of my visit at the hospital serving as her "medical assistant." This meant that I physically restrained her patients while the doctor set broken bones and sewed up wounds without any anesthetic. As she worked, I told her that I had come wanting to assess the hospital's needs and discuss how relief agencies might be able to help.

"Come with me," she said, "and I'll show you our facilities."

The half dozen "hospital beds" in the first room we entered consisted of nothing more than metal frames and springs. The appearance of one of the patients in that room horrified me. A tiny, starving child sat motionless, like an emaciated statue, atop a piece of cloth that covered a small section of the metal bedsprings. The child stared straight ahead, showing no recognition that we had entered the room. When I commented that the child looked too small and too weak even to be sitting up on her own, the doctor shocked me by saying, "This little girl is three years old; she weighs nine kilos." (Less than 20 pounds.)

My love for children trumped my horror and, without a conscious decision, I crossed the room while the doctor recited some of the things that her hospital needed. As I approached the little girl, she remained motionless, staring straight ahead, still with no evident response to my presence. It was as if raising her eyes would take more strength than she could muster. Still listening to the doctor, I reached out and absent mindedly brushed the back of my index finger up and down the child's cheek.

I recoiled in surprise the next second as a sudden, almost beatific, smile lit up that tiny face. The incongruity of this child's reaction, at that moment, in that place, so startled me that I cried silently toward heaven, *"Where in the world did that smile come from?"* Then I whirled around to look back toward the doctor who smiled sadly and simply shook her head. She thought that I was moved by the inhumane conditions of her hospital.

But I had been broken by a smile.

As we left the room to continue my tour, I promised the doctor that I would try to bring supplies on my next visit to Somalia. How could I not respond to such need?

Retracing our steps later that day, I stopped in the hallway and glanced into the first room that we had visited. When I noticed that the little girl was no longer there, I asked where she had gone. The doctor consulted a volunteer for an explanation, and then quietly, regretfully reported the response to me: "Unfortunately, that little girl died."

I was glad that I hadn't been there to see her tiny body carried out. I much preferred to remember her smile.

I would tell the story of that little girl many times in the weeks to come. The response was often the same. Organizations were convinced of the need, but they insisted on improved security before committing to work in Somalia. The refusal of faith-based organizations to get involved was especially frustrating to me. I had discovered that secular humanitarian groups, like the one I was attached to, were continuing to work both with Somali refugees and within Somalia itself. Even western construction companies and contractors were on site. After all, there was money to be made. But where was the faith community?

How is it, I wondered, that so many people are willing to die for financial or humanitarian reasons while many Christian groups insist on waiting until it is safe to obey Jesus' command to "Go" into all the world?

It soon became obvious that any faith-based agencies in Somalia would be a target and that any Somalis working for them would risk the wrath of radical elements of Islam. Knowing that, Ruth and I established our own international NGO as a way to gain entry and establish relief, health, and development projects inside Somalia. Our goal was to provide the best of care to a war-ravaged people and, in doing so, to give a "cup of cold water" in Jesus' name.

Many within the faith community applauded our hearts but questioned our wisdom. "It's too dangerous!" we were told by people who loved us. When we pointed out that Jesus commanded His followers to go into "all the world"—not only into all "*the safe places* in the world," they reluctantly agreed to let us explore the possibility. Sometimes we were warned, "If you get somebody killed doing this, their blood is going to be on your hands!"

Even so, many like-minded people flocked to our fledgling relief organization in obedience to take that *cup of cold water* wherever it might be needed. We were given seed money to equip and staff mobile health clinics and to distribute food and relief supplies.

One of the first requirements was to recruit a Somali staff—local individuals of good reputation and solid references, some of whom had worked with western agencies in the past. A couple of our first workers happened to be Somali believers; the vast majority were Muslims. At that time, there were just a few more than one hundred known believers in this country of seven million people. For Somalis, being known as a follower of Jesus opened the door to intense persecution, and often death.

We quickly realized that any Somali working with us would be suspect. According to a Somali worldview, any western organization working in Somalia was assumed to be "a Christian organization"—and any employee was suspected of being a Christian. Regardless of their religious beliefs, however, I needed a top-notch Somali staff with experience and contacts.

Following the advice of international and Somali sources, we hired staff members from each of Somalia's five or six major clans. That guaranteed that, wherever we happened to be in Somalia, we would have local contacts who could provide advice, cultural knowledge, and street smarts as we worked out details and made decisions.

While we were known as a professional relief organization, we obviously wanted to be a godly witness by operating with the highest possible moral and ethical standards.

For example, when we searched for rental property, we wanted to make certain that we were dealing with a property's rightful owner. I remember looking at one property where my Somali staff whispered a warning as soon as we walked in: "You don't want this house, Dr. Nik. This is definitely a looted compound. But don't say anything because these are really bad people. Just be nice, walk around the property, and pretend to be interested. If we leave too soon we may make them angry." Open houses being shown by hosts wielding automatic weapons adds a new dimension to real estate transactions.

We faced similar ethical questions about ownership in securing vehicles. With rampant armed hijackings, and no official system for registering or licensing cars, there was no reliable way to track a title history. It seemed that the old saying "possession is nine-tenths of the law" was the standard for ownership.

Despite the challenges that we faced in trying to launch a Christlike and ethical business venture in Mogadishu, our fledgling organization was soon operational. Early on, we flew in several nurses with enough basic medical supplies to establish mobile clinics that provided the first health care that some villages had seen in years.

Confronted by the staggering needs of the nation and sadly limited by our own meager resources, we needed more help. We also knew that there were hundreds of thousands of starving or malnourished people who could not afford to wait for the relief aid that the United Nations was promising. Given the need, we did everything that we could do, as quickly as we could.

Not long after negotiating the original ceasefire, the United Nations voted to send in a few dozen international peacekeepers to monitor the situation in Somalia. But there were never enough of them to adequately patrol even the green line in Mogadishu, let alone provide any protection or enforcement anywhere else in the country.

We were more hopeful a few weeks later when member nations of the United Nations voted to increase their commitment to Somalia. First, the United Nations announced a massive airlift of food, medical, and other relief supplies into the country. That was followed by the authorization of an international security force of several hundred military troops to accompany the supplies and provide protection for United Nations civilian personnel and any relief organizations that would partner with them to carry out the international relief mission in the country.

By the time the United Nations' major relief effort began in August of 1992, we had been in Somalia for months, networking with a dozen or more different organizations, and establishing relief and development projects of our own. Since we had established headquarters in Mogadishu and a few other places, and since our own programs were operational, United Nations' administrators recognized us as a partnering organization.

To that point, we had been working with tens of thousands of dollars in relief supplies. Suddenly, we were asked to help deliver millions of dollars' worth of international aid to the Somali people.

The rival clans agreed to grant the United Nations secure access to the Mogadishu airport and to Indian Ocean port facilities. But it became clear quickly that the agreement was a farce. Almost immediately, the relief supplies were stolen—and most of it never helped the people it was intended to help. In fact, over eighty percent of the relief goods were being stolen.

I wondered how people could be so callous. When I expressed my frustration, one of my national staff recited a Somali saying that he had heard all of his life. Sadly, it explained a lot:

> *I and Somalia against the world; I and my clan against Somalia; I and my family against my clan; I and my brother against my family; and I against my brother.*

Those were appalling words to live by, but a telling glimpse into the heart behind the face of evil—and perhaps a hint into the worldview that might actually explain the insanity.

6

God's Gift: Ruth

The most important teacher I ever had—the single greatest influence on my worldview—I first encountered at the beginning of my sophomore year in college. It was during orientation. I was trying to recruit new students to join our Christian Student Union. I was already scanning the room for prospects when an attractive freshman girl walked up. I welcomed *Ruth* (that's what her nametag said) to the college and invited her to sign up for our organization.

Ruth glanced at me for a moment, and granted me a slight smile as she very properly replied, "My father is a minister, so I am sure that I'll be active in many Christian activities on campus." With that she turned and walked away.

I was already smitten. Watching her go, I told my friends, "I'm going to marry that girl one day."

It's fair to say that I didn't know much about relationships at that time. I had been told that "opposites attract." If that old cliché was true, Ruth and I were a match made in heaven. I realized from the start that we were polar opposites; she was everything that I was not. That was probably a major factor in my falling for her.

We were both PKs. She was a preacher's kid, and I was pretty much a pagan kid.

She had grown up in a variety of places. I had spent my entire life in one little town.

She had visited dozens of states across the United States. I had left Kentucky only once before my eighteenth birthday.

Ruth seemed to fit in well in any situation. I often felt like the proverbial square peg forced into a round hole.

She struck me as a very sophisticated city girl. I was just about as country as they come.

Ruth's grasp of grammar and her mastery of the language made her voice sound elegant to me. English teachers the world over would cringe every time I opened my mouth.

She was too good to be true. I was too many things to be truly good.

She had known, loved, and followed Jesus as long as she could remember. She had read the Bible daily and regularly discussed spiritual and biblical concepts virtually all of her life. She had been involved in every activity of church every time the doors were opened. I had not had any genuine, personal faith until that first encounter with God in the back corner of the cheese factory weeks before I enrolled in college.

Ruth had personally met many missionaries. They had spoken at her church and visited in her home. I encountered my first missionary within weeks of the time I met Ruth.

Ruth went to the altar in church to accept her call to the mission field when she was still in elementary school. In sixth grade, she wrote a school paper on Africa. At that time, she knew that God wanted her to go there. I first heard of Jesus' Great Commission when I read Matthew as a college student, and I was still trying to figure out what in the world that might possibly mean for me.

To me, Ruth seemed absolutely perfect. I was not.

Total opposites? Certainly.

Made for each other? I wasn't so sure.

I was crazy about Ruth from the start, but I didn't know how to build a loving, godly relationship. It wasn't long before I realized that I loved her deeply. But that didn't mean that I knew how to treat her. I knew that she was the kind of woman that I wanted to spend the rest of my life with, but I couldn't envision the marriage that I wanted to have.

My dad, who *never* gave any of his six sons advice on affairs of the heart, said to me after he met Ruth for the first time, "If you don't keep this one, son, don't come back home."

I should have listened to him. But I didn't.

My relationship with Ruth was a rocky one, and I was to blame for that. One problem was that I had never seen a marriage that worked. I didn't have any model or example that I could emulate. Ruth and I had an on-and-off relationship for about three years. Ruth was patient and forgiving; I was confused and confusing.

As my graduation from college approached, things were far from settled. After graduation, I planned to stay on campus to work until I moved away to start seminary in the fall. Ruth had a much more exciting summer planned—she was going to spend her summer on a short-term mission trip to Zambia.

I was cutting grass on a tractor mower when I spotted her across campus the day that she was scheduled to leave for home to pack for her trip. When I waved, she saw me and walked over to tell me good-bye.

I am ashamed to admit it now, but I didn't even bother to get down from the tractor to talk to her. Knowing that she was about to begin an adventure that she had dreamed about all her life, and knowing that I would be gone to seminary when she got back, all I managed to say to her that day above the sound of the mower was, "I hope you have a nice summer."

She wished me the same, gave me a half-hearted little wave, and walked away. I think I sensed then, deep down in my heart, that I had no future with Ruth. I had fallen for her three years before, but I still didn't know how to have a healthy relationship—and now she was going halfway around the world to pursue her life dream. I had not even attempted to acknowledge or address her feelings.

And I had not attempted to acknowledge or address mine.

As I sat on the tractor and watched Ruth walk away, there was at least a part of me that recognized what I had just done. I certainly hadn't *meant* to. If you had asked me, I would have truthfully told you that it was the last thing that I would have ever *wanted* to do. Yet I did it anyway—I had broken Ruth's heart.

Maybe absence makes the heart grow smarter as well as fonder. Maybe I finally had an emotional growth spurt that summer that brought me to a deeper maturity. Maybe a summer of mindless work on campus gave me time to consider all that had happened to me in the past four years. Whatever the reason, by the end of a lonely and troubled summer, I knew that I had made a terrible mistake in the way that I had treated Ruth—and not just that last day when I didn't even say a proper good-bye. After three years of a tumultuous relational roller-coaster ride—I was suddenly terrified that the ride was over.

I desperately wanted to make things right with Ruth. But how?

I decided to start by swallowing my pride and apologizing. Soon after Ruth got back from Africa, I worked up my courage and called her. The coolness in her initial response only confirmed my fears. I pressed quickly past the greeting and small-talk about our summer experiences. I quickly launched into what felt to me like an abject apology for the unfeeling, cavalier way that I had said good-bye before her trip, for my lack of consistent commitment to our relationship, and for so much more.

Ruth didn't give any sort of audible response to what I was saying. She just let me apologize. But I did get a very clear message from what she didn't say. The conversation ended with these chilly words: "Well, thanks for calling, Nik. Good-bye." And she hung up.

I was crushed. I would do anything to get her back. *But how?*

A week later I called Ruth again and told her, "We're having a special missions emphasis week at the little church that I'm pastoring this year. And I would like for you to come and share with my congregation about your ministry in Zambia this summer—the people you met, the needs you encountered, the way you saw the Lord work, whatever you'd like to share. We will take up a love offering for the students going on next year's trip."

How could anyone called to overseas service turn down a chance to talk about her first overseas mission experience? She couldn't. Although I didn't sense any excitement in her acceptance, I gave her the date and told her that I would pick her up that Sunday morning. Ruth told me that I didn't need to pick her up, that she would be glad to drive herself. I assured her that it was "no bother" and that the church was hard to find on those unmarked country roads.

Ruth was not nearly as glad to see me as I was to see her when she climbed into my car that "Mission Sunday." She answered the questions that I asked about her Zambia trip with minimal detail. She didn't say much when I asked about her new fall classes. I did most of the talking. She listened politely. There was clearly a barrier between us that I had never sensed before.

I knew that Ruth would impress the congregation when she spoke that morning. And I thought that she did do a fine job. Still, she was quite cool after the service. On the way back to town, the tension eased a bit. By the time I let her out at her dorm, I felt that I at least had a chance. Once again, we began spending time together.

Our relationship seemed different this time around. Mostly, I was different. I felt that I was ready to make a serious commitment. Many of Ruth's friends advised Ruth not to give me another chance. Somehow, though, she believed in my commitment to her now. Later that year, when I asked Ruth if she would marry me, she said "yes."

When we went to talk with her parents, her father didn't ask me a thing. He simply turned to Ruth and asked, "What about your call to missions? What about your call to Africa?" She smiled and assured her daddy that "Nik has always wanted to serve overseas, too. We're going to be working toward that together."

That was all her father needed to hear. "If you are obedient to the Lord," he said to both of us, "you have our blessing!"

We were married the next summer in Ruth's home church. I was thrilled at the prospect of marriage. Ruth claims that she was too, but she walked down the aisle sobbing so hard that her father had to take several minutes to settle her before he could conduct the ceremony. It was a beautiful service and a wonderful evening. I still remember it as a very special time.

When we saw my mother after the ceremony, she was crying. She hugged us and said, "No matter what happens, just remember that I love you."

After Mom walked out, Ruth turned to me, obviously puzzled, to ask, "What was that all about?"

"I don't really know," I said. Then I had an intuitive flash, "But I think she's leaving Dad."

If I had said to Ruth, "We're going to Mars for our honeymoon," she would not have found that any harder to process than my casual speculation. The words that had just come out of my mouth simply made no sense to Ruth.

Her minister daddy had just married us. Ruth had never experienced the world that I grew up in. We found out later that, while the wedding guests were gathered outside the church to watch the newlyweds make their exit, my mom slipped out of the crowd and drove away—never to go home again.

My parents' marriage ended the night mine began. Looking back, I suppose what was most disturbing to my bride was the fact that I took that news in stride. It may also explain why I struggled so much to master the basics of relationships just as I did to master the basics of faith.

7

"Take My Baby!"

Two decades later, Ruth and I found ourselves confronting overwhelming need in Somalia. We distributed international aid and explored new areas in need of relief as others joined our small team. One of the core members of our growing team was a young man named J.B. He and I agreed to go on a scouting expedition into south-central Somalia. This was an area that had not seen outside visitors for many years.

One town we approached looked like an abandoned ghost-town: lifeless houses, darkened windows, dust blowing across empty streets. As soon as we appeared, however, a swarm of humanity poured out of homes and storefronts. Hundreds of emaciated villagers filled the street.

At the sound of alarmed and raised voices, I looked over my shoulder. To my horror, I saw my own hired security men cursing in Somali and swinging their rifle butts to ward off those in the surging mob who were trotting alongside and trying to reach over the sides of the truck to take our food supplies.

My initial instinct was to protest my men's violent reaction toward the very people who we had come to help. But my frustration with our guards almost instantly turned to utter dismay as I realized that many of the people surrounding us were not determined to *take* our supplies. They were, instead, attempting to *give* us the most precious things that they had.

I knew enough Somali to understand the mother frantically running beside us, crying and begging, "Take my baby! All of my other children have died. Please save this one!" She tried to thrust her infant through my open passenger window. As I sat in shock, my driver reached across and hurriedly cranked up my window to prevent any other mothers from dropping starving babies onto my lap.

Our driver accelerated through the crowd. Somehow, we avoided running over any townspeople. Only when we were several miles out of town did we stop and debrief what had happened. On the one hand, it was clear that we might have been killed for the food and fuel that we had. On the other hand, I was overwhelmed with the desperation of those mothers. I wondered what I would have done if it was my family that was starving. Would I consider giving away my son if that was the only possible way that he would live? The question haunted me.

Our team was better prepared when we entered the next village. From then on, we entered inhabited towns only after sundown. Under the cover of darkness, we would find an abandoned building where we could set up camp out of sight. Early the next morning, we would leave the drivers and some of the guards with our hidden vehicles and a few of us would hike to the middle of town, to a busy gathering place. There, without our food or vehicles serving as a distraction or temptation, we could carry on conversations with people regarding the area's recent history and inquire about its most serious needs. Once we gathered the information we needed, we could usually hike back to the vehicles without attracting more than a small following of young children who would watch us speed out of town before the rest of the community ever saw our vehicles and supplies.

As we traveled further, we encountered only more heartache. Some villages were completely empty. Evidently, entire populations had simply abandoned their homes and fled for their lives. J.B. and I found another village by following a trail of decomposed bodies, many just skeletons, lying alongside the road. I think we gained a measure of appreciation and loyalty from our Muslim staff for stopping and showing respect for the dead by digging shallow graves and providing a very simple, but religiously essential, *proper* burial for each of the first few scattered bodies we encountered. But the closer to the village we got, the more bodies there were. We simply didn't have the time or the energy to bury them all.

I vividly remember J.B. kneeling in the sandy soil, scraping out a small depression with a bayonet, wrapping what was left of a bony body in rags, gently laying the shell of a starved Somali in that "hole," piling sand and rocks on top, and then removing his cap to say a prayer over the man's body. This is a scene that I still can see today: our Muslim guards watching a white man from America respectfully burying and praying over their dead. It is a powerful image. No doubt, it was also a transcending witness.

When we found our way to an eerily silent and empty cluster of huts, we began to understand what had happened there. The bodies that we had been finding and burying along the road evidently belonged to the men of this village on the verge of starvation—husbands, fathers, and brothers—who felt that they were still strong enough, or maybe just desperate enough, to set out in search of help for their dying families and neighbors. Most of them hadn't made it very far.

The loved ones that they had left behind fared no better and probably didn't live much longer. The lush green around the village gave it the deceiving feel of a tropical paradise. Birds were singing and flowers bloomed. The silent, grass-roofed huts of typical African stick-and-wattle construction told a different story however. The rough structures showed the wear of several seasons past—clear evidence of their abandonment many months, if not years, earlier.

The scenes inside of the huts were even more haunting. What used to be family homes were now unsealed tombs.

In one hut, we discovered the bodies of two girls about the age of my sons. One of the children lay in a bed, her hand holding a brush still entangled in her hair. It was as if she had died wanting to look her best. Her little sister sat slumped on the dirt floor beside the withered remains of an old granny who was still holding an old spoon that she had been using to stir what looked like green grass in a soup pot.

That sad setting looked almost posed—as if part of some surrealistic tableau of death—with the subjects engaged in the most basic daily chores right where they had lived their lives and where they evidently had waited together for death.

Taking in the scene, there seemed to be nothing to say. Walking back toward our vehicles, one of the Somali staffers sighed deeply and soberly offered a poignant observation. "You know, Dr. Nik," he said, "they used to call Somalia a *third world country.* But now we are a *pre-world country.*" The emotional anguish that I heard in his voice was heart-wrenching.

Our expedition continued from village to village—many completely abandoned or inhabited only by the dead. Most of the people we found alive were just barely alive. It was clear from the emptiness in their eyes that they had lost all hope.

One village was full of grieving parents whose children had all gotten sick and died. We had nothing to offer them to ease their sadness and pain. Then a few days later, we found another village where the adults had all died of starvation after giving the very last of their food to keep their children alive. We transported the orphans from the second village back to the first village and prayed that there might be some solace in the instantly reconstituted families recreated there.

Two weeks into our trip, we were still hoping to reach more villages. However, the locals warned us that the roads ahead had been lined with land mines to limit the movement of opposing clans. The only safe way to go any further south or west, we were told, would be to stay off the roads and drive up the riverbeds. Since this was the "rainy" season, that too was a dangerous proposition.

At that point, we gave up our hope of completing a more extensive survey of southern Somalia. We left most of our supplies at a leper colony and departed for the coastal city of Kismayo. We knew of a sister relief agency there that could help us make our way back to Mogadishu. From there, we returned to Nairobi where we shared our heart-rending findings with representatives of the international disaster and relief community.

When I traced out our route on a map to show where we had traveled, which villages had been abandoned, where we had found people alive, and where the desperate survivors were closest to starvation, the international coalition seemed grateful for the information. They told us that our exploration party represented the first outsiders who had been in that part of Somalia since the civil war had begun in 1988—four years earlier.

What was most discouraging about that meeting was the immediate conclusion that, because of the dangerous conditions and the distance from Mogadishu, there was no way to establish distribution sites for any international response in the area that we had surveyed. Those at the meeting did, however, agree to provide some resources through air-drops where planes would fly low and slow over inhabited areas and literally drop bags of food and basic medical supplies into empty fields near the most desperate communities.

I was frustrated that we couldn't do more, but I was encouraged knowing that our efforts would at least do some good. And that encouragement lasted . . . until I heard about one of the first air-drop missions.

Evidently, well-intentioned relief workers made the mistake of informing the people in one village of the day and time of the drop. Having seen how the people swarmed to surround our trucks, I could imagine the scene on the ground as the roar of the plane's engines approached. What I could not imagine was the tragedy that occurred next. The townspeople poured onto the field and, in their excitement, attempted to catch the huge bags of wheat, rice and corn that came tumbling out of the back of the plane passing a hundred feet overhead. Scores were injured and some were killed trying to catch the relief supplies being air-dropped to save their lives.

With despair, I once again cried out: *How can anybody even help to make things better in a place like Somalia? One single failure of forethought can turn a good attempt into a tragedy! What are we doing here?*

Sometimes the problem is not the simple naïveté of well-meaning people. Sometimes the problem is the evil that would twist the best intentions into indescribable tragedy.

One morning our team delivered a truckload of food and basic health-care supplies to a small, shabby, war-ravaged village. We saw the anticipation on the faces of the starving children as we measured out each family's allotment of food and presented it to the mothers. We saw hope resurrected in grateful eyes of parents who finally had reason to believe that they just might be able to save their children. We returned home pleased with what we had done, knowing that we made a difference.

Sometime later, we learned the rest of the story. Several days after we had been there, a neighboring clan attacked and overran the poor village that we had fed. After cursing and vilifying the poor villagers for having the audacity to accept our relief aid before those who "deserved it more" had received their share, the invaders stole what was left. Before leaving, the attackers abused the women and girls of the village and then tortured the helpless and humiliated men.

I felt physically sick when I heard what had happened. But I felt far worse when I learned that the villagers who we had tried to help were warning people in other nearby villages: "You better not take any food from those people. They will get you killed!"

My anger raged at an evil that could twist our best intentions into a wicked weapon and then blame us for the resulting pain. I realized that it is a dangerous enemy who can inflict deep wounds to the hearts and bodies of both those giving and receiving aid in a place like Somalia.

I dealt with shock every time I entered or left Somalia. It was like traveling to another planet, except that the trip took only a few hours.

Going into Somalia was like stepping into the world of the Old Testament.

In Somalia, I would wake up in an insane and hostile place, a hell in the grip of evil, a world without enough food to make it habitable, a world where children could not go to school and where few of them lived until puberty, a world where parents did not expect to watch their children to grow to adulthood.

And, then, perhaps that very evening in Nairobi, I would go to bed in a different, saner world (a world that seemed more like heaven) where my wife and three sons celebrated my return at a family meal with some special dessert. This different, sane world was a place where my boys attended school, where I would referee their basketball games, where we had doctors and hospitals, where we had lights and electricity and running water and grocery stores and gas stations and so much more. I simply could not reconcile the fact that I was living in two different worlds that were located not only on the same planet, but on the same continent, in neighboring countries.

I am not certain that it was a healthy way to handle the disconnect, but I eventually learned how to flip a mental switch the moment my plane lifted off in Somalia. *"I'm headed home to Ruth and the boys!"* I would tell myself. Then I would slowly let down my defenses and relax. In the same way, I would flip the mental switch whenever I took off in the other direction. *"I'm returning to that other world again!"* I would tell myself. My senses would instinctively go into hyper-alert status in order to focus once more on the challenges of working, living, and staying alive in Somalia.

That transition wasn't always quite so instantaneous. The reconciliation of my two worlds was not quite complete. I came to realize this whenever I found myself having two almost opposite emotional responses to the most common kinds of family interactions. For example, if I overheard my boys arguing, I would feel indignation begin to swell inside, and I would want to lecture them about how grateful they should be to live in Kenya instead of Somalia where most of the children their age had died or were on the verge of death.

At other times, and sometimes just seconds later, I would look at my sons and I would suddenly feel so blessed and overwhelmed by emotion that I would begin to weep. I would want to snatch them up in a bear hug and smother them with kisses.

By this time I had made dozens of trips into and out of Somalia—staying in-country from a few days to several weeks at a time. We tried not to worry the boys with details about what we were doing, but they were certainly aware of the situation in Somalia.

After my survey trip to southern Somalia, however, having been reminded of how dangerous our work was, I felt the need to hold a serious family conference to share something close to my heart. Ruth and I gathered the boys: Shane was thirteen, Timothy was eleven, and Andrew was six.

I looked at my sons and I said,

> "Boys, when we lived back in America, even before you were born, your mama and I had to answer a very important question: *Were we willing to live our lives for Jesus?* You know that your mama made that decision as a little girl. And you've heard me tell the story of how I was eighteen before I decided that I would follow Jesus and live my life for him. Then before your mama and I got married, we made certain that we agreed and we decided that we were willing to live for Jesus together—as a couple and as a family."
>
> "Later, when we were thinking about being overseas workers, we had to answer another important question: *Were we willing to GO with Jesus and live our lives for Him in another part of the world?* We came to live in Africa after we said another 'yes' to that question."
>
> "Now, we've come to live in Kenya so we can take food and medicine to help feed and save the lives of many thousands of people—children, parents, entire families—who live in Somalia. The reason we do this is to show God's love to the Somali people who have never had a chance to know about Jesus and His love for them. But because these Somalis live in a country that is such a hard, dangerous, and bad place right now, your mama and I have to answer another very difficult question. We have always said that we were willing to *live* for Jesus. Then we decided that we would *go* with Jesus. We've said yes to both of those questions."
>
> "But now, we have to ask ourselves, *Are we willing to DIE for Jesus?*"

We didn't want to frighten our sons. We made certain that they knew that we did not expect to die. They knew that we certainly didn't want to die. We assured them that we would take every precaution that we could to protect ourselves. But after experiencing the conditions in Somalia, and understanding the stakes, we wanted them to understand the seriousness of the situation. We wanted them to know just how important Ruth and I believed it was to do what we felt Jesus had called our family to do. We were not really wanting our young sons to be willing for their dad to die; rather, we wanted them to let Jesus reign. We wanted them to trust Jesus with every detail of our lives.

As determined as we were to be obedient, it's a good thing that we didn't know then what that commitment would mean in the months and years ahead. If I had known what was coming, I am not at all sure that I would have had enough faith at that point to make the choice to stay the course.

8

Mosquitoes Win

My time in the Horn of Africa convinced me quickly that none of my educational or professional training had equipped me to face our Somali experience. I wrote a letter to the person who was most responsible for preparing me for cross-cultural living:

Dear Dad,

Since we've been in Africa, I have found that little in my formal education or professional experience prepared me to love, live, and work with Africans. But growing up in our family, the things that you and mom instilled in me—the need to take personal responsibility, the importance of treating people right, a strong work ethic, the value of working with my hands, rubbing shoulders with ordinary, everyday people—those are lessons and life skills that I use here every day. Even understanding the cycle of life, from the planting of seeds and the birth of animals, the growing of crops and the care of livestock, to the harvesting and butchering of the food we consumed—those experiences growing up help me to better understand and interact with people who cultivate fields or herd camels and goats in this part of the world.

I took for granted so many of the everyday things that I did and learned growing up. But it's now very clear to me that God intended me to be your son in order to prepare me to live among the people of the world. What I learned working alongside you on the farm and doing construction, I am now using overseas. You trained me in ways that few people are trained and you gave me what college and seminary never could have given me. I just want you to know how much I value and appreciate our family heritage. Thank you, Dad.

Love, Nik

Ruth and I had originally planned to go overseas as soon as I finished my educational training. But when my mother and father went through their divorce, my two youngest brothers and my little sister were still living at home and had to take the brunt of the acrimonious fallout. It seemed best for us to be living nearby for a while in order to provide encouragement and emotional support.

We stayed close to home after graduate school and I became the pastor of a small-town church. There, Ruth gave birth to our first son, Shane. We then moved to another church in another small Kentucky town. There, Timothy, our second son, was born.

Even though I found satisfaction as a pastor, I never really relished my role. I felt that I had the skills to be a pastor, but I never felt that continuing to pastor Kentucky churches was what God wanted me to do with my life.

Sometime in the early 1980's, we hosted an overseas speaker at our church. When he gave the altar call after his message, Ruth and I, who were in different parts of the sanctuary at the time and didn't consult with each other ahead of time, both responded by coming forward to pray and to renew our personal commitment to serving the Lord overseas. We had each felt God speaking to us about the same thing at the very same time. We made an immediate decision to begin the application process for overseas service.

I don't know how much paperwork the apostle Paul had to provide before his first overseas journey. But in the nearly two thousand years since Paul began his ministry, it seems that most denominations and ministries have developed what they consider to be a biblically-based bureaucracy. Our application process plodded along for months before we succeeded in jumping through all the hoops that finally brought Ruth and me to our final face-to-face interview with an administrative committee. This group was responsible for endorsing and approving all overseas appointments; finally, we had an opportunity to talk with them.

The committee members were clearly impressed with Ruth from the start. She told her story of being called to serve God overseas as a third-grader, how her sixth-grade writing project had helped confirm a specific calling to Africa, and how her summer experience in Zambia during college had given her a realistic picture of third-world living and erased any doubts that she might have had about her career plans.

When they asked me the same question about when I had received my call, I looked around the meeting room and simply said, "I read Matthew 28."

They thought that maybe I had misunderstood the question. They patiently explained that a special calling was required before someone could go out into the world and do this kind of work. I was not trying to be clever or disrespectful, but I responded, "No, *you* don't understand. I read Matthew 28 where Jesus told his followers, 'GO!' So I'm here trying to go."

That prompted a thirty-minute explanation about the distinction between the call to salvation and the call to ministry. What was required, I was told, was then a call to take the gospel out into the world, and perhaps even a fourth call to a specific place in the world. Then they asked me what I thought about what they had said.

I was young and naïve enough to think that when they asked me that, they really wanted my opinion. So I gave them my opinion. "Well, it appears to me," I told them, "that you all have created a 'call' to missions that allows people to be disobedient to what Jesus has already commanded all of us to do."

That wasn't the best thing to say. When no one seemed to want to respond to my statement, I looked over at my wife, and I saw that she was quietly crying. I suddenly thought, *"Oh no, I may have just cheated Ruth out of ever getting to fulfill her calling to Africa—because I didn't know the denominational code words."*

Somehow the committee voted to approve our appointment anyway. I was thrilled about that, but I simply couldn't understand the distinction that they were making between these different calls.

And, honestly, I still don't understand that.

When I share with churches today, I often suggest that people read Matthew 28. When I read that chapter, I notice that Jesus never says *if* or *whether* you go; He simply talks about *where* you go! God may have to give instructions about the location—the *where.* But there is nothing to negotiate about the command to go—God has already made our primary task perfectly clear. When I tried to explain that to the appointment committee in 1983, I just about ended our appointment process on the spot.

We received our official appointment to Malawi on August 11, 1983. We then had another few months of specialized training and preparation before we were ready to go.

We left for Malawi on New Year's Day, 1984. We arrived at the airport for our departure with a mountain of luggage. We had already crated and shipped everything that we would need to set up housekeeping for the next four years. But we had to carry with us all the clothes, supplies, and personal items that we would need until that shipment would arrive a year later.

The gate agent eyed our huge pile of stuff. "Where in the world are you going?" he wanted to know. We told him that we were going to Malawi for four years, and we explained what we would be doing. Motioning toward five-year-old Shane and three-year-old Tim, he inquired: "And those boys are going with you?"

We told him, "They certainly are!"

He looked over our shoulders to see all of Ruth's family, and all my family, gathering behind us to say goodbye. His eyes filled with tears. He began loading our luggage onto the conveyor belt. He asked our boys if they would like to take a special ride, and then he hoisted Shane and Tim up onto the last of our moving luggage. He then walked alongside them as the conveyor belt turned and went out of sight. He actually let our sons ride the baggage conveyor all the way to the backside of the Louisville International Airport terminal (this was a long time before 9/11!) so that they could see for themselves where all of their belongings would be loaded onto our plane. A few minutes later he brought the boys back to check-in with us—guaranteeing that they would never forget their first plane trip.

The goodbyes were bittersweet that day. Ruth's family was thrilled for us, of course. I think a lot of my family members were still trying to understand why we felt that we needed to do what we were doing.

I was every bit as excited and uncertain about what to expect as my pre-school sons were. I had never been overseas, had never before had a passport, and didn't know anything about international travel or jet lag.

Arriving in Malawi, we were met by about thirty cheering people —Malawi church leaders and American workers—holding banners that read: "Welcome Ripkens." It felt like a homecoming even before we knew that Africa would come to feel very much like home to us over the next twenty-seven years.

After a few weeks of studying the Chichewa language, our language coach took us around the country. We got to choose where we would live and work. Although our decision required that we begin learning a second tribal language, we chose to live among the Tumbuku people in the mountains near the city of Mzuzu, the regional capital of northern Malawi. There we helped start churches and worked with nearby Tumbuku churches. We also planted and/or oversaw many Chichewa churches.

We very quickly fell in love with the people of Malawi. They welcomed us warmly and were incredibly open to learning about Jesus. They were also among the most loving, generous, thoughtful, and hospitable people that we have met anywhere in the world. If I had to stay overnight in the bush, villagers would sometimes carry the pieces of a bed-frame and a mattress for miles over rugged trails so that I could be comfortable while I slept.

We could have happily spent the rest of our lives working among the people of Malawi. Our entire family loved the land and its people. Unfortunately, we did not have that choice.

During our second year in Africa, different members of our family began to get sick. Ruth began having severe headaches, Shane complained of a bad belly, and Tim came down with a sore throat. These ailments recurred over and over again. Finally, it was determined that we were dealing with malaria. In fact, every one of us was diagnosed with malaria.

When normal treatments failed, it became clear—much to our disappointment and sadness—that we would not be able to remain in Malawi. One morning, I woke up with terrible chills and I asked Ruth to lie back down in bed to help get me warm. As soon as she got under the sheets, she exclaimed, "Honey, your skin is practically burning me." She got back up and hurried to the hospital and brought back our doctor friend who had first diagnosed our malaria.

I thought that the doctor was joking with me when he asked, "Do you want to see Jesus, Nik?" I figured that some of my friends had put him up to this. I thought immediately, *"I know the answer to this question!"*

I told him, "Yes, of course I want to see Jesus."

He looked at me and said, "If you don't get out of this country soon, my friend, you may see him in a very short time."

9

Why Didn't I Just Keep My Mouth Shut?

We had been in Malawi less than two years. We were obviously all susceptible to malaria and getting sicker week by week. After prayer and discussion, our leadership determined, with broken hearts, that we couldn't possibly stay in Malawi. They gave us a choice. We could return to America, or we could work in South Africa where there was no danger from malaria. Given our sense of call, it was an easy choice.

When we left Malawi, our leader closed the sad occasion by reminding us, "Serving God is not a matter of location, but a matter of obedience."

Many of our family members and friends begged us to come back to the States to get further treatment. But we knew that doctors in Africa had more expertise in dealing with tropical diseases. We decided to continue our work in a different country. We wanted to be obedient to our sense of call—wherever it led.

Our move from Malawi to South Africa was far from simple. It felt like we were moving to another world.

In Malawi, it seemed that new churches were being started everywhere. Malawi felt like a modern version of the book of Acts. The Spirit of God was moving—and we had been a part of that. The spiritual hunger of the people there was overwhelming.

South Africa was a very different place. Europeans had brought the Good News of Jesus to South Africa over two hundred and fifty years earlier. Now, it seemed that there was some kind of church building wherever you went in that country. Christian religion had become so established (although admittedly not well-applied sometimes) in the culture that there was not much interest in planting new churches.

The warm welcome and instant sense of belonging that we had felt in Malawi reflected the heart and spirit of its people who were some of the kindest, most generous, accepting, and loving human beings on the planet. We arrived in South Africa at the height of apartheid, when there was an underlying and often unspoken (but always present and palpable) sense of tension, wariness, fear and anger in people and throughout the country itself. Hostility spawned and fueled by racism was like a cancerous tumor steadily eating away at the heart and soul of the nation.

I thought that I understood something of the psychology of racial prejudice and bigotry, but the racism that we found in South Africa was racism on steroids, racism multiplied to the nth degree.

We worked mostly with the Xhosa people. That meant that we would study our third African language in three years. Since most of the Xhosa were required to reside in the black homeland of Transkei, that's where we chose to live.

After we had been there for a while, I had a conversation with an Afrikaner government official. I told him where we lived. He acted a bit surprised to learn that my family had chosen to live among the black people we worked with.

Out of curiosity, and with perhaps a touch of contentiousness, I asked, "Since I am obviously permitted to live with my family in a black homeland where we minister, would one of the black pastors in the area be free to live near me in the Republic of South Africa outside of Transkei if he so chose?"

I don't know if the man had ever been asked that question before. He hesitated just a bit before he forced a smile and rather coolly assured me that I was free to live wherever I wished with my family. That was a choice I had. But it was also a choice that the black pastor did not have.

Of course, receiving that "clarification" didn't clear up all the misunderstandings related to the spoken and unspoken rules that evidently applied in apartheid. When my boys rode their bikes in Transkei, black children would sometimes throw rocks at them thinking that they were white South Africans. I would frequently get stopped and questioned by black homeland police officers who were automatically suspicious of any white man driving in that area.

There were also occasions, outside of Transkei, when white South African policeman would stop me and take me to the police station just to ask how I could let my family live with "people like that." Explaining that I loved "people like that" because every human being is in need of God's love and grace didn't seem to satisfy my interrogators.

We enjoyed a rewarding ministry, made many dear friends in both the black and white communities, celebrated the birth of another son we named Andrew, and lived in South Africa almost six years.

At that point, Ruth and I began reading the book of Acts together again. As we studied and talked about those earliest followers of Christ, we came to understand that Jesus' Great Commission in Matthew 28 meant that we needed to follow the examples of the apostles in the book of Acts. We felt strongly that we needed to go where the gospel had not yet gone, where people had little or no access to Christ. While there was certainly important work yet to be done in South Africa, neither one of us felt called to continue working in a country where Jesus had already been proclaimed for centuries.

We contacted our leadership in early May of 1991 to tell them that we were feeling led to go where there was no church, someplace where the gospel had yet to go. They listened respectfully and informed us that there was talk about exploring the possibility of new work in Sudan or Somalia. Ruth and I began researching and praying about both possibilities.

Later that May, I talked more about our thinking with one of our leaders at a conference in Kenya. He arranged for me to visit a United Nations refugee camp on the coast of Kenya. Thousands of Somalis who had fled their homeland were being detained there.

I was informed that no one in our organization was working with Muslims at that time—so there were no colleagues to give me any helpful advice. The only word I was given was this one from a veteran missionary in Kenya: "Be careful, Nik, those Somalis are 99.9 percent Muslim and they eat little Christians like you for lunch!"

I flew to the Kenyan coast and took a taxi north out of Mombasa until I reached the first refugee camp. I handed over papers granting me permission to enter "on behalf of a humanitarian organization to explore the possibility of future projects for Somali refugees."

I was only a few miles south of the Somali/Kenya border, standing just outside the gate of a camp that housed ten thousand Somalis. I didn't really know what I hoped to accomplish. I had never met or even seen a Somali before. At that point in my life, I had never met, let alone held a conversation with, a Muslim. I didn't know the Somali language or culture. And I was there all by myself because I hadn't even had enough sense to bring anyone else more experienced with me.

Before I talked myself out of doing what I had come to do, I took a deep breath and walked hurriedly through the gate. Once inside, a swarm of Somalis surrounded me, anxious to talk and tell me their stories. I was surprised at first by the number of people who spoke English. I then realized that, in all likelihood, the folks living in the squalid conditions of this refugee camp were some of most privileged of Somali society. Only that nation's best educated, professional, and well-to-do citizens had enough resources to escape the horrors of their homeland.

I soon found a friendly young college student named Abdi Bashir. He introduced me to his friends who were more than willing to practice their English language skills on an American visitor. I asked many questions and listened to their stories. Everybody, it seemed, had a story to tell.

I learned that the population of this camp was made up mostly of educated Somalis—teachers, business people, and former government workers. In general, they seemed to be motivated and capable people. Many had exhausted their personal and family resources to escape the violence of their country.

They had fled everything that they had ever known, hoping and dreaming of a better life for themselves and their families. How demeaning it must have been for them to find themselves confined and crowded in a fenced compound, living in tents, and using public latrines with no running water. They had few possessions, no financial resources, and no idea where or when they might go next. Sadly, they had no more say-so over their own future than they had had back in Somalia.

I couldn't help feeling intimidated by the warning that I had received. I sensed that I shouldn't mention that I was a follower of Jesus. My decision to abide by that advice had been reinforced when I discovered (to my horror) what had happened after one well-meaning

Christian organization had delivered ten thousand Bibles to that camp. The people had laid most of them out on the ground to make sidewalks through the mud; the rest they turned into latrine paper. Such disgraceful treatment of our holy book was just one indication of the intensity of their belief in Islam's dominance over, and their hostility toward, Christianity. And that wasn't something that I wanted to stir up when I was outnumbered ten thousand to one.

I finally decided to see what response I might get if I simply asked my engaging young friend, Abdi Bashir, "Do you know my friend Jesus Christ?"

I was totally unprepared for what happened next.

He immediately leapt to his feet and started speaking sharply to another young man nearby. Soon there were a half a dozen other men pressing around and shouting back and forth at each other. I thought that I might have triggered a riot. Here I was backed up against a metal fence topped with razor-wire with no place to go. Soon, a dozen, then maybe thirty, young men gathered around me arguing loudly, gesticulating wildly, with spittle flying.

I didn't realize that that was normal Somali behavior—Somalis are typically very demonstrative. I could hear "Jesus Christ" this, "Jesus" that. I thought, *"Why didn't I just keep my mouth shut?"*

Finally Abdi Bashir turned back to me and declared, "We don't know your friend Jesus! But Mahmoud thinks that he might have heard of him and that he may live in the other refugee camp down the road. So go back out the gate, turn left, go to the next camp, ask for Jesus Christ there, and you might find him."

I was so shaken by that experience that I decided to take his advice and leave as fast as I could. Instead of heading down the road to the other camp, I went back to Mombasa and flew home—never to return to that particular refugee camp.

That was the end of my first, less-than-encouraging experience of trying to talk with Somali Muslims about Jesus.

Back in South Africa, I told Ruth, "I have never encountered lost people like this. I wouldn't even know where to begin." Even so, we both continued to feel that God wanted us to serve among the Somali people. We shared our sense of God's guidance with our leaders. They soberly informed us that no one from our organization had ever served there—and they wondered about the wisdom of sending someone there now. The needs, however, were massive—and they invited us to embrace this incredible challenge.

Two months later we moved to Kenya to set up our base of operations. We were required to learn the local language, so we began taking Swahili classes. I contested that requirement; it seemed to me that we should start working on the Somali language immediately and that Swahili would be unnecessary. My request was denied. Somehow, despite my background, I had an aptitude for African languages. Ruth and I both passed our Swahili test—the fourth language that we had studied in seven years—after fourteen weeks, with more than a little grace from our language evaluator. Only then could we start learning Somali.

In the course of our planning, we made a quick trip to the States to consult with our mentors and to seek advice. We were both surprised and pleased to talk with a top mission leader, an expert in cross-cultural communication and one of the world's leading missiologists.

When Ruth and I walked into his office, this esteemed researcher greeted us by saying, "So you're the couple with the audacity to try to take the gospel of Jesus to Somalia?"

I assured him that we felt called by God to do that very thing. "We realize, of course, that the Somalis aren't very receptive to the gospel," I felt the need to remind him.

In response, this seemingly mild-mannered, professorial-looking diminutive scholar literally leapt up out of his chair so fast that papers scattered. I thought that he might fly across his desk at me as he demanded: "How dare you say that the Somalis are not responsive to the gospel when so many of them have never heard the gospel or been given the opportunity to respond!"

Chastised and challenged by that encounter, Ruth and I returned to Kenya to continue our preparations. Shortly after that, I made my first exploratory trip into Hargeisa in February of 1992. I quickly concluded that there could never have been adequate advice, training, or life experience to prepare us for what was to come.

10

Just Show Up

In August of 1992, the United States committed ten military cargo planes to airlift United Nations relief aid into Somalia. In the next five months, those planes delivered almost half a million tons of food and medical supplies in Operation Provide Relief. Still, nothing changed much in Somalia during 1992. Violence and anarchy still reigned in a country where the death toll by starvation surpassed five hundred thousand. Another 1,500,000 people had become displaced refugees. Many of the supplies now pouring into the country continued to be looted. Much of what was not stolen was store-housed in airport hangars. The United Nations didn't have the organizational resources to deliver the aid into the hands of the people who most desperately needed it.

The international media reported on both the massive relief response and the struggle to get the supplies to the people. After ignoring civil war and famine in Somalia for years, the world community suddenly took note of Somali's plight. Graphic images of suffering Somalis broadcast around the globe prompted a public outcry for action.

President George H. W. Bush committed American combat troops to lead the Unified Task Force (UNITAF), a United Nations-sanctioned multi-national military force that numbered 32,000 to support the relief mission. The United Nations accepted President Bush's offer on December 5, 1992. That same day the President ordered 25,000 American troops to Somalia to spearhead the newly renamed relief effort, Operation Restore Hope.

Four days later I stood on the rooftop of our rented compound in Mogadishu and watched the nearby waterfront as the first wave of United States Marines waded ashore. The event was captured live by a gaggle of camera crews and reporters.

Despite serious concerns about the fragile situation, the strong military presence did immediately resolve some of the security issues that had handicapped relief efforts for months. Stockpiled supplies could now be guarded to reduce looting. And the Somali clan militias avoided direct confrontations with the United States Marines and other international forces that helped secure delivery routes and provided military escorts for our distribution of the supplies.

In effect, the United Nations divided Mogadishu into sections. We continued to provide mobile medical clinics outside the city, but we also intensified our efforts to establish and service five feeding centers in and around Mogadishu. Our team distributed food for ten thousand people each day at each center. That meant that, beginning in 1993, we were able to keep fifty thousand people a day from starving. In addition, we continued to provide medical relief and basic survival resources.

Most of the people who we helped were actually refugees who had flooded into the city from the countryside because of drought. They had no jobs, no money, and no resources. They slept in abandoned buildings, makeshift tents and hodge-podge shelters.

When our teams first arrived in the distribution locations, people often asked first if we had any white muslin cloth. We could not make sense of that request—until we were told that bodies are required to be ceremonially wrapped in white cloth for a proper Islamic burial. We then understood that people were asking for the white cloth so that they might bury their children and relatives who had died during the night. Once that responsibility was fulfilled, the people could deal with their other needs. We quickly learned that, wherever we went, we needed to have not only food and water, but also bolts of white cotton cloth.

I learned another lesson that was even more important. This lesson helped cure me of what I might call "loving arrogance." The people I wanted to help were living in such horrible conditions that my natural response was to focus only on what they lacked. My normal questions revealed what I was thinking. My typical encounters with people would sound something like this:

> "Do you need food? We have this food for you. Is your baby sick? We have medicine. Do your children need clothes? We have clothes for them. Does your family have shelter? We have blankets for you and sheets of plastic that you can use for protection from the weather. Do you need burial cloth? We have that as well."

We soon discovered that those were not the most important questions. When we finally slowed down enough to listen, the people themselves told us what they needed most.

One day, I said to a bent-over, shriveled-up woman: "Tell me what you need most? What can I do for you first?" She looked ancient, but she may have only been in her forties if I understood the story that she began to share with me.

> "I grew up in a village many days walk from here," she told me.
> "My father was a nomad who raised camels and sheep . . . (and

she told a little about her growing up years). I married a camel herder who did the same thing. He was a good man; together we had a good life and four children . . . (and she talked some about her marriage and family). The war came and the militia marched through our village, stealing or slaughtering most of our animals. When my husband tried to stop them from taking our last camel, they beat him, and then they put a gun to his head . . . (and tears began to trickle down her cheeks). I worked hard to care for my children after my husband was killed, but the drought came. When my neighbors left for the city, some of them gave me what they couldn't carry with them. So I tried to make do . . . but there wasn't enough. My oldest boy got sick and died . . . . When the last of our food was almost gone, my children and I began walking. I hoped that life would be better here in the city. But it is not—it's harder. Men with guns are everywhere. They raped and beat me. They took my older daughters. I only have this little one left. There is no work for a woman alone. I don't know how I will take care of her. I know no one in this place. But I don't have anywhere else to go."

So many people with similar stories desperately needed more than the help that we were prepared to give. What they wanted even more, however, was for someone, anyone, even a stranger who was still trying to learn their language, to sit for a while, or just stand with them, and let them share their stories. I perhaps should have known this, but I was amazed to see the power of human presence. In my pride, I thought that I knew exactly what these people needed, but I never would have thought to put "conversation" or "human connection" on my list. Once again, I was profoundly humbled.

I wasn't able to listen to every story. There simply wasn't enough time. But the stories I did hear taught me that there was much more to these suffering Somalis than their overwhelming physical needs.

Their stories convinced me that it would never be enough merely to feed and shelter them. We do that much for animals.

Yet that was what the western governments were sending us to feed these starving people: animal food. Each day the Somalis would stand in the sun for hours so that we could dole out to them about five pounds of dirty, unprocessed wheat or the hard, yellow kernels of corn that we used to feed our animals back in Kentucky.

Those seemingly endless lines at the feeding sites were made up of individual human beings who had witnessed profound evil, endured horrible living conditions, and suffered so much heartache and loss that many of them had lost all sense of their own humanity.

Sometimes, we listened to their stories. Sometimes it was enough to remember that they had stories! By doing that, we were saying to them that they mattered. We were saying that they were important enough to be heard. Just by listening, we could restore a measure of humanity. Often, that felt more important and more transforming than one more dose of life-saving medicine or another day's worth of physical nourishment.

Some days it wasn't the humanity of the Somalis that I worried about, but my own humanity and that of my staff. It was nearly impossible for us to find the strength to get out of bed in the morning knowing that before the day was over, we would help bury twenty more children, and that there were many more starving people in this country than the fifty thousand who we would feed that day. If each soul is, indeed, a soul for whom Christ died, how would it be possible to endure the pain, the death, the inhumanity?

Clearly, we could not afford to break down every time we helped a wailing mother bury her baby. We could not let our hearts break every time we looked into the desperate eyes of a starving child the age of my sons. At the same time, we refused to let ourselves become people who didn't share the grief and pain of those around us. We struggled to steel our emotions without hardening our hearts. That was not easily done.

Wrestling daily with such difficult dilemmas made relief work as emotionally draining as it was physically taxing. Most days there was no rest. During the day, the tropical heat was devastating. Being busy kept us from thinking about the tragic pain of the Somalis.

In the dark of night, however, there was no busyness to keep us from thinking about the pain. Often, I found refuge and relief by dragging my sleeping bag out onto the flat rooftop of the villa where we stayed. There, under the stars, an ocean breeze provided blessed relief from the oppressive heat and also kept the mosquitoes at bay. That breeze, plus the view over the compound walls of Mogadishu in the moonlight, provided a stark contrast to the fury of gunfire and the flash of exploding mortars that nightly lit up the sky over the city.

Human beings are adaptable creatures. Somehow, I adapted to this world. I learned to sleep through the gunfire and explosions. But I never let my guard down. Even at night, my senses seemed to stay alert and tuned to the smallest nuance of sound or movement. I wasn't aware of it at the time, but it was impossible to relax.

We knew that everything that we were doing required risk. Over time, however, it became difficult to determine which risks were acceptable—and which risks were to be avoided. Over the past few months, we had increased our staff. Other people had joined us to supplement our Somali staff and help us administer our growing relief work. At first, we relied on western workers from other African countries who we could bring to Somalia. We assumed that people with some experience living in challenging settings would be better prepared for the situation in Somalia.

One day I welcomed one of our first American staff couples to our Mogadishu headquarters. I gave Nathan and Leah a quick tour of the compound and then took them up to the roof for a look at Mogadishu.

As I showed Nathan the water tanks and the radio antennae, Leah walked toward the edge of the rooftop to get a better look at the compound below. "My goodness, listen to that!" she exclaimed. "The mosquitoes certainly are bad here!"

My heart clenched the instant her words registered in my mind. I realized that there would be no mosquitoes in the middle of the day. As I instinctively rushed toward Leah, I began to hear what she was hearing. As calmly as I could, I said, "Leah, those aren't mosquitoes that you're hearing. Those are bullets." Before I could say more, Leah had already dropped flat and was belly-crawling back to the doorway. That was Leah's welcome to Somalia; she had to adapt in a hurry and she did it well.

We struggled to remember what was normal. We realized that we were being forced to adapt to a situation that was impossible even to comprehend. We felt certain that we were exactly where we needed to be, exactly where God wanted us to be. But, almost daily, we wondered why God would allow such suffering and pain. The human element in that pain was clear: corruption and greed and sin were obvious answers to our question. What we couldn't see quite so clearly, at the time, was the love and power of God. *Was God in Somalia? Where? What was He doing? How bad would the situation have to get before He would dramatically intervene?*

We made a conscious choice to be salt and light in a place gone mad. And we prayed that, somehow, the light would shine in the midst of this dark insanity.

11

Bubba Sings

The presence of international military forces provided adequate security for us to get more relief supplies outside of the major cities to other Somali people who so desperately needed them. The benefit gained by the presence of the forces, however, came with a price. In fact, the increasing role of the United Nations made our work more and more difficult.

As the world became increasingly aware of the humanitarian crisis in Somalia, aid poured in. The hope of the Somali people soared. At the same time, this dramatic infusion of resources led to profound economic changes. The cost of doing business and providing services skyrocketed almost overnight. Early on, we had rented our compound for five hundred dollars a month. Suddenly, our rent was five thousand dollars a month—and rising even further. At the beginning, we had rented vehicles for \$150 a month. Now, the cost was \$1,500 a month. While our organizational resources remained stable, our costs had grown by as much as one thousand percent.

The sudden visible presence of American military personnel as an integral part of the relief effort led to increasing hostility among many of the Somali people. This hostility was something that we had not encountered before. Evidently, the arrival of the troops had been seen as "a crusade." The continuing presence of the troops was seen as "an occupation." Suddenly, every Westerner was seen as suspect. Earlier, our efforts had been met with both gratitude and curiosity. Now, the reaction was often skepticism and resentment. Before, I was recognized and known well enough to walk safely around in the city alone or with some Somali staff. Now, I was seen as an invader and occupier. My western staff and I discovered that we couldn't go anywhere without armed guards. It felt as if we were wearing targets on our backs. And our humanitarian efforts began requiring significant military protection.

I was frustrated. The people we cared deeply about—the people we were working to keep alive at our feeding centers—could become belligerent in an instant. The situation was so tense that our standing security orders from the military leadership required that we arrive at our distribution points at 6:00 each morning. If, however, our military support was not already waiting for us at that time, we were instructed to leave immediately. Even the presence of the soldiers did not always guarantee a peaceful and controlled environment. And the situation could change in an instant.

Typically, the military would string razor wire to keep the pressing crowd in line as thousands cycled through our feeding centers. Our own staff assisted in keeping things orderly as well. In particular, one of our American workers was instrumental in this. He was a huge man with a soft and gentle heart. We called him Bubba. His size alone would have intimidated most potential trouble-makers. But it was his obvious and open love, and his friendly enjoyment of people, that probably had the greatest impact.

One day started like so many others. We arrived at the feeding center before daybreak. At the site was a well-armed squad of American soldiers, five tons of grain that had arrived earlier with its own guards, and a long line of hungry Somalis already waiting. It was a typical day at the feeding center—or so it seemed.

As the temperature soared, our wheat supply dwindled. It was over one hundred degrees well before noon. Hundreds of Somalis remained in line, each waiting for our workers to carefully measure out two kilograms of grain per person, the required allotment to feed up to four people for the day.

We did not notice any significant shift in tension or a lessening of patience. Looking back, it was unbearably hot and the hungry crowd had grown restless. Sometimes, a small thing can transform a crowd into an angry mob.

On this day, the trigger was an older woman with deep wrinkles. To this day, I cannot be certain about what caused her to react so strongly. Perhaps she had used up her patience simmering in the sun for hours at the back of the line. Perhaps she had some desperately hungry grandchildren who she needed to get back to. It is impossible to know exactly what happened. But after she received her allocation of wheat, she broke the established rules of the feeding site and moved toward Bubba. She looked up at him and unleashed a verbal attack. Bubba, as gentle as ever, simply smiled at her. The more he smiled, the angrier she got.

I noticed the commotion when our Somali guards suddenly tensed and turned toward the disturbance. All I could see was Bubba, head and shoulders above a gathering crowd, seemingly unperturbed, and smiling down at someone. His patient response only fueled the woman's rage. I heard her sound of fury long before I spotted the source when she launched a long stream of vile curses at Bubba. Thankfully, he didn't understand a word that she was saying.

It was now possible to understand her complaint. She was upset about the quality of the "animal feed" that was being distributed for human consumption. She was probably right in her assessment of the food. These were surplus agricultural products that United Nations contributing members didn't want, couldn't sell, and had no other use for.

As this hulking American continued to smile, the woman realized that she was not communicating. Now, furious **and** frustrated, she bent down, set her plastic bag on the ground, and grabbed two fistfuls of dirty, broken wheat, grain dust, dirt and chaff. She straightened to her full height and flung the filthy mixture as hard as she could into Bubba's face.

The crowd was deathly silent as I heard a series of loud metallic clicks that indicated that an entire squad of American soldiers had instinctively locked and loaded all weapons in readiness for whatever might happen next.

Everything felt frozen in time as everyone waited and watched for Bubba's reaction. A Somali man might have beaten the woman for such a public insult—and he would have considered his action and his anger entirely justified.

I knew that Bubba had traveled half-way around the world at his own expense to spend three months of personal vacation time to help hurting people. And this was the thanks that he received? He was hot, sweaty, and drained beyond exhaustion—and he had just been publicly embarrassed. He had every reason to be absolutely livid. Instead, he raised one hand to rub the grit out of his eyes, and then he gave the woman one more big smile.

At that point, he began to sing. And what he sang wasn't just any song.

She didn't understand the words, of course. But she, and the entire crowd, stood in silent amazement as Bubba belted out the words to the 1950's Elvis Presley rock-n-roll classic:

> You ain't nothin' but a hound dog
> Cryin' all the time

> You ain't nothin' but a hound dog
> Cryin' all the time
> Well, you ain't never caught a rabbit
> And you ain't no friend of mine.

By the time he started singing the next verse, the old woman had turned and stomped off in frustration, angrily plowing a path through the now-smiling crowd of Somalis to make her escape. Watching her go, Bubba raised his voice to send her off with rousing rendition of the final verse:

> Well they said you was high-classed
> Well, that was just a lie
> Ya know they said you was high-classed
> Well, that was just a lie
> Well, you ain't never caught a rabbit
> And you ain't no friend of mine.

Obviously, the tension was broken. Some of our own Somali guards walked over to Bubba and patted him on the back in obvious relief and gratitude as they told him, "We didn't know that you were a singer!"

"Oh, yeah," he grinned back at them. "I'm a famous singer. Back home in America, they call me 'Elvis'!" (When he finally got back to the States, Bubba actually picked up a "Best of Elvis" CD, stuck a picture of himself on the cover of the case and sent it as a gift to our Somali staff in Mogadishu. Somewhere, even today, there are a few Somalis who still believe that Elvis was a singing relief worker, very much alive and well during the early 1990's in Mogadishu.)

When I finally had time to consider what had happened in those few moments, I concluded that I had observed one of the most impressive demonstrations of Jesus' love that I had ever seen. A kind, gentle, godly example of humility and humanity had instantly defused a situation so volatile that it could have turned deadly within seconds.

Bubba had done that simply by following the seemingly insane teaching of Jesus who had instructed His followers to "love your enemies." Bubba had met angry hostility with a simple smile, and a very unlikely hymn, which God then used to change an impending crisis into a sacred moment of Christ-like testimony. In that moment, I learned some good lessons about cross-cultural relationships. What I had mistaken at first for naiveté, I came to see as nothing less than the love of Jesus.

For twenty years, that event was my most vivid memory of Bubba. I think I was captivated by the humor and the positive outcome. When I thought of Bubba, that is the day I remembered. While working on this manuscript, however, another memory surfaced. I wonder now if I had repressed it. Suddenly, another memory came to mind.

It was another day at the same feeding center. Several thousand starving Somalis stood in line under the searing tropical sun. Another squad of American military men provided security.

A Somali boy who was about twelve years old walked up the far side of the feeding line toward our distribution point. Some people in the waiting crowd seemed to stir and stare as he moved past them. As he neared the front of the waiting line, I realized that he was carrying some kind of a weapon at his side.

An American soldier spotted the danger about the same time I did and shouted out an order: "Drop your weapon, son!"

The boy ignored the command and kept walking. Three or four times the soldier repeated his order. I heard several soldiers cock their rifles. The boy kept coming, a finger inside the trigger guard of what looked like an old, beat-up AK-47. He held the gun tightly, but it was still pointed toward the ground.

Everyone else stood frozen in time. As the young boy neared us and began to raise his weapon, several soldiers shouted, "Drop it!"

When the boy failed to do so, one of them shot him in the chest, killing him instantly.

The child fell at Bubba's feet.

The security force, as trained, stood in place and visually scanned the area for additional gunmen. None of the Somalis in line made a move to go to the boy. The whole confrontation, from beginning to end, had lasted less than thirty seconds.

As Bubba looked down at that crumpled, lifeless twelve-year-old body, he began to weep.

Suddenly, a cluster of Somali men gathered around Bubba. Instead of looking at the boy or mourning his death, they began to chastise Bubba for his tears. This is what they said to him:

> "Stop your crying!"
>
> "This boy was a fool! If he had wanted to kill these soldiers, he should have shot at them from a distance!"
>
> "The boy died because he did a stupid thing."
>
> "He deserved to die."
>
> "Don't embarrass yourself, or us, by crying like a woman. Men don't weep over things like this!"
>
> Within moments, they demanded that Bubba return to helping distribute grain. They made it clear that they were "tired of waiting and wasting time over this foolish dead boy."
>
> For two decades, I had blocked out the violent horror of that memory. Somehow, I had chosen instead to remember the story of Bubba serenading the old Somali woman with a

classic Elvis tune as "one of the most impressive demonstrations of Jesus' love and grace that I had ever seen."

Upon reflection, however, I see another example that I couldn't quite grasp or face for many, many years. Like the biblical account of Christ's anguish over Jerusalem, I now see in my mind's eye two mourners in Mogadishu that day.

I realize that both Bubba—and Jesus—wept over the death of that young boy.

The rapid expansion of our relief work in those first months of Operation Restore Hope could not have happened without the steady stream of excellent short-term volunteers who augmented our full-time staff.

I continued making trips in and out of Somalia, Northeast Kenya, Djibouti, and Ethiopia to manage the work among Somalis. At the same time, Ruth was in Kenya recruiting and coordinating travel for scores of volunteers, managing the finances for a rapidly expanding relief agency, raising three boys while simultaneously learning how to grow and administer an international relief agency out of our family home. She spent her time calming American families who had loaned us their loved ones for relief work in a war zone. All the time, she was wondering where in the world her husband was, if he was safe, and when he might come home to Nairobi.

Supervising five feeding sites, distributing food and medical relief to numerous villages, providing fresh-water wells, seeds, and farming tools to outlying communities, and traveling through different regions of Somalia exposed me to countless suffering people. We felt proud of what our organization had been able to do, but there was so much more that needed to be done. There was so much hurt that we could not heal.

In the spring of 1993, Ruth and I returned to the States for a conference. We met with some of the people who had prayed for us and we spent time with supporters to report on our work and to seek additional advice.

During that same stateside visit, we made a quick trip to Kentucky to see family and friends. The day I visited home, Dad treated me to lunch at the little downtown restaurant. I hadn't been there for years. As I followed my father through the door, a number of his retired friends slowly rose to their feet and began applauding. I was confused. I didn't understand what was happening. Several of the men slapped me on the back and shook my hand. As Dad and I made our way to an empty table, I heard some of the men say, "Well done" or "Good job."

As we settled into our seats I asked: "Dad, what in the world was that all about?"

My father wasn't the most demonstrative or communicative parent in the world. In all the years that we had been in Africa, I had received one piece of correspondence from him. When I pulled the envelope out of the mail box and recognized his handwriting, I immediately suspected that something terrible had happened. Without opening the letter, I walked home from the post office; I figured that I would need Ruth's strength and help in dealing with whatever bad news the letter contained.

Ruth knew that something had to be wrong the moment I walked in the door of our house. I showed her the letter and I told her that I had been afraid to open it. Together, we ripped open the envelope.

There was a single piece of paper that read in its entirety: "Dear Son, I thought I'd write—Dad."

This was the same man who had verbally expressed his love for me only one time in my life—as far back as I could remember. One time, we had placed a trans-Atlantic phone call home from Africa for some reason. We made the connections and held a very brief conversation with Dad before I signed off by telling him, "I love you, Dad." He responded to that by replying, "I love you too, son." I was so shocked that I quickly hung up before he could take it back!

This was the man I was looking at across the table in the restaurant. I asked him again, "What is going on with these people? Why did they react like that when we walked in?"

He smiled at me with a look of unmistakable pride in his eyes. He said, "Well, Nik, I guess it's because I told them what you've done."

"What did I do, Dad?" I said slowly. I wasn't sure that I wanted to hear his answer.

"Why . . . I told everyone how you brought all those troops from all over the world to save Somalia."

"DAD!" I exclaimed. I then lowered my voice to a whisper: "I did no such thing!"

He looked at me and said, "Didn't you go into that country before anybody else?" *I was one of the first to go back in, yeah.* "Did you stay there when everybody else was leaving?" *Well, I stayed and tried to help when I saw how bad things were, that was true.* "Did you write articles and tell people how terrible conditions were in there—how the Somalis were starving and how the bad guys were keeping the food from reaching the people who needed it most?" *Well . . . I tried to do some of that . . . sure.*

In his mind, it was perfectly clear: "So you helped Americans and people in other countries learn what was going on there, and they responded, first with relief aid and then with troops to help that country."

I could see that there was no point in trying to dissuade him. In Dad's eyes, and what he had evidently convinced a bunch of his friends to believe, was that I had been the primary person responsible for convincing President Bush, then President Clinton, and finally other international leaders (none of whom I had ever spoken to) to send thirty-two thousand troops to Somalia in a massive, multinational relief effort. My father wanted to place the credit for all of that on my shoulders. Now the folks of my hometown thought they had reason to be proud of me.

I couldn't blame my father for not wanting his son to be yet another "prophet without honor in his own country."

However, I couldn't escape the irony either.

My dad and his friends in rural Kentucky wanted to credit me with doing so much to "save Somalia." But the honest truth was that sometimes, more often than I wanted to admit, when I was on the ground in the Horn of Africa, horrified by the overwhelming needs that I saw all around me, I couldn't help wondering if my efforts, and those of all the wonderful people working with our organization, were actually making any difference at all. Or if we ever could.

12

Tears for Somalia

My father's friends in Kentucky weren't the only people now watching the developments in East Africa with interest and concern. The media attention on Operation Restore Hope moved the long-term heartache and horror that was Somalia's history to center stage in the American consciousness. As word of the scope of the need spread, the generosity of faithful friends and supporters in the States and around the globe enabled our work to expand rapidly. Sometimes, we felt that our work had become too big to manage.

We had launched a modest mom-and-pop relief venture. It had mushroomed into a professional multi-national organization that employed as many as one hundred and fifty Somali and thirty-five full-time western staff members stationed in four different countries. For the first several years, Ruth administered the entire operation from a small office in our home in Nairobi.

While most of the relief that we distributed came from the United Nations, our bare-bones organization greatly appreciated and needed the steady stream of funds generously given by believers. This support enabled us to recruit personnel and fund what had become an expensive endeavor.

Even beyond that support, what made the biggest difference in those days were the thousands of people who also supported us by praying for the Somalis and for their physical and spiritual needs.

Our swiftly increasing monthly expenses and payroll meant that I had to carry as much as $100,000 cash (in one-hundred-dollar bills) on each trip into the country. I would divide the money into three or four different bundles hidden in different places in my gear and on my person. If I was robbed, I hoped that my attackers would be so thrilled with the first stash they found that they would quit looking and leave me with most of the money. I am thankful to say that I was never robbed.

Nevertheless, when my supervisors learned how I was transporting funds into Somalia, they were horrified and they informed me that I was not allowed to do that anymore. I asked if they had a better plan. There was no financial system operating in Mogadishu, and no legally recognized or transferable Somali currency. The only option, I argued, was to continue with my financial strategy or to end our work and pull our team out of the country.

They had nothing better to suggest, so I kept doing what I had been doing—without their authorization, but with their full knowledge and unspoken blessing. We never came up with any other workable system for handling funds during the entire six years that our organization conducted relief work in Somalia.

One of the key reasons our organization was able to accomplish so much and keep working in Somalia for so long was because of our committed Somali staff—almost all of whom were Muslims. Because we provided employment where there were few jobs, and because they saw that we were helping so many of their people, the Somalis who worked for us, and most of those we helped, were willing to overlook the fact that we were Westerners—and, by definition, infidels.

Our Somali staff was the cream of the crop. The few believers we employed or interacted with were godly people. And our Muslim staff included some of the most sacrificial people I have ever met. Because the unemployment rate was about ninety percent, we were able to hire quality people from a variety of backgrounds—former college professors, nurses, agriculturalists, nutritionists, veterinarians, water engineers, businessmen, educators, and accountants. Our relatively low pay scale was considered a princely sum in Somalia in those days. We attempted to spread our money as far as possible to help as many families as we could.

My Somali chief of staff and right-hand man, Omar Aziz, became a dear and trusted friend. He was one of the most street-smart *and* compassionate individuals I have ever known. One day he came into the office weeping. I didn't know what had happened or how I should respond in a culturally-appropriate manner. I did what seemed natural; I waited out his tears.

He soon wiped his eyes and told me why he was so upset. He had been on an errand, walking down a street near his own neighborhood when he spotted a malnourished woman sitting in the shade of a small tree, leaning against the trunk, nursing a baby. Omar Aziz greeted her as he passed by. She returned his smile, but her baby never stopped eating to look at him.

When Omar finished his business and returned the same way less than an hour later, he noted the same peaceful scene—the same woman under the same tree with the same baby in the same pose. But as he strolled by this time, he heard the infant whimpering. He glanced in that direction and immediately sensed that something was wrong. The tiny child cried and squirmed in its mother's arms, but the woman seemed oddly still. For just a moment Omar assumed that the woman was asleep. As he stepped toward her, however, he realized the truth. In the time since he had last walked down this street, the young mother had died! He walked over to the woman, bent down to gently lift the baby from its mother's arms, and tried to comfort the child.

He could find no identification papers for the woman, so Omar walked around the neighborhood, knocking on doors, searching in vain for someone who might know her. He managed to round up enough people to help give the woman a proper burial, but no one seemed to know her well enough to take the child.

By this time tears were streaming down Omar Aziz's face again as he said, "I don't know what to do with the baby!" Then he exclaimed in an anguished voice, "My poor country! What is going to become of us?"

(What became of that baby made for a happier-than-expected ending to a tragic story when Omar Aziz found another nursing mother whose baby had just died. That woman was thrilled to care for this child.)

I knew that Omar had witnessed many scenes that were more shocking than the one he encountered that day. But when people are forced to deal with a daily barrage of human suffering and inhumane violence, the emotional response is never predictable. Sometimes, it is possible to remain calm and relatively detached. At other times, sometimes without warning, the dam breaks and there is emotional turmoil. The trigger for these emotional floods is not always dramatic. It might be something as simple as seeing yet another orphaned baby. At other times, it is the cumulative result of countless microscopic nicks and cracks caused by the constant reminders of brokenness all around. Sometimes we would be moved most by small deeds of kindness or tenderness.

When the pressure and sadness became unbearable, I knew that it was time to get out and spend time in Nairobi with my family. Our staff rule was to not keep spouses apart for more than a month at a time. Ruth and I tried to live by that same rule. I knew that Ruth was my anchor.

And I needed an anchor more than ever to protect me from a serious danger that is probably intrinsic to professional relief work. I was often forced to choose which villages we would go to, and where we couldn't go because of limited staff and resources. Many of my daily decisions determined who lived and who died. These decisions were weighty and terrifying. It was an overwhelming responsibility. Our projects were affecting thousands of people. There was always a latent temptation to lose perspective and think about the power that we held in our hands. But we worked hard to remember—and to remind one another—that only our Creator God has ultimate power over life and death. We knew that such authority was never ours to assume.

All the same, if there was food and water for ten villages—and there were twenty desperate villages in the area—choices were required.

Quickly, I learned that I could never divorce my decisions from my prayer time and my relationship with God. I guarded against assuming a level of responsibility and authority that was not mine to assume.

No matter how consumed I was with the incredible opportunities and overwhelming demands in Somalia, it was that essential connection with Ruth and the boys that helped keep me grounded. The way they welcomed me home every time I landed in Nairobi reminded me that my God-given roles as husband and father were essential to my ministry too.

Ruth was an equal partner in our venture. When I was away in Somalia, I devoted my full attention to our relief work. Back in Nairobi, Ruth had become the ultimate multi-tasker. In my absence, she mothered *and* fathered our three boys and assumed responsibility for maintaining a busy household. She did all of that while running our base of operations.

When we lived in a Somali area of Nairobi early on, four times a week Ruth made a ten-mile round trip by car to purchase enough drinkable water to fill four twenty-gallon plastic tanks that she then transported back home for our family. While she could fill the tanks right in the car with a hose, she could not lift the twenty-gallon water tanks out of the car when she got home. So she would siphon the water into smaller containers that she could carry and store in the house. Securing water was just one of many logistical challenges that had to be dealt with day after day.

Our home was more than a household. It was eventually an operational hub and international headquarters for a multi-national company engaged in corporate business activities conducted in four different countries. Ruth kept it all running smoothly by acting as lead encourager and mentor for those who came to function as our company's CEO, COO, CFO, Personnel Director, Chief Communications Officer, Senior IT Manager, Executive Secretary, Corporate Travel Agent, and Head Maintenance Department Engineer. (In the early days, she performed all of those jobs herself.)

The most important role she played for me was that of a wise and trusted counselor, a personal therapist who offered spiritual support, encouragement, a listening ear, and much more of what some organizations now lump together and call *member care.*

The Kenyan church where our family worshiped in Nairobi served as another spiritual harbor where I could safely anchor and unload whatever emotional and spiritual baggage I had brought home. A small accountability group of four believing brothers who regularly met with me whenever I got back to Nairobi served much the same purpose.

During my recovery periods in Nairobi, Ruth would also bring me up to date on the most pressing company business, financing, and logistic and personnel issues. We would try to strategize and set priorities for the next few weeks. Then she would drive me to the airport and put me on a plane heading into a war zone once again—knowing that all she could do was pray and trust God with my care for however long it would be before I returned home again.

13

Broken and Poured Out

The violence in Somalia increased in 1993. The situation seemed to grow more chaotic with each passing month. In early June, twenty-four Pakistani peacekeepers were killed. In August of 1993, in an effort to regain control and squelch the growing violence, the United States Army Task Force Ranger was dispatched to Somalia to root out rebel forces. Task Force Ranger's assault on the Olympic Hotel in pursuit of the rebel leaders in a seventeen-hour battle in October resulted in the loss of eighteen American soldiers. Eighty-four American soldiers were wounded. (We later learned that over seven hundred Somalis were also killed.) This engagement—which could be heard from our headquarters a mile away—was later named the "Battle of Mogadishu" and made famous by the book and movie entitled *Blackhawk Down*.

The frequency and intensity of violence waned for a time following that tragedy. Prospects for peace and any hope for a final resolution of the conflict, however, seemed hopeless. After repeated failed attempts to bring the warring clans together, the United Nations began to question the wisdom of involvement in Somalia. From my point of view, their message was clear: "Somalis are not worth the effort, the cost or the lives. The price is simply too high to save people who do not even know how to say *thank you.*"

We were most concerned about the 1.7 million people who had been displaced by years of brutal civil war, drought, and famine. They were now being victimized further by anarchic clan violence, political turmoil and complete societal collapse. Because of the United Nations relief resources and the work of many relief agencies, most of the refugees who had flooded into Mogadishu were now receiving the necessary nutrition required for survival. But that was only short-term progress. Somalia would obviously require enormous resources to recreate a functioning nation again—and that process would clearly take a long, long time. Even while the United Nations was tediously deciding to extend its Somali commitment for another six months, our organization committed to continue with our work as long as we were able to get into the country and as long as the violence didn't escalate to the point where we could not do our job. We were determined not to let evil overcome good.

A short stateside furlough for our family from December of 1993 into the first few months of 1994 gave us a respite from the physical fatigue and the emotional stress of almost two years of living in the Somalia crucible. This time of rest once again provided us with the opportunity to connect with our supporters and to consult with advisers.

When we spoke about Somalia during our time in America, we felt intense, and often conflicting, emotions. I was resolute in my commitment to respond to the suffering of Somalia. Clearly, the needs of Somalia were immense, and I was passionate about what we were doing. I was also intensely proud of our efforts. We had started our team from scratch, and we had quickly become an effective international relief organization. We had employed significant numbers of Somalis, and we had distributed millions of dollars' worth of aid to meet the survival needs of tens of thousands of desperate families.

In terms of the physical needs of Somalia, our team was having an amazing impact! When I considered the spiritual needs of the Somalis, however, my assessment of our efforts was not as positive. In fact, other than the personal relationships that we had established with our Somali friends and coworkers, there was little that I could point to that I would call "success" in the realm of meeting spiritual needs. I felt deep concern—and even guilt—about that.

The Jesus who I encountered in Scripture taught His followers to provide food for the hungry, water for the thirsty, healing for the sick and wounded, and care for the suffering and persecuted. That was our explicit purpose in Somalia, and I felt that we had done those things well.

At the same time, Jesus also instructed His followers to go into all the world and make disciples. We had done well with the "going into all the world" part of His assignment. But when it came to the "making disciples" part of our purpose, we had failed.

We could not find a way to tie together the two great themes of Jesus' call. As strange as it might sound, it was easy to meet physical needs in Somalia. Addressing the spiritual needs, however, seemed impossible. Sharing Jesus with people was our deepest desire. That was both our passion and our goal. That was at the very heart of our assignment—and that was our God-given task. Yet, often, it seemed impossible to overcome the barriers that stood in our way.

Even today, I admit that there are no easy answers to this crucial struggle. How is it possible to give bold verbal witness to Jesus in a country where sharing Jesus is against the law? How is it possible to lead friends to become followers of Christ knowing that their newfound faith could lead to their deaths? We had debated questions like these long before we ever got to Somalia—but, suddenly, they were not theoretical questions any longer. Suddenly, we were talking about real people and real lives. If sharing with a friend could lead to my friend's death—will I share my faith anyway? And am I willing to live with what might happen next? These questions were profoundly disturbing, and we fought with them night and day.

From the time Ruth and I had felt called to Somalia, we had sought insight and wisdom from anyone and everyone. We talked with leaders of large relief organizations. We spoke with believers from a variety of agencies. We talked with people who seemed to know about prayer and the ways of God. Time after time, we would ask: "How can we effectively demonstrate and share the love of Christ with people who have no idea who Jesus is? How do we make a spiritual impact in a place so hostile to the faith? How do we exhibit a winsome witness for Jesus among people who feel justified in reviling and persecuting His followers? How will people recognize the love of Christ in us if we never tell them whose love it is that motivates us? How can God's love overcome their hate?"

Most of the people that we talked to had very little to offer. Some said they would think about it or pray about it—and get back to us. Clearly, we were not the only ones disturbed by the questions. And we were not the only ones without good answers.

During this time in the States, however, some of my mentors provided tremendous help when they said, "Nik, we have seldom, if ever, encountered a place like Somalia. Living for Christ in that kind of world is something that we have never attempted. I guess that's why we have left you on your own out there. Together, we need to figure this out."

Oddly, I was not disappointed to hear my mentors and colleagues admit that they did not have answers to my questions. In fact, I found it liberating. I felt that we had been given the freedom to go out on our own to explore possible strategies needed for people of faith to live and work in a place like Somalia. Since there was no strategy that we were required to follow, we felt free to make our own way.

At that moment, Ruth and I felt free to dream about finding, or if necessary, *developing* discipleship materials and practical guidelines for people like us—people who were living and working in some of the world's most difficult places—people who were desperately wanting to share God's love in those places. On the one hand, there were no easy answers. On the other hand, we were thrilled to have the opportunity to try to find some of our own.

Before acting on that newfound freedom in Africa, we spent a little more time in Kentucky with family. After my experience with my dad on our last visit, I thought that maybe I would have time now to talk more with him about Somalia. I knew that he would be interested given the "Blackhawk Down" incident and America's recent withdrawal of most of its military forces from Somalia. I asked my dad what he would tell his friends now that the United States military had been forced out of Somalia.

Dad gave a sad shake of his head and replied, "I've already told them. I said that if the United States military had just listened to you, they would still be there, they probably would not have gotten kicked out, and everything would probably be settled there by now!"

I had to laugh. Once again I hesitated to burst Dad's bubble of fatherly pride, so I didn't tell him that some days I still wondered if anything I had done in Somalia or with Somalis had made any difference at all.

I noticed little change when we returned to Kenya and I made my next trip into Somalia early that spring. Needy people still required assistance. Opposing clan leaders still were not willing to reconcile. Despite the horrible sameness of the situation, the United Nations had authorized another six-month extension of its relief operations. That meant that our organization still had plenty of work to do.

I did see more ships in the harbor and more traffic on the streets. More trade goods were arriving. A few shops had even opened for business. At the same time, things seemed much less secure now that the United Nation's military footprint in the country had been reduced by more than half. As a result, the areas where we could safely travel and the places where our work was approved were fewer in number. I sensed that we might have only weeks or months before the United Nations would pull out of the country. It seemed clear to me that there wasn't much hope left for Operation Restore Hope.

Of course, our work did not require a United Nations resolution. No earthly authority had sent us to Somalia. And no earthly power made it possible for us to be there.

We were obeying a higher directive.

Still, we appreciated and benefitted from the international aid that had poured into the country. Sadly, that aid disappeared almost as quickly as it had come.

We thought that we had everything we needed when, almost overnight, the United Nations finally took notice of Somalia. We were hopeful when the United States and coalition troops showed up in force. Now the whole world seemed to be slinking away quickly and quietly from this still-broken land and its devastated people.

Even people of faith seemed to be losing interest in Somalia. Evidently, it is hard to maintain commitment in the face of failure and loss and sacrifice. We could feel our support slipping away.

Yet God was not finished with Somalia.

I had not been back in Africa long when I received an invitation that led to one of the most meaningful spiritual experiences that I ever had in Somalia—in my entire life actually. It came about when a good friend working with another organization invited me to participate in a special service with four Somali believers who worked for various relief organizations.

Seven of us, three Westerners and those four local believers, met at a pre-arranged time in the privacy of an abandoned, shelled-out building in the heart of Mogadishu—each of us coming alone from different directions. Once we had gathered and affectionately greeted one another, my friend led in a time of prayer and fellowship. We shared a light meal together. Then, as Jesus' followers have done for almost two thousand years, we shared the Lord's Supper in remembrance and celebration of Christ's willing and sacrificial death on the cross in our place, in atonement for our sins.

We ate the bread in memory of His body, broken for us. I wondered how often, down through the ages, believers had broken bread together here in the capital city of this now-broken country. I had no way of knowing, but I suspected that this hadn't happened there for years. (And looking back nearly two decades later, I believe that it is altogether possible that the Lord's Supper has not been observed in Mogadishu since.)

We drank the grape juice in remembrance of Christ's blood, shed for us. I wondered how many unnamed and unknown Somali believers had faced persecution, suffering, and death in this country for their faith. I felt honored to worship at the Lord's Table with these four brothers who were willing to risk their own blood, their own bodies, and their very lives to follow Jesus among an unbelieving people group in this unbelieving country.

Never before had I felt the true cost and significance of Jesus' Last Supper with his disciples. This was a high and holy moment. It was also a moment that raised serious concern for our four believing brothers. The furtive and wary looks on the faces of my Somali friends served as a powerful reminder for me—a reminder not just of our Lord's death and sacrifice two thousand years ago, but also a reminder of His continuing and constant love, His faithfulness, and His presence in the lives of brave and faithful followers today.

Unfortunately, that meaningful Lord's Supper experience took on even greater emotional poignancy for me not long after that on a horrible August morning.

14

Too Great a Cost

The morning was like so many others. I sat in a briefing room listening to a military commander describe the current situation in Somalia. Conditions changed daily, and these updates were a regular occurrence. The meeting was drawing to a close when a colleague burst into the room. Normally, it would not have been proper to interrupt this kind of meeting, but he was obviously shaken by something that had happened. Interrupting the military commander, this is what he said:

> "Most of you know that our organization has worked in Somalia for decades. I have just been informed that, this morning, four Somali believers we have worked with have, in separate incidents, been ambushed and killed on their way to work. Our office has already received an ultimatum telling us that if our organization doesn't pull out of Somalia immediately, everyone who works for us will be killed."

With tears running down his face, he added, "We have no choice but to leave!" With that declaration, he turned and left as quickly as he had come.

A wave of dread washed over me. Even without hearing more details, I somehow felt that I knew more than my friend had shared. Hoping against hope that my suspicions were unfounded, I quickly learned that the four Somalis assassinated that day were the same four believers who had shared the Lord's Supper with us just weeks before. In what was clearly a coordinated assassination plot, all four attacks had been launched within minutes of each other on the same morning.

A radical Muslim group claimed credit. To add further cruelty, the murderers had stolen the bodies of the men they had assassinated. Not one of the bodies was ever found.

The day after the assassinations, I walked through the streets of our Mogadishu neighborhood with armed guards trailing along in my wake. Everywhere I looked, I saw destruction and suffering. As I thought about my murdered friends, I suddenly became so angry at the evil that I cried out to God like an Old Testament prophet wanting to call down destruction from on high.

"Why don't you just destroy these people, Lord?" I demanded to know. "They have already killed almost all of your children in this country. Not one of these people deserves your salvation or your grace!"

The Spirit of God spoke to my heart in that instant: *Neither do you, Nik! You were no less lost than they are—but, by my grace, you were born in an environment where you could hear, understand and believe. These people have not had that opportunity.*

God reminded me of a truth from Scripture, *"Even while you were still a sinner, Christ died for you."* Then another thought came to mind: *And Christ died not only for you, Nik, but for every Somali in the Horn of Africa.*

For a long time, I had known that I was not worthy of Christ's sacrifice. I understood that. I knew that my salvation was a result of God's grace. I knew all of that . . . intellectually.

But suddenly I understood at a deeper level. I saw my own sin more clearly. I saw my own evil heart. And I realized that without Jesus, there is simply no hope . . . for anyone. In Somalia, it was easy to put people into categories: good, bad, evil, godly, selfish, giving, ungrateful, kind, hateful. We attached the labels almost automatically. But, here in this moment, I saw the lost condition of every human being without the grace of Christ.

My anger, I believe, was an appropriate response to the evil. Indeed, God Himself hates evil with a righteous fury. Those of us who claim to represent Him, however, need to distinguish between the sin and the sinner. That was a daily struggle for me, and some days it was especially difficult. Honestly, two decades later, that continues to be a struggle.

I had to work hard to remember that neither Islam nor Muslims were the real enemy here. *Lostness* was the enemy. The enemy was the evil that viciously misleads and traps people like lost sheep without a shepherd. The Somalis were the victims. They were not the source or even the cause of the evil in their land. They were victims suffering evil's grim effects.

In the days following the deaths of my four friends, I worried about every Somali believer who had ever been connected to our organization. Their numbers were relatively few and we had been careful not to be open about our connections. But I had grown close to most of them, loved them like family, and dreaded the thought that a continuing relationship with outsiders might make them the next targets. I was horrified by the thought that I might be the cause of pain in their lives.

Amazingly, it wasn't only Somali believers who were in danger. Soon, three of our Muslim guards came to me, terrified, when their names inexplicably appeared on a list of "Somali Infidels/Traitors" published by a local terrorist group. This list had been distributed to every western compound and tacked up around the city. It claimed to identify individuals suspected of having converted to Christianity, those who were sympathetic to or interested in the Christian faith, and those who were close friends with Christians. All of these people, the list said, deserved to be killed.

These three Somali employees rushed into my office holding one of the lists: "Dr. Nik! Dr. Nik!" they pleaded. "You know that we are good Muslims!" I agreed that I did indeed know that. They insisted that I had to do something about this list with their names on it, and they handed me a large sheet of paper.

I told them that I didn't know anything that I could do to help.

"But it's a terrible mistake!" they insisted. "We're Muslims, not Christians. You could tell them that their list is wrong!"

The men were so insistent, so frantic with fear, that I finally asked them what they thought I could possibly do about a terrorist hit list. These Muslim employees pleaded with me to go to the headquarters of the terrorist group and testify to the fervency of their Islamic faith.

The thought was utterly insane. I imagined walking into an Islamic terrorist headquarters vouching for the validity of the faith commitment of my Muslim staff members. I almost cynically laughed out loud. I thought again about how impossible it would have been to be prepared and equipped to live in this insane world.

Their suggestion seemed utterly absurd. The men, however, were completely serious. I reluctantly agreed to try. We drove to the local stronghold of the most militant Islamic group in the entire country. I walked in alone. With all the sarcasm that I could muster, I "thanked" them for sending this hit list to our compound. I pointed at the names of my three Muslim employees and explained: "But this has to be a mistake. These three men listed here are not only valuable employees, they are also good Muslims. They go to the mosque every week; they pray toward Mecca five times a day. They keep the fast during Ramadan, and one of them has even been on the Hajj. You don't want to kill these men; they are good and faithful Muslims. You need to take their names off of your list."

The militants actually thanked me for clearing up the matter and promised to scratch the names of my employees off of their list. I was stunned by their reasonable response. When I turned to leave, I stopped, looked back, and inquired, "Can you tell me . . . why would you publish a list of one hundred and fifty names when you know that there aren't that many Christian believers in the entire country of Somalia today?"

I realized immediately how stupid that comment was. I should have just kept my mouth shut.

But they went ahead and answered my question anyway. "You're right," they admitted. "We believe that there are probably no more than forty or fifty Somali Christian traitors left in our country. But we also know that if we list the Christians that we already know about and add to the list those that we are suspicious about, then we have a good chance of getting everyone."

It was a cold and calculated strategy! And it was a strategy that was confirmed by a chilling exchange that I read in a local newspaper a day or two later. A militant Islamist had written a letter to the editor asking: "Why bother killing Somali Christians—wouldn't it be a more effective strategy just to kill the Westerners that they associate with who might convert them?"

The editor responded this way:

> "Killing Westerners," he wrote, "might turn them into martyrs. So it is not cost effective to kill western Christians whose deaths might possibly inspire additional committed believers to come to our country and take up each martyr's mantle."
>
> "If, however, we kill off their converts," the editor predicted, "the western Christians will be afraid and they will go

home." The editor's conclusion was chilling: "These western Christians will not be able to watch their converts be killed. When their converts are killed, the western Christians will leave."

As much as I wanted to object, I knew that there was truth in the editor's words. At the time of those four assassinations, there were approximately seventy committed western workers serving with relief groups in and around Somalia. Two months later, there were four of us still working with Somalis.

To this day, I do not know why I didn't walk away too. I do remember thinking that leaving, at this point, would mean that the sacrifices that my friends had made for Jesus in Somalia would have been wasted. I thought of my four friends. I thought that, somehow, my staying would honor their memory and give value to their deaths.

Despite the counsel of many, our international organization recommitted to staying in Somalia. We said that we would stay as long as we felt God might use us to make a difference. Our experience to this point had convinced us that nothing but the love of Jesus—not international aid, or western culture, or a certain kind of government, or diplomacy, or military force—could heal the cruel wounds of this sad and suffering land.

When we started our work in Somalia, there were only a tiny number of believers there. Early in our work, that number had increased a little. By the time that these four friends had been murdered, though, we knew only a handful of Somali believers who remained alive. I'm not sure what we expected in terms of success when we started our Somali work—but I can assure you that it didn't look like this.

When we had started our work, there were barely enough believers in Somalia to fill a small Kentucky church. Now there were not enough to fill one pew.

We had come, obedient to God's call, to meet the needs of hurting people, unaware that the Lord had called a scattered remnant of individual believers to Himself before we arrived. Sadly, despite our best hopes and dreams, we had been unable to personally witness new believers coming to faith. Worse yet, we hadn't arrived early enough to help connect, strengthen or disciple the faithful few.

We had arrived in time to witness their demise.

Still, despite the fact that most Somali followers of Christ were either killed or fled the country, we stayed because we were convinced that Jesus was still there. Long ago, Jesus had explained that whatever we, as His followers, did for "the least of these"—the hungry, the thirsty, the sick, the naked and the persecuted—we did to Him. We believed that we were ministering to Jesus in the *least of these* throughout Somalia.

15

When Your Best Is Not Enough

During these dark days, we felt that our Somali neighbors valued us for who we were, for what we said, and for what we did. Sometimes, we even sensed that they noticed the values that motivated our work. At least, we hoped that they did.

For example, we sometimes encountered Somalis who were surprised that we wouldn't take bribes to feed certain people first or to decide which village we would help next. Their culture had convinced them that everyone can be corrupted. One day a group of grateful Somalis from a coastal village came to us and said, "You would not accept any bribes to come to our village. Then, after your people did feed us, you refused to take any payment for it."

That was all true, so I nodded. I had no idea what would be said next. They continued: "You know that as Muslims we can't eat certain foods. They are unclean for us. So we brought this for you." They opened two huge coolers to reveal seventy-eight fresh Indian Ocean lobsters. The man continued: "You can't consider this a bribe because you have already fed us, so this is a thank you gift for your people from our village. We understand that you Westerners love lobster."

We enjoyed a lobster feast—and we deeply appreciated their gift especially because it was based on behaviors and values that they had noticed in our lives and work.

We were also encouraged when Somalis noticed and appreciated the serious commitment required by our relief work. In fact, there were times when Muslim people even recognized the power and reality of the One we ultimately served. Often, in times of great danger, my Muslim staff members and friends would ask me to pray for them. At other times, during a medical crisis, our Muslim nurses would stop emergency treatments, saying, "You always pray for our sick people. So, first, ask God for help, and then we will continue treating this child." We would stop and pray, simple and sweet prayers, public and out loud. Then, the medical treatment could continue.

We hoped that we were creating a little circle of light in the vast void of darkness. But many days we wondered. I still believed that the Lord had sent us to this place. But where was the spiritual fruit of our labor and sacrifice? There had been no Christian church, no Body of believers, anywhere in Somalia before we arrived. Now, years later, the situation seemed even worse. Now, there were almost no individual members of the Body left. I wondered if there was any hope that good could triumph over evil in Somalia.

When the United Nations pulled its staff out of the country in the spring of 1995, no one knew what to expect. In fact, little seemed to change for the average Somali. Poor people still struggled to acquire the basic necessities of life. Opposing clans still fought. Some days were probably better. Others were worse. After all that these people had suffered for years, the mid-1990's were hardly the best of times nor the worst of times for Somalia.

The departure of the United Nations did, however, change the nature and scope of our work. With less attention on the needs of Somalia, financial support decreased quickly. We also lost easy access to transportation and security. It was a painful and dangerous time for us on several scores. We were forced to release employees who had served us well for years. In many cases when I let employees go, I tried to ease the pain by giving them a cash incentive of five hundred dollars after they had submitted a plan to set up a small business. That was a princely sum for Somalis in those days—enough for a prudent and resourceful man to open a shop or launch a small business that could support his family.

I could see the handwriting on the wall: the opportunity for us to work anywhere inside Somalia seemed to be coming to an end.

That realization was especially difficult for me to accept. The people in our organization had invested blood, sweat, and tears, with so few tangible results. Certainly, we had eased suffering and saved tens of thousands of lives. But for how long? And to what end? Was Somalia better off now than when we had first arrived?

I honestly didn't know the answer to that question. And my struggle at this point brought me to a profound spiritual crisis. I knew that God had never promised to reward obedient sacrifice with measurable success. At the same time, I wondered why our sacrifices had yielded so little. Maybe, I wondered, there were results that we could not see. Still, these were dark days.

I stubbornly, and perhaps pridefully, resisted giving up and leaving. I feared that leaving would be a way of saying that evil had won. I held tight to the psalmist David's conviction that the weeping and tears might linger for the night, but that joy would come in the morning. Sadly, after six years in Somalia, each morning brought only more tears.

For perhaps the first time in my life, I was dealing with something that I could not fix. Prayer and obedience and hard work and good training and godly intentions and sacrifice—none of it seemed to make a difference. The situation had changed so slowly and so little in Somalia since I had made my first flight into Hargeisa. I wondered if it might take all eternity for God Himself to make things right in Somalia. I am embarrassed to admit it now, but I even wondered if maybe this problem was too big for Him.

Everything in my background told me that if I trained better, worked harder, prayed longer, sacrificed more, and sowed more widely, God would grant an abundant spiritual harvest. But that did not happen in Somalia.

We knew that we had been obedient. We were proud of our team and its hard work. But when I tried to catalogue the results of our efforts—the unfinished business, the shortage of spiritual fruit, all of the things that we couldn't accomplish—doubts and questions filled my mind. Had our efforts been worth the time, the money, and the energy invested? Was this worth the price that we had paid?

There was no way to know, of course, that very soon these hard questions would become even more personal.

16

Death Follows Me Home

Our second son Timothy had battled asthma since he was seven. It typically flared up when we moved and his body had to adjust to a new environment. But he had experienced no serious attacks since we had moved to Nairobi—until a 1996 school trip to Mombasa. He stayed in a damp hotel room where the mold triggered a severe reaction. One of the chaperones on the trip rushed him to a hospital emergency room where the medical staff quickly got his breathing stabilized. When the teachers reported the incident to us after the trip, we immediately followed up with doctors.

The doctor assured us that Tim was recovering fine, but he said that we were right to be concerned. The good news was that Tim's lungs and heart had grown strong from fighting off asthma-causing infections for years. He was now a robust and healthy young man. The bad news was that Tim was so resilient and his body so good at fighting off asthmatic events that, by the time he evidenced serious symptoms from another attack, he might already be on the verge of cardiac arrest.

We took the doctor's warning very seriously. We even stocked up on epinephrine pens that could be used at the first sign of an episode. But there were no further episodes for over a year.

Very early on Easter Sunday morning in 1997, Tim woke Ruth and me up. It was 1:30. By the time he stumbled into our bedroom, Tim was already having such difficulty breathing that he couldn't talk. We had never before used an epinephrine pen, but I immediately stuck one in his thigh. There was no noticeable improvement in his breathing. I gave him a second one. Nothing seemed to change.

I rushed Tim out to the car—leaving Ruth with the other boys—and drove toward the closest emergency room. Halfway to the hospital, Tim went into cardiac arrest.

The dark streets of Nairobi were deserted. I could find no one to help until I spotted a man coming out of a darkened shopping center. I quickly blocked his car with mine and jumped out to explain what was happening. I demanded that he drive my car to the hospital while I climbed into the back seat and frantically administered CPR on my son. Thankfully, Tim's heart began beating almost immediately, and he started breathing again. When we reached the hospital, the medical staff began emergency treatment for Tim. In the meantime, Ruth was making her way to the hospital.

By this point, Tim was unconscious, but breathing. As Ruth, Shane, and some friends began to arrive, we huddled to pray. When we next saw the doctors, their eyes told us what had happened even before they spoke a word.

Tim was gone. He was sixteen years old.

Time stood still as we leaned over the bed to hold him. In that moment, something inside me died. Even in that moment, we were sure about Tim's place in heaven. That reality was a certainty for us. But I was overwhelmed by my own loss. Ruth used the word "resurrection" that night; I was fixed on the crucifixion. The pain was unbearable.

Because there was nothing else to do, we returned to our home and began making calls to our family members in the States to tell them what had happened on this early Easter morning.

Later that morning, we sat with our other sons and talked about what had happened. I said, "We did not choose this horrible thing that has happened. And I don't know how we are going to live through it. But we are going to make sure that we don't waste Tim's death. Somehow, we will do our best to honor God through even this."

Our loved ones in the States were heart-broken, but they were so far away. We knew that they loved us, but it was hard to feel the comfort of family members who were eight thousand miles away. Most of our family members did not even have passports. Ruth's brother, however, began making immediate plans to travel to Nairobi. He would be on a plane the next day.

The sad news spread quickly and triggered a worldwide outpouring of love. Friends who lived close flooded into our home. (Between the day of Tim's death on March 28 and our departure for the United States in June, we did not prepare a single meal for ourselves. Every meal for almost three months was provided by friends and neighbors.)

We could have taken Tim's body home to Kentucky for burial, but we knew that he would have had other wishes. As a high school sophomore, he was already telling us that he didn't want to go back to America for college, but wanted to remain in Africa and become a teacher. Africa was his home.

Knowing that, we decided to bury Tim at his school in Nairobi. It seemed like a miracle when the school administration granted our request and agreed to set aside a little plot of ground. We considered it an even bigger miracle when the government officials approved our request.

The funeral was scheduled for the following Saturday. During that week, our home was filled with people every hour of every day.

Neighbors, Tim's fellow students, colleagues, and friends from our Kenyan church enveloped us in their love and care.

Probably the biggest surprise of the week came on Thursday when Omar Aziz, our senior Somali staff member still living in Mogadishu, appeared at the front door. I was stunned to hear him say: "I have walked here from Somalia. I had to come to help bury *our* son, Timothy."

As soon as he had received word of Tim's death, this dear Muslim friend had started a five-day odyssey. He had walked through minefields, deserts, and mountains. He had crossed rivers and national borders. He had hitched rides and he had ridden on cattle trucks. And he then arrived at our home hundreds of miles later with only the clothes on his back.

I have never been quite so humbled. And I have never seen such a demonstration of friendship.

Omar Aziz would sit between Ruth and me at the funeral.

The funeral took place in the school's outdoor amphitheater. Hundreds of people packed the hillside seating. Much to our surprise, our oldest son sang with his school choir. Ruth's brother, the high school chaplain, and our Kenyan pastor each shared during the service. There were other words of testimony and shared memories from Tim's classmates, friends, and teachers.

The theme of the day was God's love and grace. That clear message was heard by everyone who came: young people from all over Nairobi, our Hindu and Muslim neighbors, shopkeepers from the surrounding community. After the service, we heard a common refrain. People would say to us: "Your son had been talking to us about Jesus" or "Tim befriended our daughter (*or* our son.)" How heartening to discover, after the fact, the witness that Tim had been to so many people!

After the service, we buried Tim's body about fifty meters down the hillside from the amphitheater.

We had been held up by the love and care of friends. God had proven Himself to be faithful. We were confident in His promises. Still, we were empty and broken, crushed by grief and loss. The pain that we had felt for years in Somalia had now come close. From the outside, we probably looked like we were doing fine. Inside, we were in despair.

We began to make plans for a trip to America to rest and visit with family. Before that happened, however, we found ourselves on the receiving end of another distressing eight-thousand-mile phone call. It was Ruth's father telling Ruth that her mother had passed away. Another death. More crucifixion pain. Our sad hearts were even heavier because we couldn't even make it back to America for her funeral.

Before returning to America, I felt the need to make one last trip to Mogadishu to say some good-byes. Omar Aziz met me when I landed. I gathered with the few staff members who were still doing relief work. They knew that, soon, the entire operation would come to an end.

I thanked them for their years of faithful service helping our company help their people. I also thanked them for sending Omar Aziz to us in our time of grief over Tim's death. I described how surprised and moved I had been to see him standing at my door. I told them what comfort and joy his presence had been at the funeral.

Omar took that opportunity to talk about his journey to Kenya.

"There is one thing I don't understand about that funeral," Omar admitted to his Somali friends. "Nik and Ruth buried Timothy—a son who they loved with all their hearts. During the service many people were talking about Tim. People were singing. People were crying. But everyone there seemed *to know* that Tim was in paradise! Why can't we Muslims know that our loved ones are in paradise when they die? Why is it that only these followers of Jesus know exactly where they are going after death? We bury our people. We weep. We walk away. And we do not know where our loved ones are. Why? Why have Jesus' followers kept these things from us?"

His words were a powerful, though perhaps unintended, witness to his own people. But his words were a severe challenge to me. Why, indeed, had Jesus' followers kept such things from Somalis for over two thousand years?

I was concerned that perhaps Omar Aziz had said too much. I feared that perhaps he had gone too far with his words. I was afraid that he too might become a victim of Somali violence, perhaps even at the hands of our own Muslim staff.

Everyone in the room, however, shifted their attention to me, as if waiting for me to answer the question that now hung in the air. *Why **had** Christians ignored Somalia for centuries and kept Jesus to themselves?*

They expected an answer. I didn't have one.

Instead, another question burned in my heart. It was a question for God: *Why, Lord, when we are ending our work here, are their hearts finally ready to ask the right questions?*

I had no answer to that question either. Then it was time to leave.

In those final moments, I told my staff how proud they should be about their years of hard work helping to feed and clothe so many Somali people. I reminded them of how many lives they had saved. Then I said, "I would like to bless you. Would it be alright if I prayed for you?"

They were eager to have that happen. I shared with them the blessing that Moses recorded in the sixth chapter of the book of Numbers, ancient words that seemed especially pertinent for a people in a land not all that different from Old Testament times.

I held out my hands in the manner that Muslims often pray and I offered aloud this benediction for some of my best friends in all the world:

"May the Lord bless you and keep you. May the Lord make His face to shine upon you, and be gracious unto you. May the Lord lift up His countenance upon you, and give you peace. Amen."

On the way to the airport, I talked with Omar Aziz about what he had said about Tim's funeral. I reminded him that he had been dreaming about Tim during his time in Nairobi. Evidently, Tim kept coming to Omar in a dream. When Omar had shared that with me, I had told him the Old Testament story of Samuel and Eli. I told him how the boy kept having a dream that the old priest was calling him. Samuel would get out of bed to find out what Eli needed. Every time, Eli insisted that he hadn't called and he sent Samuel back to bed. Finally, the priest realized that Samuel was actually hearing the voice of the Lord, so he instructed the boy to tell God that he was listening and ready to hear what God would say.

Now, I reminded Omar Aziz again of Samuel's story. I said, "I believe that God has been speaking to you for many years, through a lot of different people, Omar. He is calling you to Jesus. In these difficult days for Somalia, you may be the last and only chance that your people have to find Him."

That was the challenge I left with my friend as we said good-bye.

On the flight back to Nairobi, I wrestled with the doubts that haunted me day and night. *After all the time, the expense, the energy, and the sacrifice expended by so many people, what (if anything) had our years in Somalia really accomplished?*

I thought of the story that Jesus had told about the farmer sowing seed. We had done just that; we had sowed seed. Over thousands of days, through thousands of deeds and thousands of natural spiritual conversations in the context of everyday Somali life, we had cast our seeds far and wide. For six long, hard, dry years we had watched and we had waited. My relationship with Omar Aziz was a reminder that a few individuals might have taken note, that we might have successfully planted a seed here or there. *But how and when could those seeds ever grow? Who would be there to water and tend the field? Who would be there to reap the harvest—if there ever was a harvest?*

As I looked down from the plane, I saw a hostile land consisting mostly of dry, lifeless desert and hard, rocky terrain. *Where is the fertile ground that Jesus talked about in His story? I am so tired of the rocks, the hard ground, the weeds and thistles. Where in Somalia is the good soil? Is there any good soil? Could a seed ever grow here?*

Our souls were weary. It was clear that we were coming to an ending of some kind. There had been so much loss and pain. As we returned to America, the questions would not let me rest.

Was it worth it or not? Aren't those fifty thousand people we fed every day eventually going to die anyway? What could we have done differently? What should we have done differently? Can faith in Jesus survive, let alone thrive, in such a hostile place? And where do we go now and what do we do next?

Tim's death had changed us. After all that we had been through, we wondered if we were still willing to risk ourselves and our family to do what God had called us to do. Honestly, I thought that question had already been settled—but, now, I wasn't sure.

I finally understood how Jesus' disciples must have felt on that dark, despairing Saturday between the cross and the empty tomb. Even in my own dark time, I did not doubt the depth of Jesus' love in His willingness to die for me on the cross. And, even in my dark time, I did not doubt Jesus' resurrection.

But here was my struggle: I couldn't see the relevance or the power of Jesus' resurrection in Somalia. I couldn't point to any evidence of good overcoming evil. I couldn't see where love was overcoming hate.

17

A New Path

We instinctively knew that things were going to be drastically different now. We were painfully aware of how much had changed—and of how much more we had changed. It was a truism, but we understood what it meant to say that we could never really go back home again. Even so, through the grace and care of God's people, our family found a place.

Our alma mater invited Ruth and me to live and serve on campus during our furlough year. That opportunity would put us close to family and provide us with meaningful work. Being on this campus—and being once again with people we loved so dearly—eased our adjustment and aided our healing.

Once again our immediate family benefited from Ruth's God-given people skills. For years in Nairobi, Ruth had made our home a safe haven, a refuge, and a recovery ward for emotionally bruised and battered friends. In the same way, on our old campus, Ruth created the same world—but this time, for us. Soon, a group of committed Christian college students filled our home for times of food, fun and fellowship. Perhaps unknowingly, the students ministered to our entire family in profound ways. The students' energy, love, and passion for Christ healed and helped us.

Over time, I was able to revisit and process some of the experiences, issues, and challenges that I had wrestled with in Somalia. Painfully, I relived vivid memories of dark and discouraging times when I had felt anger, frustration, and despair.

I began to understand that I had often survived the insanity of Somalia by pushing my questions and struggles out of sight. One way to deal with impossible things is simply not to think of them. I realized that I had done that for years. In the moment, there simply wasn't time to figure things out. I guess I suspected that there would be time to do that somewhere in the future. And, now, suddenly—and clearly—I understood that this was that time.

Now in a safe place—and surrounded by loving people—I forced myself to deal with the questions. *Can God truly overcome evil? Is love really more powerful than hate? How can a person maintain even a small hope in a dark place? How is it possible for faith to survive in an insane environment like Somalia's? How can someone live the abundant, victorious life that Jesus promised in our world's hardest places? Can Christianity work outside of western, dressed-up, well-ordered nations? If so, how?*

Once again, I realized how woefully unprepared and ill-equipped Ruth and I had been to try to do what we did in the Horn of Africa. We had landed in Mogadishu, the capital of a militantly Muslim country, in the midst of a brutal civil war without knowing a thing about: (1) living in a setting of persecution, (2) being a witness to people who knew nothing of Jesus and were hostile to the information, or (3) teaching new believers how to survive in a hostile culture. We had never imagined the insanity of evil that we would encounter in Somalia. And we had certainly not been trained to deal with it.

It wasn't that our sending agency had sent us out ignorant and unqualified. The problem was deeper than that. In our local church upbringing, we had never experienced anything that had prepared us for Somalia. The way we learned and grew and matured in our faith would not have prepared anyone for Somalia. It was no comfort for us to realize that we weren't the only ones so unprepared.

Our new family of college students played an invaluable role in our emotional healing and in helping us process the discouragement and despair tied to our memories. We were open with the students about our life stories. They wanted to know more about our sense of calling to make Jesus known overseas—and about how we had felt that calling both as individuals and as a couple. We were honest about our mistakes and our fears, our foolishness and our limitations. We were also honest about God's power to work even in our mistakes. The students were moved when we told them about God's activity in Malawi and South Africa.

Many of these students were seriously considering serving God in some capacity overseas, so we felt compelled to give them a realistic picture of what they might experience. We candidly conveyed the good, the bad, and the ugly side of such a calling. In doing that, we were forced to deal with our own feelings as well.

It was fun to tell them the warm and inspiring stories of missionary success. But we also talked about the insanity of evil, the inhumanity of people, and the pain of failure. We described horrors that had shaken us. We admitted our doubts and our struggles of faith. We challenged them to ask the same hard questions that tormented us: *Was the good news of the gospel powerful enough to overcome the forces of evil in our world's darkest places? And if it was, why had we seen so much crucifixion in Somalia and experienced so little of the resurrection?*

We felt safe enough to be transparent with these college students. We warned them that if they did answer the call to serve God in some other part of the world, there would probably come a time (or many times) when family and friends, and maybe even their home churches, might question their sanity. Sometimes, the questions would be difficult to answer: *"Why go around the world to share Jesus when there are so many lost people here?" "Why risk your life, waste your time, invest your energies, or expend so many personal and Kingdom resources to try to change the minds and hearts of people who don't want to change, and don't even think they need to change?"* We encouraged the students to ask these troubling questions now, in this safe place, before making their decision about God's call.

Those of us who have grown comfortable with the teachings of Christ have allowed His teachings to lose their edge. So much of what Jesus taught makes no sense from a human perspective. *Love your enemies. If you want to be great, first learn to be a servant. If someone smacks you across the face, turn your head and let him slap you on the other side. If someone steals your coat, offer him your shirt as well. If you want to live, you need first to die to yourself.* The complete list of Jesus' crazy-sounding teachings is a lot longer than that.

To me, the most startling thing Jesus ever said was when He assigned His followers the task of going out in pairs to share His good news with lost people. He said that He was sending them "as sheep among wolves." Still, He expected them to prevail. In the history of the world, no sheep has ever won a fight with a wolf. The very idea is insane.

We talked a lot about that with our students. We said that Jesus still calls His followers today to go out and live "as sheep among wolves." We said that we had consciously chosen to do that when we went to Somalia. And we talked about how what we had done there felt completely insane. We also admitted that, at this point, it looked like the wolves had won.

We never felt free to say those kinds of things when we spoke at churches about our work. But that wonderful group of college students gave us the opportunity to be open and honest about our deepest personal struggles.

Ruth and I also shared with them our struggle about our next steps. We wondered if we might be willing to return to Somalia if that became possible. We wondered (out loud) if we would be willing to go again "as sheep among wolves." If that were to happen, however, we didn't want to be *stupid* sheep among wolves! And we certainly didn't want our ignorance, our lack of preparation, or our foolish and unintentional mistakes to endanger other sheep.

We asked our family of college students to pray that the Lord would show us where we should go, who we should talk to, and what we needed to learn in order to be better prepared sheep the next time. During that time, Ruth and I began to seriously explore our future options. We wondered how God would prepare us to be better prepared sheep among wolves.

Ruth and I felt like the disciple Peter when Jesus was ready to set His face toward the danger and death that He knew was waiting in Jerusalem. Many of His fearful followers turned back and deserted him. When Jesus asked the other disciples if they, too, might leave Him, Peter replied, "Where else would we go?"

Ruth and I were captive to the conviction that, if Jesus is not the answer to the human condition, there is no answer.

As we prayed and waited, one thought would not leave our minds. If we wanted to learn how to live in places like Somalia, then we would be wise to visit *places like Somalia*! At this point, it sounds like an obvious conclusion. At the time, however, the thought was startling. Were there other places in the world where believers were forced to live under persecution? Had believers been able to do that? How? How had believers survived brutal hatred and hostility? And, if such people were out there somewhere, would it be possible to find them and learn from them?

As we continued to pray and study, we began to ask questions. We stumbled on a single thought that captured our hearts: *Surely, wherever believers have suffered, and still suffer, for their faith, we could find wise and faithful people who would be willing to share their spiritual survival strategies and other faith lessons learned from the hardship they have faced. Perhaps their personal, practical, tested, biblically-based counsel could help us. And maybe their wisdom could help other believers like us minister more effectively in impossible places such as Somalia. Is it possible that faith might thrive in such places?*

The idea was life-giving. We had no idea, however, how to make it happen. We also had no idea where to start.

Ruth and I didn't have the resources or the wisdom to do this by ourselves. We began to fashion what became a *Persecution Task Force* to advise and partner with us on this endeavor. We soon enlisted an impressive panel of experts—experienced leaders from our own sending agency, former teachers and personal mentors, and missiologists from several different denominations and seminaries. We were thrilled that they were willing to help us develop a plan. We would visit believers who have lived in persecution, sit at their feet, and learn from them.

We began making a list of countries where we thought we would find persecution. We consulted "The World Watch List" issued annually by Brother Andrew's (of *God's Smuggler* fame) organization, Open Doors International. We compared that list with those of other organizations with a special concern for the persecuted church around the world. With the added input of our advisory team, we soon had a target list of forty-five countries where we thought we would find significant persecution of believers.

In some cases, we knew that we might have to find refugees who had already left their countries. But, whenever possible, we wanted to meet and interview believers in their own cultural contexts. We wanted to listen to believers who were, somehow, surviving and thriving in persecution and being salt and light in hard places.

Unable to fund our dream, our sending agency allowed us to take a two-year leave of absence to pursue our project. We maintained our association with the college and began raising funds to support ourselves and to launch an independent research venture. As much as we would want to claim that this new project was our idea, we are certain that is was the gift of God. We were convinced that there were answers out there for our questions. Now, we had a glimmer of an idea where we might find them.

Our task force members helped us develop a research tool that would, hopefully, work cross-culturally to elicit the information that we needed to gather. Ruth and I began planning the first of our research trips. Given the recent collapse of communism in the U.S.S.R. and other Eastern European nations, and the well-documented religious oppression in that part of the world for most of the twentieth century, we concluded that Russia and some of its neighbors might be a logical and productive place to begin.

We began developing a list of potential contacts in Russia and neighboring countries. We wrote letters, made phone calls, sent e-mails and quickly collected a list of the names of people who could or might talk to me, or at least find people who would. We discovered someone who I had never met who agreed to host me in Russia and another stranger who was willing to serve as my interpreter. Ruth finalized my itinerary, purchased my plane tickets, and applied for the necessary permits for me to visit a half dozen former Iron Curtain countries.

18

Seeking Answers in the USSR

I had never visited a communist country or a former-communist country. I had no idea what to expect in Russia. For the past fifteen years, I had lived in a culture where, simply because of my skin color, I was automatically identified as "an outsider." Oddly, I felt as conspicuous in Moscow as I had felt in Nairobi or Mogadishu.

My *differentness* struck me in Russia the moment I exited the plane. The Moscow airport was no larger and only slightly more "modern" than some major African airports that I had seen, but the feel of the place was coldly impersonal, institutional, and lacking in what I had come to know as African hospitality.

The calendar indicated that it was July, but the weather was gray and cold, just like the airport. The downtown tourist hotel felt no different. I felt even more unsettled when I left the hotel and walked through the city's central business and government district, past the Kremlin and through Red Square. I was unable to make eye contact with a single person; no one would look me in the eye. I realized that what made me different was not the color of my skin, but the colors covering my skin! My clothing was ordinary and plain, but it stood out in contrast to the browns and grays that everyone else wore.

It seemed that everyone was aware of me. Rather than staring openly, however, they glanced at me furtively out of the corner of their eyes. The instinctive wariness of the people seemed to me more symptomatic of a worn and weary sadness of soul than any real hostility. However, that first exposure to the psyche of the Russian public made me wonder what, if anything, I would learn from my interviews which were scheduled for the following day.

Because I was unfamiliar with both subways and Russian signs, my cross-town journey the next morning was an adventure. Somehow, I managed to find my way to my appointment at the national church headquarters for one of Russia's largest protestant denominations. The western worker who had been my contact had arranged for me to meet with several Russian believers. He had also promised to be my translator. At the last minute, I was told that, due to a medical emergency, there had been a change in plans. I was entrusted to the capable care and translation assistance of Viktor, an older Russian pastor who had been a national leader in this same denomination prior to his retirement.

Viktor introduced me to several denominational leaders who briefly greeted and welcomed me. Then he and I began to interview two believers who had been invited there. I was interested in their personal lives and wanted to learn how decades of communist rule had affected their lives as followers of Jesus.

In an effort to establish rapport, I shared some of my own faith journey. I briefly talked about my sense of God's call. I shared about making a commitment to serve in Africa, and briefly described my time in Malawi, South Africa, and Somalia. I explained how the persecution in Somalia had been so severe that an entire generation of believers had been killed or forced from the country. I sadly noted that we had no idea how to help believers grow in that kind of environment. And, then, I concluded my story by telling them that we had seen many believers die because of their faith. I confessed our discouragement and sadness about returning to America.

"So," I explained, "I have come to Russia to learn from believers who have served Christ in difficult circumstances. I want to learn spiritual lessons from you. I want to know how you have survived and grown and shared your faith. I want to learn from your experience and wisdom."

At that point, the two men began to talk. These first two interviews lasted the entire day. The men talked about the systemic persecution that the communist government and Russian society had inflicted on believers for almost eight decades of the twentieth century. The men recounted their own experiences and they told the stories of other believers and family members.

Both men had grown up in families where the grandparents had been active and committed church people before the revolution. With official sanction, the communist youth organizations and the educational system worked to alienate children from their believing parents and grandparents. In school, the men explained, teachers would hold up a Bible and ask kindergarten students if they had ever seen a book like this one in their homes. If the children said that they had, a local party official would pay a visit to the home before the children even finished school that day.

The men talked about pastors and lay people who were imprisoned—and family members who disappeared in the Soviet Gulag never to be heard from again. When I asked what had enabled them to maintain their faith through years of hardship and persecution, I heard stories of family members whose examples had inspired the community of faith. I heard other sad tales of people who had compromised and recanted their beliefs.

The government required pastors to show up once a week for an appointment with a designated party official (or "minder") who would ask for information on visitors and anything else of note that might have happened the previous week. Sermon topics had to be approved, and eventually officials would offer "suggestions" about all manner of church activities. Church leaders who were willing to make compromises—small ones at first, but bigger and bigger concessions over time—were sometimes allowed to keep their positions, continue their weekly services, and stay in the government's good graces. Those who weren't so "cooperative" were typically replaced by a more compliant clergyman of the party's choosing. Sometimes churches were simply shut down and the leaders disappeared.

It was a productive and informative first day. All of my questions had been answered. Beyond my questions, I heard words that were even more helpful when I stopped asking questions and simply asked the men to tell me about their families, their lives, and their own personal spiritual journeys. Viktor and I both were already looking forward to coming back the following morning for another round of interviews.

When we arrived the next day, we were asked to take a seat in the lobby of the building. There, we waited. For a long time, we waited. No one invited us into the office. No one brought us tea. Viktor, at first, apologized for the delay. The longer we sat there, however, the more agitated he became. "I don't know what is happening!" he told me.

I had a sneaking suspicion that I did.

Finally a receptionist came into the lobby to inform us that I would not be allowed to complete any more interviews. I was told that I was no longer welcome in their headquarters and that we needed to leave the building immediately.

As word went around the denominational headquarters that we had been ordered to leave the building, the people who had been scheduled to talk with us that day became so upset that they called Viktor and offered to meet with me outside the office, in secret, despite their superiors' orders. Even some who had been reluctant to meet with us before suddenly wanted to meet now. The next morning, before dawn, we found ourselves in an apartment. The man wanted to have his interview before leaving for work in the morning. We were interviewing other people long after mid-night. My original trickle of pre-arranged interviews became a flood.

The reason that our welcome in the denominational headquarters had been rescinded became quickly clear. I had made no secret of my motives and intentions: I wanted to discover if, and how, faith was affected by persecution. Those first two interviews had taken place in offices with the doors open. People walked freely in the hallway while we talked. If they had wanted to stop and listen, they could have. Evidently, when some of the leaders heard both my questions and the answers that were being offered, they had serious reservations about what we were doing.

According to my first secret interview (and this was later confirmed by Viktor and other interviews), several of the denominational leaders were currently engaged in negotiations with the new, post-communist Russian government for the return of church buildings and property that the old communist regime had confiscated. They were also pressing their case for financial restitution, as well as the same kind of annual support from the government that the Russian Orthodox Church received.

Because some of the new government officials had also been part of the old communist system, the church leaders evidently didn't want to do anything that might negatively affect their bargaining position. Even after the fall of communism, it was evidently not safe to talk openly about faith and religious persecution.

A sense of righteous anger began to surface in the interviews that followed: "For decades," several people said, "our government tried to prevent us from practicing our faith. Now our own church leaders want us to keep quiet! At least with the communists, the motive was clearly spiritual oppression. This issue now is all about money and finances. If we let that silence us, we should be truly ashamed."

n't know the exact reason, but those "secret" interviews felt nd were much more informative, than the ones that we had been permitted to do at the denominational headquarters. The subjects opened up and talked about how they, and many other known believers, were automatically suspected of disloyalty. They claimed that, especially during the years of President Jimmy Carter's administration, Russian believers, and particularly Baptists, were assumed to be spies for the American president whom the whole world knew was a born-again Baptist. Believers in the Soviet military found it hard, if not impossible, to earn promotions. And Russian Baptists, during the Carter years, were given only the lowliest, most mundane military tasks.

Pastors and church lay leaders were arrested and imprisoned. Their wives were pressured to divorce them; children were discouraged from writing to their imprisoned fathers. The sons and daughters of known believers would be kept after school to be questioned and badgered by a panel of teachers who denigrated the family's faith. Sometimes children were called up in front of school-wide assemblies and publicly ridiculed by both school officials and classmates for their family's "backward, traitorous and anti-communist beliefs." Unless they denounced their parents' religion, most young people from believing homes were not admitted to the university and were allowed to pursue only the most menial jobs or careers. The strategy of the government was clear: it would do anything to keep faith in Jesus from continuing beyond the current generation. Their biggest concern was the genealogy of faith.

By the time we finished several fourteen-hour-days of interviews, I was amazed that any believers had maintained their faith in the former USSR. The opposition was relentless. The fact that so many had both survived and remained strong and faithful moved me deeply.

Viktor began to embrace my mission as his own. He said, "Other people from the headquarters want to talk with you, but I think tomorrow there is someone I want you to meet. I don't know him well myself, but I know something of his testimony. He suffered much for his faith. And I think you need to hear his story!" Intrigued, I quickly agreed to be ready at five o'clock the next morning to meet Viktor and a friend of his with a car, "because this brother," he said, "lives many kilometers from Moscow."

Before we parted for the evening, I told Viktor that I had seen evidence that someone had been in my hotel room while I was gone the day before. I felt certain that someone had searched my room.

Victor looked at me, glanced around to see that no one was listening, and then nodded. "No doubt that happens with most foreigners," he said softly. "And that is one reason why we will never do any of these interviews here at the hotel."

Early the next morning, Viktor and his friend picked me up. We began a four-hour drive through the countryside north of Moscow. On the way, Viktor told me what he knew about Dmitri, this fellow believer who had suffered much for the faith. For the rest of the trip I listened to Viktor and his friend recount their faith journeys and life stories.

We finally arrived at a small Russian village and stopped in front of a tiny dwelling. Dmitri opened the door and graciously welcomed us into his tiny home. "I want you to sit here," he instructed me. "This was where I was sitting when the authorities came to arrest me and send me to prison for seventeen years."

I settled in and listened with rapt attention as Dmitri related his unforgettable personal story over the next few hours.

Dmitri told me that he had been born and raised in a believing family; his parents had taken him to church as a child. Over the decades, he explained, communism slowly destroyed most of the churches and places of worship. Many pastors were imprisoned or killed.

By the time he was grown, Dmitri told me, the nearest remaining church building was a three-day-walk away. It was impossible for his family to attend church more than once or twice a year.

"One day," Dmitri told me, "I said to my wife: 'You'll probably think that I am insane . . . I know that I have no religious training whatsoever, but I am concerned that our sons are growing up without learning about Jesus. This may sound like a crazy idea . . . but what would you think if just one night a week we gathered the boys together so I could read them a Bible story and try to give them a little of the training they are missing because we no longer have a real church?'"

What Dmitri didn't know was that his wife had been praying for years that her husband would do something like that. She readily embraced his idea. He started teaching his family one night a week. Dmitri would read from the old family Bible. Then he would try to explain what he had just read so that his children could understand.

As he relearned and retold the Bible stories, his sons soon began helping with the task. Eventually, the boys and Dmitri and his wife were telling the familiar stories back and forth to each other. The more they learned, the more the children seemed to enjoy their family worship time.

Eventually the boys started asking for more: "Papa, can we sing those songs that they sing when we go to the real church?" So Dmitri and his wife taught them the traditional songs of their faith.

It seemed a natural progression for the family not only to read the Bible and sing, but also to take time together to pray. And they began to do that.

Nothing could be hidden for long in small villages. Houses were close together and windows were often open. Neighbors began noticing what was going on with Dmitri's family. Some of them asked if they could come and listen to the Bible stories and sing the familiar songs.

Dmitri protested that he was not trained to do this; he wasn't a minister. His excuse didn't seem to dissuade his neighbors, and a small group began gathering to share in the reading and telling and discussing of Bible stories and to sing and pray together.

By the time the little group grew to twenty-five people, the authorities had noticed. Local party officials came to see Dmitri. They threatened him physically, which was to be expected. What upset Dmitri much more was their accusation: "You have started an illegal church!"

"How can you say that?" he argued. "I have no religious training. I am not a pastor. This is not a church building. We are just a group of family and friends getting together. All we are doing is reading and talking about the Bible, singing, praying, and sometimes sharing what money we have to help out a poor neighbor. How can you call that a church?"

(I almost laughed at the irony of his claim. But this was early in my pilgrimage. I could not easily appreciate the truth that he was sharing. Looking back now, I understand that one of the most accurate ways to detect and measure the activity of God is to note the amount of opposition that is present. *The stronger the persecution, the more significant the spiritual vitality of the believers.* Surprisingly, all too often, persecutors sense the activity of God before the believing participants even realize the significance of what is happening! In the case of Dmitri, the officials could sense the threat of what he was doing long before it even crossed his mind.)

The communist official told Dmitri: "We don't care what you call it, but this looks like church to us. And if you don't stop it, bad things are going to happen."

When the group grew to fifty people, the authorities made good on their threats. "I got fired from my factory job," Dmitri recounted. "My wife lost her teaching position. My boys were expelled from school."

"And," he added, "*little* things like that."

When the number of people grew to seventy-five, there was no place for everyone to sit. Villagers stood shoulder-to-shoulder, cheek-to-cheek inside the house. They pressed close-in around the windows on the outside so they could listen as this man of God led the people of God in worship. Then one night as Dmitri spoke (sitting in the chair where I was now seated), the door to his house suddenly, violently burst open. An officer and soldiers pushed through the crowd. The officer grabbed Dmitri by the shirt, slapped him rhythmically back and forth across the face, slammed him against the wall, and said in a cold voice: "We have warned you, and warned you, and warned you. I will not warn you again! If you do not stop this nonsense, this is the least that is going to happen to you."

As the officer pushed his way back toward the door, a small grandmother took her life in her hands, stepped out of the anonymity of that worshiping community, and waved a finger in the officer's face. Sounding like an Old Testament prophet, she declared, "You have laid hands on a man of God and you will NOT survive!"

That happened on a Tuesday evening—and on Thursday night the officer dropped dead of a heart attack. The fear of God swept through the community. At the next house-church service, more than one hundred and fifty people showed up. The authorities couldn't let this continue, so Dmitri went to jail for seventeen years.

I knew, because Dmitri was sitting right in front of me in his own home, that this particular persecution story was ultimately a story of survival and victory. This story would obviously have a happy ending. But that didn't mean that the story was going to be "nice" or easy to hear.

Indeed, it was a painful story. Dmitri spoke quietly of long, heart-wrenching separation. He spoke of sweat, blood, and tears. He talked about sons growing up without their father in the house. He described a poor, struggling family enduring great hardship. This was not the kind of inspirational testimony that we love to celebrate; this was raw, biblical faith. This was the story of one man who refused to let go of Jesus and refused to stop telling the Good News to his family and neighbors.

As if that was not enough, the rest of Dmitri's story would be one of the most remarkable and life-changing testimonies I have ever heard. . .

19

A Prison Sings

The authorities moved Dmitri a thousand kilometers away from his family and locked him in a prison. His cell was so tiny that when he got out of bed, it took but a single step either to get to the door of his cell, to reach the stained and cracked sink mounted on the opposite wall, or to use the foul, open toilet in the "far" corner of the cell. Even worse, according to Dmitri, he was the only believer among fifteen hundred hardened criminals.

He said that his isolation from the Body of Christ was more difficult than even the physical torture. And there was much of that. Still, his tormentors were unable to break him. Dmitri pointed to two reasons for his strength in the face of torture. There were two spiritual habits that he had learned from his father, disciplines that Dmitri had taken with him into prison. Without these two disciplines, Dmitri insisted, his faith would have not survived.

For seventeen years in prison, every morning at daybreak, Dmitri would stand at attention by his bed. As was his custom, he would face the east, raise his arms in praise to God, and then he would sing a HeartSong™ to Jesus. The reaction of the other prisoners was predictable. Dmitri recounted the laughter, the cursing, the jeers. The other prisoners banged metals cups against the iron bars in angry protest. They threw food and sometimes human waste to try to shut him up and extinguish the only true light shining in that dark place every morning at dawn.

There was another discipline too, another custom that Dmitri told me about. Whenever he found a scrap of paper in the prison, he would sneak it back to his cell. There he would pull out a stub of a pencil or a tiny piece of charcoal that he had saved, and he would write on that scrap of paper, as tiny as he could, all the Bible verses and scriptural stories or songs that he could remember. When the scrap was completely filled, he would walk to the corner of his little jail cell where there was a concrete pillar that constantly dripped water—except in the wintertime when the moisture became a solid coat of ice on the inside surface of his cell. Dmitri would take the paper fragment, reach as high as he possibly could, and stick it on that damp pillar as a praise offering to God.

Of course, whenever one of his jailors spotted a piece of paper on the pillar, he would come into his cell, take it down, read it, beat Dmitri severely, and threaten him with death. Still, Dmitri refused to stop his two disciplines.

Every day, he rose at dawn to sing his song. And every time he found a scrap of paper, he filled it with Scripture and praise.

This went on year after year after year. His guards tried to make him stop. The authorities did unspeakable things to his family. At one point, they even led him to believe that his wife had been murdered and that his children had been taken by the state.

They taunted him cruelly, "We have ruined your home. Your family is gone."

Dmitri's resolve finally broke. He told God that he could not take any more. He admitted to his guards, "You win! I will sign any confession that you want me to sign. I must get out of here to find out where my children are."

They told Dmitri, "We will prepare your confession tonight, and then you will sign it tomorrow. Then you will be free to go." After all those years, the only thing that he had to do was sign his name on a document saying that he was not a believer in Jesus and that he was a paid agent of western governments trying to destroy the USSR. Once he put his signature on that dotted line, he would be free to go.

Dmitri repeated his intention: "Bring it tomorrow and I will sign it!"

That very night he sat on his jail cell bed. He was in deep despair, grieving the fact that he had given up. At that same moment, a thousand kilometers away his family—Dmitri's wife, his children who were growing up without him, and his brother—sensed through the Holy Spirit the despair of this man in prison. His loved ones gathered around the very place where I was sitting as Dmitri told me his story. They knelt in a circle and began to pray out loud for him. Miraculously, the Holy Spirit of the Living God allowed Dmitri to hear the voices of his loved ones as they prayed.

The next morning, when the guards marched into his cell with the documents, Dmitri's back was straight. His shoulders were squared and there was strength on his face and in his eyes. He looked at his captors and declared, "I am not signing anything!"

The guards were incredulous. They had thought that he was beaten and destroyed. "What happened?" they demanded to know.

Dmitri smiled and told them, "In the night, God let me hear the voices of my wife and my children and my brother praying for me. You lied to me! I now know that my wife is alive and physically well. I know that my sons are with her. I also know that they are all still in Christ. So I am not signing anything!"

His persecutors continued to discourage and silence him. Dmitri remained faithful. He was overwhelmed one day by a special gift from

God's hand. In the prison yard, he found a whole sheet of paper. "And God," Dmitri said, "had laid a pencil beside it!"

Dmitri went on, "I rushed back to my jail cell and I wrote every Scripture reference, every Bible verse, every story, and every song I could recall."

"I knew that it was probably foolish," Dmitri told me, "but I couldn't help myself. I filled both sides of the paper with as much of the Bible as I could. I reached up and stuck the entire sheet of paper on that wet concrete pillar. Then I stood and looked at it: to me it seemed like the greatest offering I could give Jesus from my prison cell. Of course, my jailor saw it. I was beaten and punished. I was threatened with execution."

Dmitri was dragged from his cell. As he was dragged down the corridor in the center of the prison, the strangest thing happened. Before they reached the door leading to the courtyard—before stepping out into the place of execution—fifteen hundred hardened criminals stood at attention by their beds. They faced the east and they began to sing. Dmitri told me that it sounded to him like the greatest choir in all of human history. Fifteen hundred criminals raised their arms and began to sing the HeartSong that they had heard Dmitri sing to Jesus every morning for all of those years.

Dmitri's jailers instantly released their hold on his arms and stepped away from him in terror.

One of them demanded to know, "Who are you?" Dmitri straightened his back and stood as tall and as proud as he could.

He responded: "I am a son of the Living God, and Jesus is His name!"

The guards returned him to his cell. Sometime later, Dmitri was released and he returned to his family.

Now many years later, I listened as Dmitri told his story of his own unspeakable suffering and God's steady faithfulness. I found myself thinking of a time in Somalia when I envisioned creating some discipleship materials that might help believers in places of persecution, believers like Dmitri. What a ridiculous idea that seemed now. *What could I possibly ever teach this man about following Jesus? Absolutely nothing!*

I was overwhelmed by what I had just heard. I held my head in my hands. I cried out in my heart: *Oh God, What do I do with a story like this? I have always known of your power—but I have never seen your power on display like this!*

Lost in my own thoughts, I realized that Dmitri was still speaking. "Oh, I'm sorry," I apologized, "I wasn't listening!"

Dmitri dismissed my concern with a small shake of his head and a wry smile. "That's okay," he told me. "I wasn't talking to you." He went on to explain, "When you arrived this morning, God and I were discussing something; your visit interrupted that. So right now, when I saw that you were busy with your own thoughts, the Lord and I went back to finishing that conversation."

In that moment, I knew what I had to ask next.

"Brother Dmitri, would you do something for me?" I asked. I hesitated to continue, but his eyes moved me forward: "Would you sing that song for me?"

Dmitri pushed himself up from the table. He stared into my eyes for three or four seconds. Those seconds felt like an eternity to me. He turned slowly toward the east. He stiffened his back to stand at attention. He lifted his arms and began to sing.

I don't know Russian, so I didn't understand a single word of his song. But I didn't need to. The words probably didn't matter. As Dmitri raised his arms and his voice in praise and sang that song that he had sung every morning in prison for seventeen years, the tears began to flow down both of our faces. Only then did I begin to grasp the meaning of worship and the importance of HeartSongs.

I had come to Russia looking for answers—wondering if faith could survive and even grow in the world's most hostile environments.

Dmitri became one of my first guides on my journey. *I began to sense that this journey was not about developing discipleship materials, but about walking with Jesus in hard places. I felt drawn to this life that Dmitri had lived: knowing Jesus, loving Jesus, following Jesus, living with Jesus.*

I met many other believers on that trip to Russia. Hearing Dmitri's story must have inspired Viktor too. He became almost feverish in networking and finding other people who we needed to talk to—unearthing stories that we needed to hear.

After years of discouragement over the lostness of Somalia, these Russian stories of spiritual endurance in the face of persecution filled me with a sense of hope. That budding hope took me completely by surprise.

One morning Viktor arranged for me to meet with a group of his friends—several Russian pastors, some evangelists and church planters, and some elders—a cross section of his church. I listened in wonder as these believers almost casually recounted being sent to prison for "five years," "three years," or "seven years" and being "beaten," "forced to sleep naked in a cold, damp cell" or "having nothing but moldy bread and boiled cabbage to eat for months." These same men shared joyful memories of "the time when my wife and son visited me in prison," "when I was placed in a cell with another believer who could encourage me as I encouraged him," and "how the church cared for the needs of my family while I was in prison."

When we stopped to eat lunch, I gently scolded the group, saying: "Your stories are amazing. Why haven't they been written down? Your stories sound like Bible stories come to life! I can't believe that you haven't collected them in a book, or recorded them in some video form. Other followers of Jesus around the world could hear your stories and be encouraged by what God is doing here among those who are persecuted."

They seemed confused by what I was saying. Clearly, we were not understanding each other. Then one of older pastors stood and motioned for me to follow him. He led me over to a large window in the front room of the home. As we stood together in front of the window, the old gentleman speaking passable, but heavily accented, English said to me: "I understand that you have some sons, Nik. Is that true?"

I told him that it was true. He nodded and then asked me, "Tell me, Nik. How many times have you awakened your sons before dawn and brought them to a window like this one, one that faces east, and said to them, 'Boys, watch carefully. This morning you're going to see the sun coming up in the east! It's going to happen in just a few more minutes. Get ready now, boys.' How many times have you done that with your sons?"

"Well," I chuckled, "I've never done that. If I ever did that, my boys would think I was crazy. The sun *always* comes up in the east. It happens every morning!"

The old man nodded and smiled. I didn't understand his point.

I didn't understand his point, that is, until he continued: "Nik, that's why we haven't made books and movies out of these stories that you have been hearing. For us, persecution is like the sun coming up in the east. It happens all the time. It's the way things are. There is nothing unusual or unexpected about it. Persecution for our faith has always been—and probably always will be—a normal part of life."

His words took my breath away. Though I understood what he was saying, I wondered if it was true. Certainly, I had never heard this before. In fact, there was a part of me that wanted to object to his claim. I wondered if the certainty of persecution meant that evil had the upper hand. And, then, I wondered if it was insane to believe that faith could actually flourish where persecution always is normal and ordinary, like "the sun coming up in the east."

I had always assumed that persecution was abnormal, exceptional, unusual, out of the ordinary. In my mind, persecution was something to avoid. It was a problem, a setback, a barrier. I was captivated by the thought: what if persecution is the normal, expected situation for a believer? And what if the persecution is, in fact, soil in which faith can grow? What if persecution can be, in fact, good soil?

I began to wonder about what that might mean for the church in America—and I began to wonder about what that might mean for the potential church in Somalia.

20

The Genealogy of Faith

I heard more stories in Russia. For example, I was told about an incident that happened in the early 1950's when three charismatic pastors were organizing house churches. While they were experiencing exciting growth in the larger movement and regularly adding new house churches, each individual house-church "congregation" consisted of the same ten or twenty people week after week, year after year. For security reasons, many of the house churches consisted entirely of people who were related to one another and were, therefore, known well enough to be trusted.

In that setting, I imagined how teenagers or young adults might understand the church and the Body of Christ. Their entire faith experience had been defined by a lifetime of weekly worship in the front room of the house with mom and dad and a few other relatives. In their eyes, that was church. There was no awareness of a larger Kingdom of God, no knowledge of what God was doing in other house churches—or even in other countries. These young people were surely in need of spiritual peers and a larger sense of community, but they likely felt isolated, lonely, and discouraged.

The three pastors who were helping to lead this movement realized what was happening, and they decided to try something. They came up with a very bold (some people would say *foolish*) idea. They planned and organized a youth congress in Moscow and invited all of the young, unmarried members of their various house churches—from eighteen to thirty years of age—to meet and encourage one another. They hoped that there would be some spiritual cross-pollination between the different house-church groups and that these younger believers might learn what God was doing on a broader stage.

What some people judged to be "foolish" about the idea was thinking that a week-long meeting of almost seven hundred young believers in Russia during the early 1950's could possibly escape the notice of the communist government. Sure enough, the authorities did take notice. When the event was over, all three organizing pastors were arrested and sentenced to prison for three years each.

The people who were now telling me the story claimed that the pastors would have eagerly suffered the same punishment over and over again, because, as they explained it, "The Holy Spirit fell on that conference."

The primary purpose in bringing the young people together was to gather the scattered parts of the Body of Christ in one place. The goal was to hear what God was doing with other people and to simply enjoy the experience of Christian community. At the beginning of the conference—evidently without much forethought or planning—the young people were given an interesting challenge. None of them had owned a Bible. They had never had hymnbooks or songbooks or recordings of religious music. So, in an off-handed way, the three pastors decided to determine how much Bible truth was present in that group of young people.

They said, "This will be like a game. Every day this week, we want you to gather in small groups. And we want to see how much of the four New Testament Gospels—Matthew, Mark, Luke, and John—you know and have memorized. In your groups, see how much of the Gospels you can recreate. And then do the same thing with songs and hymns. Let's see how much of that can be reproduced by memory."

At the end of the conference, when they compared and combined the efforts of all the different small groups, the young people had recreated all of Matthew, Mark, Luke and John with only a half-dozen mistakes. They had also recreated the lyrics of more than twelve hundred songs, choruses, and hymns of the faith from memory.

It became clear to me in an instant why and how the Christian faith had survived and often thrived under decades of communist oppression in the Soviet Union. I also understood what had enabled so many Russian believers to remain strong and faithful.

On the day I heard the story about that conference, I was able to visit with some young people. The younger ones were excited about the chance to meet a real, live American; they wanted to practice their English language skills. Many of these young people were the grandchildren of the pastors who had been telling me the stories from those earlier days. I asked the grandchildren of the men who had so proudly told me how much Scripture and how many lyrics the young people in the house churches had been able to reproduce back in 1950's: "Tell me, how much Bible do the young people in your churches know today?"

They looked at each other and rather sheepishly admitted, "Not much."

I didn't want to put them on the spot or embarrass them by asking how much of Matthew, Mark, Luke, and John they might be able to quote. So I asked them how many different stories from the Gospels they could think of and list. They came up with a handful.

"How many books of the Bible can you name?" I asked.

"Only a few," they said.

I don't know if those young people were embarrassed by their responses to my questions. I did see, however, what the Russian church had lost in its first decade of "freedom." Under communism, the church had found a way to survive and often thrive. Scripture and holy song was its lifeblood. Now, in a much freer day for the church, Scripture and holy song did not seem nearly as important. This coda to the earlier story was sobering and sad.

Many of the stories that I heard in Russia celebrated God's faithfulness and provision.

One pastor was arrested and placed in prison, while his wife and children were sent to live (or die) in Siberia.

One wintry night in their remote, dilapidated wooden cabin which now served as their home, the three children divided their family's last crust of bread, and drank the last cup of tea in the house before climbing into bed still hungry. Kneeling to say their prayers, they asked, "Where are we going to get some more food, Mama? We're hungry! Do you think Papa even knows where we live now?" Their mother assured them their *heavenly* Father knew where they lived. For now, He was the one who would have to provide. They prayed and asked for God's provision.

Thirty kilometers away, in the middle of the night, God woke up the deacon of a church and instructed him, "Get out of bed. Harness your horse, hitch the horse to the sled, load up all the extra vegetables that the church has harvested, the meat, and the other food that the congregation has collected, and take it to that pastor's family living outside the village. They are hungry!"

The deacon said, "But, Lord, I can't do that! It's below zero outside. My horse might freeze and I might freeze!"

The Holy Spirit told him, "You must go! The pastor's family is in trouble!"

The man argued, "Lord, you've got to know that there are wolves everywhere. They could eat my horse and if they do, they'll then eat me! I'll never make it back."

But the deacon said that the Holy Spirit told him, "You don't have to come back. You just have to go."

So he did.

When he knocked loudly on the door of that rickety cabin in the pre-dawn darkness the next morning, the banging must have terrified the mother and her children. But imagine their joy and amazement when they fearfully, hesitantly opened the cabin door to find one very small, very cold member of the Body of Christ standing on their front step. His food-laden sleigh was behind him. He held a huge sack and announced, "Our church collected this food for you. Be fed. When this runs out, I'll bring more."

Long after I heard that story, I kept thinking about God's final instruction to the deacon: *"You just have to go."*

You don't have to come back. You just have to go.

As it turns out, he did come back. Even so, the instruction is so clear. *You just have to go. You just have to go. Even if there is no clarity about your return, you just have to go.*

The memory of that deacon's courageous obedience lives on in his story. The story has been told by his family for generations. And the story is also told by the extended family of those who were saved by his gift. The story celebrates one man's obedience and God's miraculous provision.

Viktor took me to meet Katya on one of my last days in Russia. Based on the records she had, the events that she described took place in 1917.

Katya said that she was seven years old when her protestant pastor grandfather received one day's notice that the police were going to arrest him and lock him up. He used what little time he had to get his affairs in order and to bury the family Bible in the field behind his house. His hope was that the authorities would not be able to confiscate the Bible when they took him into custody. It didn't seem to me that Katya personally witnessed the arrest or saw the police take her grandfather away to jail.

Several weeks later, his family was granted permission to come and bring the old pastor clothes, food and money to last him through the harsh winter. Katya described how "armed guards watched carefully as brothers, sisters, children, and grandchildren lined up to say good-bye to this man of God through the barbed-wire fence."

I interrupted her to ask: "Have you ever told this entire story about your grandfather to your family?"

She told me that she didn't think she had. I then suggested: "Before we go on, call your daughter and your son-in-law in from the kitchen and call your grandchildren in from outdoors."

I had been hearing these life-changing stories long enough by that point to recognize that this was a special opportunity. "Your family needs to hear this story," I told her, "from the time you were born, about your grandfather, about your life and your faith over the years. So let's just let your family sit in here with us and listen as you and I talk."

She was living on a small pension and was pleased when I offered to send one of the children to the shop for tea bags, sugar, milk and cookies.

Soon, after we had all had a cup of tea and some cookies, Katya's four grandchildren and their parents filed in and sat on the floor of the little parlor room. I asked Grandmother Katya to start over from the beginning. As she talked, I found myself paying as much attention to her family's reactions as I did to the old woman's story.

She told again of her own grandfather's arrest and imprisonment, the family's visit to the prison camp, the armed guards, the family lining up at the fence to say their good-byes. Katya went on to say, "When I carefully reached my little hand between the sharp strands of the fence to touch my grandfather, I did not know that I would never see him again."

She said that none of the family could have imagined that he would be martyred two weeks later. But they know that he was.

Katya had been given copies of the official police and prison reports. She unfolded those documents and passed them around for us to examine.

Katya remembered that the last person at the fence was her grandmother. When the old woman's hands touched her husband's hands for the final time, Katya's grandmother felt a little piece of folded paper which she clenched tightly in her fingers and quickly slid into one of her pockets out of sight.

In the privacy of her own home, Katya's grandmother pulled the message out of her pocket. The note explained where Grandfather had buried the family Bible. It also instructed her to dig it up, gather the extended family together, and read the pages that he had written, folded, and hidden inside the Bible's front cover. That's what Katya's grandmother did. "There must have been thirty family members all together," Katya told us, "as my grandmother opened the Bible, unfolded the paper that Grandfather had left there, and read his last message to us all."

Katya described her grandfather's letter as sort of a spiritual last will and testament to the family. "And the very final thing he wrote at the end of his letter," said Katya, "his very last message to the family was that we should all read and forever remember Revelation 2:10—here's what I require of you, that you should 'be faithful unto death.'"

Seventy years later, not only did Katya clearly recall her grandfather's final words, she told us that other people in her community still approach her on the street to remember her pastor grandfather, to tell her how much they admired him, and to thank Katya and her family for his example of faith that is still honored and talked about all these years later.

As Katya finished her story, I watched her daughter and son-in-law get up and embrace her. Her daughter said, "Oh, Mama, we never knew all that." The grandchildren crowded around to hug Katya's neck and kiss her cheeks and tell her how brave she was as a little girl.

Being a part of that special family scene was an especially holy moment for me. I felt that I had just witnessed the genealogy of faith that Katya's grandfather had provided for her seventy years earlier. It was now being passed on to strengthen the faith in that family's fourth and fifth generations.

The Moscow airport didn't feel any warmer when I left the city than it had when I arrived. Most of the Russians I passed still had that tired, down-trodden look. They still lowered their gaze and avoided eye contact.

But my own heart was encouraged. I don't know that I would have been able to explain why at the time. Looking back now, I know that my time in Russia—and my time with the believers that I had met—had changed me. Or, at least, my experiences there had started to change me.

I realized that it would take a lifetime to process what I had heard, to connect the dots, and even to begin to understand what I had learned. I had started my trip with a long list of carefully-formulated questions that I intended to ask. By the time I met Dmitri—my fifth interview—I realized that my questions were not the key to what I was seeking.

I wouldn't find the truth I was searching for in the simple, direct responses to my precisely-worded questions. The wisdom, the guidance, and the insights had come beautifully gift-wrapped in layers of narrative and personal stories that believers had shared with me before and after I asked my questions.

I had arrived in Moscow with great anticipation and much uncertainty.

I left feeling sure of one thing: that I was on the right track, even as I realized that my journey had just begun.

My next stop was the Ukraine, a place that would turn out to be as different from Russia as spring is from winter.

21

Learning to Live; Learning to Die

The spirit of the Ukrainian people was such a contrast to what I had seen in Russia that I noticed the difference as soon as I deplaned in Kiev. The people working in the airport and in the hotel were openly gracious and helpful. Where the Russian people had seemed shackled to a past that they weren't certain was gone for good, the Ukrainians that I met seemed to relish a newfound sense of freedom with high hopes for a better future. They walked with heads up and a spring in their step. They made eye contact and smiled when I passed them on the streets. The people I interviewed weren't just willing, but rather anxious, to tell me about the impact of communism on their faith and to share their renewed hopes and dreams for the future.

One of the first Ukrainian believers I talked with was a pastor in his late fifties, a national leader in his denomination. He excitedly recounted a recent experience that epitomized the rapidly-changing spiritual climate in that part of the old Soviet Union. "Just last week," he told me, "the leadership of the Ukrainian army invited me to pray for them in a public military ceremony. I agreed. Before I prayed, I reminded those military men that not long ago they and our other government authorities had considered me an enemy of the state. I reminded them that a few months ago they were trying to arrest me. Now they were asking me to pray for them. So I was thrilled to stand before them to pray and to thank God for the great changes that He is bringing to our country!"

The optimism and pride evidenced by the people that I met in Kiev when they talked about a newly independent Ukraine, however, hadn't erased their memories of the devastating hardships that they had endured through long decades of communist rule. In fact, those hard memories may have inspired the optimism that was now present. Recent changes were being received with joy.

Some of the stories of faith that I heard in the Ukraine sounded similar to what I had heard in Russia. Many of these stories were both inspiring and disturbing. I don't know whether the oppression of Ukrainian believers had been any harsher than that in Russia. But in the storytelling, the Ukrainians seemed more open about the horrific details of their suffering.

I met a Ukrainian man by the name of Kostyantyn who was willing to talk with me. He also wanted me to meet his son, Alexi, who was himself a well-known leader in their denomination. As we talked, I learned that Kostyantyn had been imprisoned for many years for his faith during the time of communist rule. His son volunteered to translate for his father in order to make it easier for the older man to share his story.

Kostyantyn was not a minister. He was, however, such an active layman in his church that the local authorities evidently decided that he and two other elders in his congregation would benefit from some re-education in a Soviet labor camp. During his incarceration, the regional authorities cracked down on many area churches and arrested over two hundred pastors who were then sent to the same camp. Quickly the rumor spread around the camp that because these pastors were considered a serious threat to the state, they were to be kept separate from the other prisoners. The labor camp guards had been instructed to administer the harshest possible treatment so that none of the pastors would survive imprisonment.

Evidently, the authorities didn't want to execute these pastors. What they did, instead, may have been worse. The pastors were issued the most rudimentary tools (broken shovels and sharpened sticks) and assigned the task of digging a trench in the frozen ground. They would be punished each day if they did not make adequate progress.

Of course, the daily goal was impossible to achieve. When the pastors were escorted back to the barracks each night, they were stripped to their underwear, doused with ice water, fed stale crusts of bread and water for supper, and then herded back into freezing cells to sleep for the night.

There was no formal torture. There were no beatings. But, according to Kostyantyn, more than two hundred pastors died within three months because of disease and other "natural causes." Kostyantyn knew that the pastors had been sent to the gulag and, for all practical purposes, condemned to die because they had refused to deny their faith. Their courage and conviction gave Kostyantyn the strength to survive his own personal ordeal. He determined never to forget their faithful examples.

By the time Kostyantyn was himself released from the camp, he learned that his wife had died and that his teen-aged son Alexi had been living for years with relatives. He was re-united with his son, and together they visited his wife's grave. The next Sunday, Kostyantyn took Alexi to church with him. That was the day when Kostyantyn learned that not all ministers had made the same decisions as the brave pastors that he had seen die at the labor camp.

The new pastor of his old congregation had evidently made some concessions to the communist authorities in order to keep his job.

And on Kostyantyn's first Sunday back at church with his son, the pastor was about to make yet another compromise.

The man stood in the pulpit and looked sadly out over his people. He hesitantly, almost apologetically, announced that the government had established a new law. Starting immediately, and from that day forward, no one under the age of twenty-six would be allowed to attend a worship service in a church. His voice cracked with emotion. He said that he felt bad about the new ruling. He also said that if the people of the congregation wanted their church doors to remain open, they would be required to abide by the law. He instructed everyone under the age of twenty-six to leave the building immediately.

Knowing that someone present in the congregation that morning would be reporting to the authorities, Kostyantyn stood with his son when Alexi rose to leave. As the two of them walked out of the sanctuary together, Kostyantyn vowed never to enter that church again. He explained, "It was no longer the church that I had attended and known before. And the gospel that minister preached certainly was not the faith that I had gone to prison for!"

As Kostyantyn finished telling me his faith story, I noticed that his son was weeping. Alexi was now a middle-aged man. He knelt before his father. Kostyantyn stroked his son's hair as if Alexi was once again a small boy. Alexi looked up at his father and declared "I am so proud of you, Father! I never knew all that you went through."

The older man smiled sadly and said, "I didn't think you needed to know. We didn't know if those difficult days would return. And I didn't want to hurt you. But I'm glad that you know now."

Even though Alexi had never known the details of Kostyantyn's ordeal, he had always known *enough* about his genealogy of faith that his father's convictions and courage had inspired and influenced his own decision to become a follower of Jesus, to accept his own call to the ministry, and to become a spiritual leader of his people.

As Kostyantyn learned, not every pastor maintained the strength of his convictions in the face of communist opposition. According to stories I heard both in Russia and in the Ukraine, compromising church leaders were dealt with in a variety of ways. In some cases, when a pastor was imprisoned for standing by his convictions and continuing to preach the gospel, local governmental authorities appointed another, more cooperative minister to fill the pulpit and lead the congregation. However, when the new communist-appointed pastor arrived for his first Sunday morning worship service, church members (often the older women) would show their disdain by linking arms and blocking his way to the pulpit. If he was able to push through to the pulpit, the women would take their usual places in the pews and join the rest of the congregation in singing the hymns. Then, when the new pastor (whom they felt had compromised his faith to stay out of prison) stood to deliver his government-approved sermon, the same women would silently stand and turn their backs on the preacher. They would face the rear of the sanctuary until he finished the sermon and it was time to sing the closing hymn.

Throughout the former Soviet Union, many church leaders refused to compromise their faith. This conviction so impressed and inspired the congregations that believers today still remember and honor those pastors. Now, in weekly worship services throughout the old USSR, congregants typically stand to honor the *office* of pastor whenever their minister enters the sanctuary. Until the pastor walks up onto the platform to take his place behind the pulpit, they remain standing in respectful silence for what is clearly a moving and meaningful tribute.

As a guest speaker in some of those churches, walking in and standing alongside my Russian and Ukrainian brothers being honored in that way, I felt utterly unworthy. I felt that I should have stepped down from the platform as if my own presence there would have cheapened the moment. I felt that I was experiencing an honor that I had never earned or paid for.

There were other pastors who never really had a choice about whether or not they would live. In arresting them, the authorities essentially decided that these pastors were going to die. Their only choice, at that point, was deciding whether they would die honoring their faith and their Lord or denying His name. Today, the churches in Russia and the Ukraine remember those who stood strong. By honoring that faithfulness, believers endeavor to value the painful lessons learned under persecution.

One question came to my mind often: *How did so many Russians and Ukrainians keep their faith strong over decades of communist oppression of believers?* The professional researcher in me wanted to discover simple, practical, measurable, and objective answers to that question.

But I wasn't only a professional researcher. I was also a still-grieving father. I was a wounded would-be healer. I was a failed relief worker who had so helplessly watched thousands of starving people die. My objectivity was hard to maintain. Often, in interviews, I would simply blurt out: "How did you (or your family, or your church, or your people) learn to live like this? How did you learn to die like that?"

One of the first men I said that to answered me by telling me this story:

> "I remember the day like it was yesterday, Nik. My father put his arms around me and my sister and my brother and guided us into the kitchen to sit around the table where he could talk with us. My Mama was crying, so I knew that something was wrong. Papa didn't look at her because he was talking directly to us. He said, 'Children, you know that I am the pastor of our church. That's what God has called me to do—to tell others about Him. I have learned that the communist authorities

will come tomorrow to arrest me. They will put me in prison because they want me to stop preaching about Jesus. But I cannot stop doing that because I must obey God. I will miss you very much, but I will trust God to watch over you while I'm gone.'"

"He hugged each one of us. Then he said: 'All around this part of the country, the authorities are rounding up followers of Jesus and demanding that they deny their faith. Sometimes, when they refuse, the authorities will line up whole families and hang them by the neck until they are dead. I don't want that to happen to our family, so I am praying that once they put me in prison, they will leave you and your mother alone.'"

"'However,' and here he paused and made eye contact with us, 'If I am in prison and I hear that my wife and my children have been hung to death rather than deny Jesus, I will be the most proud man in that prison!'"

When he finished his story, I was stunned. I had never heard that kind of thing in my church growing up. I had never encountered that in my pilgrimage. I was sure that I had never been told that a father should value his faith over his family.

Almost immediately, though, I caught myself and I thought of some biblical examples of that very thing. *I guess that is part of our story,* I silently concluded. But it's a part of the story that we have kept very hidden.

This was one more thing that sounded insane to me. *Is this really the way that God intends for His people to live? And am I so certain about the resurrection that I would actually be willing to live that way—and maybe even be willing to die that way?*

Another time, I asked the same question of another storyteller: "How did you learn to live and die like this?" This man responded this way:

"I remember when my parents gathered our family together and my father said, 'Children, all over this district the communist authorities are slowly starving to death believers who refuse to deny their faith. If our family has to starve for Jesus, then let us do so with joy.'"

What was I to do with a story like that? I could only imagine what that experience—what the words of that father—had meant to that family.

That "How did you learn to live and die like that?" question was not only answered by those two stories. It was also answered by many other testimonies that I heard in Russia and in the Ukraine. In fact, whether I specifically asked that question or not, it was answered in almost every story I heard.

It was even answered in the story of the old women who stood up (literally) for their convictions and turned their backs on their compromising ministers.

How did so many Russian and Ukrainian believers remain strong in their faith through almost a century of communist persecution? How did they learn to live and die like they did? Time and time again, I heard the same words: "We learned it from our mothers, our grandmothers, and our great-grandmothers. We learned it from our fathers, our grandfathers and our great-grandfathers."

As my time in the Ukraine was drawing to a close, I recalled those final days in Russia, especially the conversation when I had been told that persecution was as normal "as the sun coming up in the east." I wondered if my Ukrainian friends would have the same view of persecution.

I was with yet another group of believers listening to their stories of prison, persecution, and God's provision for His people. Once again I was struck by the power of the testimonies and stories that

I was hearing. As we came to the end of our time together, I asked: "I just don't understand why you haven't collected these stories in a book? Believers around the world ought to hear what you have been telling me here today. Your stories are amazing! These are inspiring testimonies! I have never heard anything like them!"

An older pastor reached out and took my shoulder. He clamped his other hand tightly onto my arm, and looked me right in the eye. He said, "Son, when did you stop reading your Bible? All of our stories are in the Bible. God has already written them down. Why would we bother writing books to tell our stories when God has already told His story. If you would just read the Bible, you would see that our stories are there."

He paused and then he asked me again, "When did you stop reading your Bible?"

Without waiting for me to answer, he turned and walked away. There was no friendly smile, no encouraging pat on the back, and no kiss on the cheek.

His convicting question still echoes in my mind.

22

Fear or Freedom?

Much of what I heard from believers throughout Eastern Europe over the next several days echoed the stories that I had been told by the Russians and Ukrainians. But the most disheartening place I visited, which will go unnamed here, was a former communist-bloc nation where the church actually suffered little overt persecution.

That seemed like a positive thing, until I found out why that was true. My interviews there revealed that, from the beginning of communist rule, this nation's churches quickly and completely embraced the verses that Paul wrote in Romans 13 about honoring and obeying the authority of earthly rulers. In fact, the churches emphasized those verses so much that they ignored and failed to obey many other Scriptures, including some of the central teachings of Christ.

For example, once that nation's churches had made their go-along-get-along strategy for survival a central tenet of their faith, they pretty much forgot the very last instruction Jesus gave His followers—to go and make disciples. Since the government concluded that the church posed little threat and would probably soon wither and die, there was no need for concerted persecution to control the believers. These compromised churches had shackled themselves.

These believers had failed to share their faith or speak for themselves. They had failed to speak for others when thousands of Jews were slaughtered just blocks from their church's headquarters. They allowed the communist leadership to share space inside their denominational offices. Why would they ever face overt persecution when they had already surrendered almost everything?

One small protestant group in another former Iron Curtain country had fallen into that same trap—for a time. Gradually, over decades of severe persecution, they had allowed the government to dictate how, when and where they would worship. All the while, these believers resented their loss of religious freedom under communism. One of their pastors applied to the government for permission to study theology in England. *Miraculously* (and there seemed to be no other explanation), the communist government had granted the permission.

After three years of study, this pastor returned home. In a meeting with fellow pastors, he reported on his experience. "The ONLY important thing I learned," he told his colleagues, "was that we are free! We are free, because our freedom comes from God, and not from our government. We need to start acting like we are free!"

Over the next year, these pastors struggled with the meaning and possible application of this seemingly radical idea. During that year, they fasted and prayed. They tried to understand how this freedom related to the teachings of Romans 13. In the end, about half of the pastors signed a carefully-drafted letter that they then sent to their repressive communist government. It said, in essence:

Our Bible instructs us to respect and accept your authority over us and the people of our country. For years now, we have done that. But our Bible also teaches us to distinguish between the authority granted to governments and the authority that belongs to God.

In the letter, they tried to articulate that difference. They assured the authorities that there was no intent to oppose or overthrow the government. But, respectfully, they also explained that they would obey God and do what God tells his followers to do in His Word. They explained that the Holy Spirit was giving them the freedom and the strength to do this. From that day forward, they stated, they were determined to fulfill the biblical and historic role of their faith—to proclaim the gospel, to plant churches, to witness to their beliefs in the public arena, to baptize new believers, and to worship together when and where they chose.

The church leaders mailed their letter. Then they waited, no doubt with fear and trepidation, to see what might happen. To their surprise, the government did nothing in response. The only significant change that resulted from claiming their freedom was that they were now able to exercise that freedom. Eventually, they became part of the Body of Christ again.

In talking with several of the leaders who had signed and sent that declaration of freedom to their government, including the old pastor who had gone away to study theology three decades earlier, I shared some of the stories that I had already heard in the former USSR. After I told them the story of Dmitri in prison singing his HeartSong every morning, they immediately got excited. They said that there was another believer who I needed to talk with before leaving their country. "You simply ***must*** talk with him!" they insisted. He lived just down the street from the church where we were interviewing at the time.

Up four flights of creaking stairs, in a tiny apartment, we met a white-haired, stooped-over, shell of a man. It was clear that, earlier in his life, he had cast a longer shadow. He invited us into his apartment. The aged furnishings made the room feel like a museum.

Tavian, the old man who lived there, took us back in time as he recounted his personal history. He said that during the days of Soviet occupation, in the post-World War II decade before his country established its own communist government, he had been part of a charismatic underground movement that rose from within the country's traditional Orthodox Church. They called themselves "The Army of God." Reading their Bibles, they discovered what Jesus had said about the sending of the Holy Spirit to enable His followers to carry out His will on earth. They came to understand that this same Holy Spirit would empower them to do the work of Christ's Body—with or without the blessing of the Orthodox Church or the permission of the government.

When they began to put those beliefs into practice, they, of course, attracted the attention of others. The established national church opposed their efforts. Soviet occupiers declared that they were dangerous. And their own new communist government accused them of being traitors. Tavian and many other believers were arrested and imprisoned. The established church was party to this incarceration.

Tavian recalled many incidents of physical and emotional torture. Soviet indoctrination experts came from the USSR to train this satellite nation's police and prison officials. The different forms of torture were simple, but effective. For example, large amounts of salt were added to the prisoners' food, while, at the same time, water allowances were reduced. Other times, prisoners were hung by the wrists; their feet were unable to touch the floor. Sleep deprivation was also common. For days on end, prisoners would be kept awake. They were beaten every time they started to fall asleep—or topple out of the chair.

As was the case in other communist countries, the authorities tried to destroy the soul or at least the self-identity of those they saw as a threat. It took great energy for a prisoner to retain the smallest remnant of his or her original personality. Many lost that battle. Some prisoners were isolated in cells for years. At other times, jailors would pack fifty people in a cell designed to hold four people.

Tavian spoke about the abuse in a straightforward, matter-of-fact way. The pain in his voice became clearer, however, as he told how leaders of his traditional church had betrayed and informed on the underground renewal movement. I heard even deeper anguish as he described the helpless grief when he learned that his wife had died.

With a very different voice, however, he spoke of something that had helped him to stay strong.

"I wrote many songs," he told me. "God gave me words and melodies to strengthen and soothe my soul."

"How many songs did you write?" I asked.

He smiled and replied, "Around six hundred!"

That confirmed what I had already been told by the believers who insisted that I meet this man. They had already told me that Tavian's name was known by believers all over their country. Before communism, the Orthodox Church had used the ancient music of their tradition in worship. Protestant believers normally transliterated western hymns and songs of faith to sing in their worship. Since Tavian had been released from prison, however, believers were now singing much of this old man's worship music in their worship services every Sunday morning.

Naturally, I asked if he would sing one of his songs. Tavian sang two. As he sang, I understood how he had been able to silence his captors and persecutors as he sang the power of God into their lives.

As I exited his building, I imagined Tavian arriving in heaven one day, being met by a choir of angels singing one of the HeartSongs that he had composed while in prison for Jesus' sake.

In a different Eastern European nation, I encountered another believer who shared an instructive and thought-provoking story.

Eugen told me that during the days of communist rule in his country, he had been interviewed by a Westerner representing the magazine of a Christian organization that supported believers who were persecuted for their faith. When this reporter had asked Eugen how he had been treated by the communist government, Eugen had said that the local authorities tormented him and physically assaulted him. He said that sometimes they would try to intimidate him by stopping right in front of him and staring until he stepped aside to let them pass.

Eugen told how someone (he suspected the same policemen) had punctured his tires with a screwdriver and smashed his windshield with a hammer. He told how his children were regularly ridiculed in front of their classmates for coming from a believing family. Keeping his children after school, school administrators would tell them: "It is because your father is a minister that you are being embarrassed in front of your classmates. That is also why you don't have any friends." The communists evidently believed that if they could demean and discredit the parents' beliefs, they could turn the children against their parents. And, if they could do that, the churches would die within one generation.

The western reporter who had heard Eugen's story was appalled. He told him, "What the government is doing to you and your family is not right! We need to tell your story in our magazine so we can get people to pray for you!"

"Oh, please don't do that!" Eugen had exclaimed. "These things that have happened to me and my family are normal here. It is only a small cross for us to bear. Someday, if you hear that I am imprisoned, tortured and being threatened with death, maybe then you could make our story public. Maybe then, your government could intervene for us and maybe then people could pray for us. But not now! We don't want to embarrass our persecutors and cause more trouble by making a big deal out of such small things."

The reporter and his well-meaning organization heard that word from Eugen, but they refused to accept it. Despite what Eugen had said, they believed that they could (and that they should) do something to help. Eugen's story was published. To protect Eugen and his family from retribution, the magazine printed a disclaimer: "The names of the people in this article, as well as the name and location of the city, have been changed. But the details of the story are true. This is how believers are treated by the government of ___________." (And, amazingly, the disclaimer identified the actual county by name!)

The magazine made up a name for the central character in the story. They made up names for his wife and children. Totally at random, they used the name of a town in that same country. Choosing the name of the town completely at random, the publishers had no idea if any believers actually lived in that place. They decided that it would be perfectly safe to use randomly-chosen names and places in the magazine article.

The authorities in Eugen's country came across a copy of the magazine. In all likelihood, they read the disclaimer. Even so, they went to the city named in the article and investigated. They almost immediately discovered more than a dozen, previously unknown, illegal house churches operating in that area. They promptly arrested and imprisoned people from each of those churches.

Eugen, whose interview had indirectly led to this tragedy, was horrified and heart-broken. Years later, he shared this story with me in an effort to keep the same thing from happening again.

That is why I have waited over a decade and a half to put these stories in print.

Eugen's warning is crucial. In fact, I determined then and there to tell this cautionary tale to others in an effort to support and help fellow believers around the world in places where they suffer persecution for their faith. My hope is that this story will illustrate in a powerful way something important: if we tell the stories of believers in persecution in real time, if we are not very careful, we can actually increase their persecution. The Bible instructs us to pray for our spiritually-oppressed brothers and sisters. Sometimes, it is not helpful or wise to go beyond that instruction and share their stories. Even with the best of intentions, we cannot always be sure about the outcome of our sharing.

It is one thing to suffer persecution for Jesus' sake. My own personal experience in Somalia, as well as these amazing and powerful stories that I was hearing, convinced me that God is able and willing to use that kind of persecution for His glory. Causing people (even unintentionally) to be persecuted because of our foolishness or carelessness, however, is a different matter. What a tragedy for persecution to be wasted!

When I had left Somalia, I had resolved not to do that. According to Jesus, His followers would be "sheep among wolves." But there was no reason for His sheep to be unnecessarily foolish or careless. That was one of the reasons that I had started this journey: to learn wisdom from the experiences of others. As encouraged as I had been by what I had heard so far, I knew that there was much more that I needed to learn.

23

Refusing to Be Silenced

I will call my next storyteller Stoyan. The name means "stand firm" or "stay," and it is a common Eastern European name. Stoyan was about sixty years old, energetic and friendly. We met in the capital city of his country. After my usual explanation of who I was and what I was doing, Stoyan began telling me his story.

He began by talking about his parents. After the end of World War II, the communists began consolidating their power throughout his country. Eventually, they took control of the government. For decades, the authorities oppressed believers. When Stoyan was twelve, they imprisoned his protestant pastor father. His father remained in custody for ten years.

"At first," he said, "they held him in a secret police place in our city." "Every morning one of the guards would take some of his own human waste and spread it on the piece of toast that he brought to my father for breakfast."

Stoyan reported that the emotional and psychological impact of this persecution was even worse, and left deeper scars, than any physical mistreatment. Nine discouraging months passed with no word about his father. Stoyan's mother finally received notification that her husband was being transferred, with a group of other prisoners, to a distant labor camp.

The jailers allowed the families a one-hour visit before the transfer. Stoyan and his mother went to the well-known torture facility of the secret police on their assigned day. They were ushered out onto a football-sized field along with many other families who had come to see their beloved husbands and fathers and sons.

"Most of the prisoners rushed out to talk with their relatives from the other side of a long row of tables lined up to separate visitors from the inmates," Stoyan recalled. "But my father did not appear. My mother and I sat and waited. We waited for a long time. Finally, when our hour of visitation was almost up, another prisoner, evidently a trustee, walked through the visiting room door carrying what looked like a bundle of rags. He strode toward us and laid that bundle on top of one of the tables."

"My mother took my hand," recalled Stoyan, "and together we walked up to the table where, only because of the piercing blue eyes staring out at me from those rags, did I recognize this skeletal figure of a man as my father."

"I took my father's hand in mine and I put my face close to his. I whispered, 'Papa, I am so proud of you!' I was thirteen years old."

"Mama knew what my father would want most, so she slipped a little pocket New Testament under his wool cap. The jailer saw what she had done. He rushed over and took the little book, and then he summoned his commander. The officer took one look at the book before furiously throwing it to the ground. He screamed at my mother, with a great crowd of people around us, 'Woman, don't you realize that it is because of this book and because of your God that your husband is here? I can kill him, I can kill you, and I can kill your son. And I would be applauded for it!'"

Stoyan was remembering something that had happened decades earlier. But he recited the words as if they had been spoken yesterday. "My mother looked at that prison officer and said, 'Sir, you are right. You *can* kill my husband. You can kill me. I know that you can even kill our son. But nothing you can do will separate us from the love that is in Jesus Christ!'"

Stoyan said, "I was so proud of my mama!"

After the communist government had transferred his pastor father to the gulag outside of the city, the authorities exiled the rest of Stoyan's family to a remote gypsy village in a distant corner of the country. The police knocked on the door late one night and gave Stoyan, his mother and his three younger brothers an hour to pack. They were allowed to take two suitcases each. They were loaded on a midnight train bound for a place that they had never been.

At some point on that lonely train-ride, frightened and feeling like they had lost everything, Stoyan's younger siblings began to cry. They pleaded with their mother: "What's going to happen to our house? Mama, where are we going to live now? How will Papa know where we are? What are we going to do? What's going to happen to us?"

Stoyan's mother had no answers for her traumatized family. All she could do to reassure them was to say: "God will have to provide, little ones."

Then she led them in singing a hymn. After they finished singing, as the train drew near its destination, a stranger approached the fearful family huddled together and spoke to the mother: "Are you the family of the pastor who has been imprisoned?" (As he asked the question, he referred to the pastor by name.)

"Yes, we are," she told him.

The man said, "Our church was meeting last night. During our prayers, the Holy Spirit told us to take up an offering, and for me to bring it on this train, to give it to you, and to escort your family to your new home." He handed her a small cloth bag and lowered his voice to say, "Here's enough money for six months. We will bring more when this runs out."

Over the remaining years of his father's imprisonment, Stoyan's family was allowed two visits. Each visit was for one hour each time. Somehow, the pastor and his family managed to survive. It wasn't easy for any of them.

Three times a day, Stoyan was required to report to the local police station. In 1955, the communist authorities expelled him from the university. Stoyan's father, like every evangelical pastor that the government had imprisoned, had been accused of being an American or British spy. Stoyan's father was called "a political prisoner." Because of his family connection, the secret police stamped "Enemy of the Republic" on Stoyan's university record, and declared him ineligible to graduate. He was then conscripted into military service. There, he received no promotions and was allowed to do only menial work in a supply unit.

More than ten thousand "political prisoners" died in Stoyan's country during those years. There was little hope that his father would survive his ordeal. Near the end, his guards made one last cruel attempt to break him. They informed the pastor that he was scheduled for execution. They took him outside, tied him to a pole, and offered him one last opportunity to deny his faith. If he would not deny his faith, they told him, he would be shot.

He straightened his back, stood tall and declared, "I will not deny Christ." The guards became furious with him. Evidently, they did not have the authority to carry out their threat of execution. And, evidently, they had actually been given very different orders. They continued to insult and curse him even as they began to untie him. Then, much to his surprise, instead of escorting him back to his cell, they took him to the prison wall, unlocked a gate, opened a door and literally threw him out of prison without a word of explanation. He was so shocked by what had just happened that he didn't know what to do.

It finally dawned on him that he had been released. He began to walk. Much later, he found his way to his family's new home. It was a Saturday when he arrived, and no one was home. He then found the church and discovered his family and other church members praying for him at the altar. After a joyous reunion, he was finally able to preach again.

One Sunday, a few months later, an elderly woman asked the pastor for help. He did not know her. She told the pastor that she had a diabetic son—a son who had recently gone blind and was now close to death. He needed medication to manage his agonizing pain. Unfortunately, as a believer, there was no way for her to get that medicine for her son. Stoyan's father promised to try to help acquire the medication. And eventually he was able to do that.

When he took the medicine to the old woman's apartment, she led him into the bedroom to introduce the pastor to her son. She was grateful for the medicine, and she wanted the pastor to pray for her son.

When Stoyan's father entered the room, he got the shock of his life.

The blind, invalid, middle-aged man lying helpless in the bed before him was the prison guard who had spread human waste on the pastor's breakfast toast every morning for the first nine months of his imprisonment.

"Oh, Lord! Do not let me fail you now!" Stoyan's father prayed beneath his breath. Without identifying himself or saying anything that might give away the connection, the pastor granted his former tormenter forgiveness in his own heart, helped the old woman administer the medicine to relieve the man's pain, prayed for her son, and then returned home awed by a new and deeper understanding of God's grace. In fact, he was so overwhelmed by God's grace that the experience changed his life and the lives of his family members.

By the time of his father's release from prison, Stoyan had completed his military service. He had found work in a foundry and had started pursuing his theology studies through a correspondence school. His goal was to become a pastor himself. His plans were delayed, however, when the police broke into his apartment and destroyed his books and the sermons he had written.

By 1962, Stoyan had completed his correspondence degree and had become a pastor himself. That led to his firing from the foundry, after which he earned another theology degree by correspondence.

By 1966, he had acquired two illegal Bibles in his national language. This gave him the idea to start an underground center for smuggled materials in his home. Over the next two decades, he translated over twenty Christian books. The authors of those books are well-known: Corrie ten Boom, David Wilkerson, Billy Graham. Stoyan organized an underground publishing network. The details of his work and the methods used by his organization to print and distribute thousands of books throughout Eastern Europe still remained a secret when I met him in the summer of 1998.

He told me that the secret police had suspected his activities. One time, they had even arrested him and thrown him in prison. Unlike his father, however, his imprisonment lasted months rather than years. The authorities would have kept him longer if they had caught him in possession of illegal religious materials. But they never did.

Stoyan told me hair-raising tales of close calls and miraculous escapes. One time, he received a last minute warning that the police were waiting for him at his house. He left his wife in the woods overnight with a carload of books so that he could arrive home innocently empty-handed. Another time, a police officer actually sat on a stack of Bibles wrapped in brown paper while he directed a squad of his men on a futile, hours-long search of Stoyan's house.

By the time I had listened to Stoyan for two full days, I wished we had a month to talk.

I was struck by the progression that I had observed on this trip.

> In Russia, I had found a wary and weary people who were still hiding their stories—not only from the world but from each other.
>
> In the Ukraine, I discovered believers celebrating a spring-like freedom. They were starting to tell their stories openly, and they were doing that with joy.
>
> Now in Eastern Europe, where fallen walls no longer cast shadows, the curtains had opened so wide that citizens were again free to cross their countries' borders. Here, believers, like Stoyan, seemed to bask in the sunshine. They were beginning to reflect on the experiences and memories of seasons past.

Despite decades of extreme hardship, Stoyan's stories were joyful and hopeful. He was convinced that people flocked to Christ in greater numbers during difficult days of persecution because that's when they could recognize how God sustains and strengthens His followers through times of trouble. He said that he had learned that family is the believer's greatest reservoir of faith and resistance in the face of persecution. And he explained that, surprisingly, freedom had brought a new set of challenges that had blurred spiritual battle lines.

As my interview with Stoyan drew to a close, I knew that it was going to take a long time to process the wisdom, insights and conclusions that this one man had drawn from his life-treasure of faith experience.

When I mentioned that to Stoyan, and thanked him for his time, he smiled modestly and replied, "I thank God and I take great joy in knowing that I was suffering in prison in my country, so that you, Nik, could be free to share Jesus in Kentucky."

Those words pierced my soul. I looked Stoyan straight in the eyes.

"Oh, no!" I protested. "No! You are not going to do that! You are NOT going to put that on me. That is a debt so large that I can never repay you!"

Stoyan stared right back at me and said, "Son, that's the debt of the cross!" He leaned forward and poked me in the chest with his finger as he continued, "Don't you steal my joy! I took great joy that I was suffering in my country, so that you could be free to witness in your country."

Then he raised his voice in a prophet-like challenge that I knew would live with me forever: "Don't ever give up in freedom what we would never have given up in persecution! That is our witness to the power of the resurrection of Jesus Christ!"

Those words from Stoyan haunted me as I flew back to the States. *Had I given up in freedom what he and others had refused to surrender under the worst forms of persecution? Had I?*

I kept hearing the voices that I had heard in the interviews. I kept seeing the faces. So many life stories had been packed into such a short time. *I had been at this for less than a month. Was that even possible?* My mind was full with all that I had found—and all that I had seen and heard and experienced.

True to form, I opened my heart to my family, then to my colleagues and partners, then finally to the college students who had become our newly-adopted family.

Only a few weeks later, the students gathered in our home. I tried to provide a brief overview of my travels, but soon they were asking to hear the stories. And I began to tell them the stories.

I told them about Dmitri and his HeartSongs. I told them about

Katya and her grandfather's instruction to "be faithful unto death." I told them about the deacon who was faithful when he hitched his horse to the sleigh to deliver food in the blizzard. I told them about the Russian pastor who had explained that persecution was "like the sun coming up in the east." I told them that I was beginning to understand that "persecution is normal" for millions of believers around the world.

My recollections included confessions as well. "I don't know how I have lived to be forty-five years old," I told them, "without realizing the implications of this. You would think that I would already understand this; I lived in Africa for fifteen years! And I have studied Scripture! I know that Jesus told His followers that they would suffer for His sake. So none of this should be a surprise to any of us."

"But, somehow, it is a surprise," I said slowly.

I then told them about the Ukrainian pastor who had chastised me by asking when I had stopped reading my Bible.

The students were broken and convicted to hear about the Russian youth who could recite and reproduce the first four books of the New Testament almost in their entirety at that Moscow youth conference back in the 1950's. When I offered the sad observation "that the Russian church had lost in its first decade of 'freedom' what Soviet believers had managed to hold on to under communism for most of the century," I think that many of the college students made an immediate personal application.

It was late and time to draw things to a close. But no one seemed inclined to leave. I kept telling stories.

I told them about Tavian and the six hundred songs that he had written in prison—songs that were now being sung in churches all over his country every Sunday morning. I talked about HeartSongs of our faith, and I noted that many people in the interviews had cited favorite music and Scripture as a powerful source of spiritual strength during times of trial.

I played a recording of Dmitri and Tavian singing their HeartSongs. The students wept with me.

I told the students the story of Stoyan and his family—and I told them how his father's suffering and his mother's courageous faith had provided a genealogy of faith that had shaped his own remarkable life. And then I told them about my final exchange with Stoyan, and I confessed to those college students that I had felt the need to ask for God's forgiveness for "giving up in freedom what Stoyan and so many others had never given up in persecution."

It was even later now. The students, however, refused to leave. Ruth and I went upstairs to go to bed, leaving behind the students who were singing, and praying, and crying.

The students returned the next week with more friends. They asked me to tell stories again—the same stories that they had heard the previous week. Clearly, God has placed something holy in our hands.

I certainly had not found all the answers that I was looking for. What's more, I had returned home with even more questions. But in Russia and in Eastern Europe, I had found a new hope. It was small, but it was hope.

I had left Africa after Tim's death wondering how my faith applied—or if it applied—in brutal places like Mogadishu. Ruth and I had gone to Somalia in obedience to Christ's instructions to His followers "to go into all the world to make disciples." We did that confidently believing in what the Bible proclaims about the resurrection power of Jesus. Six years later, I had fled home doubting that power—and wondering if perhaps evil was stronger than God.

If that kind of resurrection power couldn't be found in the world today, I had a problem. If that kind of resurrection power was not present and alive, I had important questions to answer—questions that shook me to the core: *What was the point of the last fifteen years of my life? And what was I going to do with the rest of my life?*

We had ostensibly set up our Persecution Task Force and designed a set of research goals to help us learn how to make disciples in those places in the world most hostile to Christianity. That was our expressed goal. Beyond that, I knew early on that my quest was much more personal. I left for Russia with a question I desperately wanted to answer: *What if what the Bible teaches about the power of my faith is not true today?*

Coming home from Russia, however, a different question was in my heart. It was a question that grew from those remarkable, life-giving interviews. It was a question that hinted of hope: *What if the resurrection power available to Jesus' followers in the New Testament is just as real for believers in our world today?*

I wondered if that could possibly be true. Driven by that question, my journey continued.

24

Secret Rendezvous

From the beginning of our persecution interviews, Ruth and I knew that if we wanted to learn how spiritual faith could survive in tough times in hostile places, a visit to mainland China would be essential. Deciding to travel to China was easy; planning and executing the details of the trip proved to be a much more difficult challenge.

We had never worked in China. We had never traveled to that part of the world. I personally did not know one person in China. We reached out to organizations and agencies with work in China, in hopes of connecting with someone who knew someone who might have contacts in China. We needed a group or an individual with credibility and trust among Chinese believers. We needed someone who would be able to open doors for us.

Our search was difficult and closed doors were common. Some people we thought could help told us that they couldn't—or, for some reason, wouldn't. It was a challenge even to communicate our intentions and our goals, let alone to orchestrate the logistics of travel and personal contact. Ruth and I spent weeks writing e-mails, making phone calls, and asking for assistance.

Finally, we were told of a man named David Chen. Born in China, he had been educated in North America. He had become a pastor and a seminary professor. Even better, he had made over one hundred trips of his own into China where he regularly provided theological and Bible training to leaders of Chinese house churches. He had also conducted his own life-long study of the growth of Christianity in China under communist rule.

David told us that he was planning another visit to China that fall. He said that he would vouch for me with his contacts and encourage their cooperation. If things worked out, it was possible that David and I could even travel together.

That old axiom, *"It's not what you know, but who you know,"* proved to be true. David's introductions and endorsement opened the door to an extensive network of believers throughout China. Those believers, upon David's trusted recommendation, agreed to open themselves and, in some cases, their homes and house churches to help me. Within days, detailed plans for my seven-week trip began to fall into place.

I received my initial introduction to China and Chinese culture in Hong Kong. David Chen, who would meet up with me in mainland China later on my trip, had given me a crash course in Chinese heritage and the history of Christianity in his native land before I had left America. He had put me in touch with a number of believers in Hong Kong who had agreed to talk with me about how the local churches had been impacted by the government changeover which had taken place just the year before. After more than a century and a half as a British colony, Hong Kong was now under the control of China.

The Hong Kong believers I met said that there had been a lot of speculation and worry as that long-awaited (and, for many, much-dreaded) transfer of power had come. In fact, uncertainty and fear about the future had been so prevalent that in the years and months prior to the communist takeover in July of 1997, seventy-five percent of the city's protestant pastors had emigrated from Hong Kong. Many of these pastors, claiming political and/or religious refugee status, had gone to Taiwan, and many had gone to countries in the west.

The lay-leaders and believers who had been left behind said that, so far, the Chinese authorities had lived up to their promises. They were allowing Hong Kong to continue operating under a very different style of government—a style that was more western and capitalistic, less authoritarian, and even somewhat democratic. According to the Hong Kong believers, the biggest problem that they faced now was how to deal with the sudden loss of trained and experienced leadership among the city's churches. I found it interesting, and even disturbing, that so many of the pastors had left Hong Kong.

Never in my life had I felt so conspicuous, so alien, so completely out of place as I did walking along the back streets of Hong Kong. It surprised me how much that bothered me and it made me wonder a bit about what might be in store over the next few weeks at my various destinations around the mainland—none of which would be nearly as "westernized" as Hong Kong.

My unexpected culture shock reinforced the concern that I had when David Chen had first told me that it would be a good idea if we went into mainland China separately. David knew that every time he made the trip, he increased the risk that he might be suspected and arrested by the Chinese authorities for his work with the house churches. Since I had never been to China, he assured me that there would be little chance that I would be detained. However, if this was the time they finally caught him and I happened to be travelling with him, or if they decided to investigate him because he was traveling with an American, they might somehow discover the real purpose of his visit. I would likely be caught in the same web, and I would probably be refused entry or expelled from the country.

"I'll catch up with you soon enough," David said. "Until then, you'll be safer without me. The people who are meeting you at your first couple of stops speak excellent English. They will be able to interpret if any people they have lined up for interviews don't speak English. The young couple meeting you at the train station in your first city will take good care of you. At the end of your three days there, they will give you instructions about how to make contact at your second stop."

"But how will I recognize them?" I asked.

David smiled. "Don't worry," he said. "They will find you."

But I pressed for more assurance: "But how will they . . ."

David's laughter interrupted me. "Don't worry, Nik," he insisted. "They will know!"

Standing on the loading platform at the main Hong Kong railroad station, waiting to board my train to the mainland, I concluded that half of the population of China must have been in the city on holiday and were now heading home, hauling heavy bags of whatever they had purchased in Hong Kong.

I suddenly realized why David had laughed when I asked how the people meeting my train would recognize me. At a towering height of 5'11" I found myself looking over the tops of thousands of heads, as far as I could see, all covered with straight dark hair. There wasn't a single African, European, or Latino in sight. It was just China and me packed into that train terminal.

The entire crowd suddenly surged toward the slowly-opening doors of the nearest railroad car. Fortunately, I was among the first passengers squeezed onto the train. I managed to claim a seat in a passenger car that filled far beyond its intended capacity.

When we reached our southern Chinese city, the train emptied so fast that I had no chance to get my bearings. I simply followed the flood of humanity as it carried me through the station. I had no alternative but to trust David Chen's instructions and pray that his friends were as reliable as he had said. Sure enough, within seconds, I felt someone brush up against me and subtly pat my hand as I walked by. Turning, I noticed a young Chinese couple who made eye contact and silently motioned for me to follow them out toward the street. At the curb they hailed a taxi, tossed my single bag into the trunk, and gestured for me to climb in the back seat.

My greeters gave the driver directions. We started on what was a relatively silent forty-minute taxi ride to somewhere in the city that I suspected would not be our final destination. Sure enough, after waiting for our taxi driver to leave, my hosts led me through a confusing, meandering maze of streets for several blocks. Then they slowed their pace. They carefully scanned the empty streets before and behind us, and then stepped quickly through an unlocked door into the tiny foyer of what was some sort of residential building. Only after they led me up three flights of stairs, ushered me into their apartment, and closed the door behind us did they finally relax enough to speak freely.

Daniel and Lydia Wang explained that later that evening, after dark, they would accompany me back downtown to one of the government-owned "official" tourist hotels where foreign visitors were required to register and stay. Until then, they explained, their apartment would be a much safer place to talk. Lydia served tea and cookies as we began to talk.

The Wangs described their role as leaders of a local house church in a regional network of affiliated congregations. That was how they had met David Chen.

I expressed my appreciation and respect for David and explained my own connection with him as a valued advisor. I went on to summarize the purpose of my visit to China and shared a sampling of the Russian and Eastern European stories that I had gathered in those places. I also told them a little about my own background, including my time in Africa. Of course, I also included some of my Somali struggles and how those struggles had led me to China.

In an effort to be sensitive to the situation, I told them that I appreciated and understood the reasons behind their caution. I explained that in Somalia believers could be killed simply for associating with outsiders. I assured Daniel and Lydia that I would gladly follow whatever security precautions they wanted to establish and that I didn't want to put them in any unnecessary danger.

They explained that our surreptitious route to their apartment that afternoon was because local authorities seemed to have ratcheted up the surveillance level in recent months. A number of their house-church colleagues had reported being followed.

"Do you think we were being followed?" I wanted to know.

"We don't think so," Lydia replied. "But we won't be certain for a few more days."

"What do you mean?" I asked her.

"If anyone happened to be following us today, they would just keep watching as long as you are here, in order to discover what you might be doing and what's going on," Daniel explained. "They would be content to continue gathering evidence until you leave. Then, if there was going to be any trouble, that's when they would come back and arrest us."

When Lydia saw the look of concern on my face, she smiled and tried to reassure me: "Don't worry. Daniel and I were very careful going to and coming from the station today. We didn't notice anyone. We're pretty sure that we weren't followed."

"And even if we were followed and discovered," Daniel added, "there is little chance that it would be a life or death situation like it might be for your friends in Somalia. So don't worry. Here in China, most believers who get arrested, even our evangelists who face the serious charge of starting an illegal house church, are usually sentenced to no more than three years in prison."

I was stunned by the casual way that he said those words. And I was more than worried; I was alarmed. I was alarmed not simply for myself, but by the thought that my visit could actually result in my hosts' imprisonment.

"Why didn't you just tell me not to come because it might be too dangerous for you?" I asked.

"We were willing to accept the risk," Daniel assured me.

"If I had known, though, I'm not sure that I would have accepted that risk," I told him. That response seemed to surprise them both. I went on to explain the lesson that I had learned in Somalia about the importance of making sure that any persecution to be endured came for Jesus' sake.

"What I mean," I explained, "is that if you get in trouble with the authorities for worshiping or witnessing for Jesus, God can and God will honor that. When the people closest to you—your family, your friends, your neighbors, and even those authorities familiar with your case—see and understand what you did and how that was a result of your commitment to Jesus, God can use that for His glory. That might even lead to other people thinking about God."

"But if you get arrested for associating with me (or any other westerner) simply because someone spotted you meeting me at the train station or walking down your street—and if someone just happened to notice us entering your apartment building together, I'm not sure that God will bless that in the same way."

"For one thing, many people who know you might never understand that your persecution was for Jesus' sake. If you are arrested for worshipping with other believers, the reason for your arrest is clear. But there could be many motivations for associating with a foreigner. For example, people might be told that you did that for financial gain, or people might assume that you were working on a plan to leave the country. They might even think that you were involved in something political."

"So how would the Lord be able to use that to point people to Jesus? The Bible assures us that God can use *anything* for good, but I don't think that He wants to reward us when our unnecessary actions make that more difficult for Him to do."

"What I learned during my time in Somalia" I continued, "was that I never wanted my words, my actions, or my work to be the cause of anyone's suffering. Being persecuted for my sake is NOT the same as being persecuted for Jesus' sake. Causing suffering for my sake, especially if that suffering is the result of a thoughtless, uninformed, or downright stupid decision or action on my part, would be sad and unnecessary. It would be wrong. It might even be a sin."

Daniel and Lydia seemed intensely interested in what I was saying. They also seemed troubled.

Lydia spoke up first: "I understand and appreciate what you are telling us. It makes sense. But what Daniel didn't say when he told you why we were willing to take the risk—and what you need to understand—is that we would never tell someone like you, a visitor, not to come. We just couldn't do that! We wouldn't do that."

I wasn't quite sure that I understood her point. So I followed up: "Why not?"

"Because not welcoming a visitor would go against everything we *believe*. It would go against everything we *are!*" She went on to explain that hospitality is a high value, one of the very highest values in Chinese culture. Telling someone not to come would be unthinkable. Any Chinese person would consider that both embarrassing and wrong. She explained: "It would never be appropriate to turn down the request of a visitor or a guest."

Suddenly I understood the issue that we were dealing with. I had been trained to be aware of the different values among different cultures and people groups. The Chinese obviously highly value hospitality (as do Arabs and many other Muslim cultures). Disregard for that value would be considered a terrible offense.

In that moment, it also dawned on me that these kinds of questions were not unique to any one culture. As the Wangs talked, I found myself thinking of things that I had learned as a child, experiences that I had had in Somalia, and stories that had been shared in my recent visits to Russia and Eastern Europe. I suddenly wished that I could get everyone in the same room at the same time! And I began to wonder if these lessons and insights might be transferable from one culture to another. I suspected that they would be.

Listening to Lydia talk about the high value of hospitality in her culture, I thought about an experience from my days in Somalia that highlighted the difference in values between cultures.

> In sub-Saharan Africa, relationship is such a highly regarded value that for many tribal Africans that value often takes precedence over *truth*—which most westerners usually consider the higher of the two values. That difference in perspective can create serious misunderstandings, unnecessary conflict and sometimes even tragic consequences. An African might choose to massage or shade the truth, or withhold important information, because he doesn't want to cause offense. He might refuse to say something that others might not want to hear.
>
> When that happens, it would be easy for an American to see the African as deceitful and untrustworthy, even lacking in moral character. The African, however, might feel that he has actually demonstrated the highest integrity and trustworthiness by honoring what he had always been taught to believe was the more important cultural value. For him, consciously saying something that he feared could damage or strain a relationship would have been the far greater wrong.
>
> I encountered that kind of cross-cultural misunderstanding shortly after we began working in Somalia. I sought

security advice from the newly-hired Omar Aziz. I asked if he thought that it would be safe for me to go to a certain section of the city for a meeting that I needed to attend. Did he think that there would be enough danger that I should cancel my plans?

Omar Aziz told me that I should be fine.

I left for the meeting. As I approached my destination, a firefight broke out. I heard gunfire on my right and my left. I ran for my life. When I reached the safety of our compound and reported what had happened, other Somali staff told me that I should never have been in that part of the city alone. They said, “Everyone knows that is one of the most dangerous areas in all of Mogadishu.”

I was furious. The next time I saw Omar Aziz, I accused him of almost getting me killed. I demanded to know why he had lied to me. I demanded to know why he would place me at such risk.

His immediate, indignant response to my charges floored me. He believed that he was giving a complete justification when he said, “I don’t know you well enough to owe you the truth!”

For Omar Aziz, *relationship* earned and elicited *truth*. In my background, *truthfulness* was crucial for the development of any *relationship*. We both saw a strong connection between the two, but we saw those two things very differently.

Once we understood and accepted the difference in our cultural values, we began to realize that we both desired the same thing. Omar Aziz wanted a relationship that was strong and deep enough to survive the most difficult truth. Truth and honesty, for me, was the essential foundation upon which to build a good relationship.

Once we understood and honored each other’s values, we developed one of the deepest friendships I have ever had. I knew that I could trust Omar Aziz with my life—and I often did. He knew that I cared deeply for him, and I proved that to him on many occasions. We discovered that relationship and truth were both crucial—and that they did not ever need to be in conflict. We both got what we wanted and our lives were richer for it.

I shared that memory with Lydia and Daniel. I told them that I believed that with good effort at honest communication, and a little more cross-cultural understanding and sensitivity to our different values, most conflict could be avoided or resolved.

Then I continued: "So let me make a suggestion that will allow you to honor and maintain your commitment to your cultural value of hospitality. Let me suggest a way to do that without unnecessarily compromising your personal security situation or endangering others in your house-church movement. When you are contacted by an outsider the next time . . ."

"Wait!" Lydia excitedly interrupted. "We have friends who need to hear what you are saying. We will call them and invite them over. Then you can tell us all at the same time."

I listened as Daniel and Lydia each began to call their friends. They told them, "We have a Westerner visiting us this evening. He has been telling us some very interesting things that you need to hear."

Soon, fifteen of Daniel and Lydia's house-church colleagues joined us in their tiny apartment. Daniel briefly introduced me to their friends and quickly summarized my background and my intentions for this visit to China. He told his friends that I had come to learn from them how faith had not only survived, but had literally exploded, multiplied and spread throughout all of China despite decades of communist rule and the unrelenting opposition from both national and local authorities.

As quickly as possible, I tried to bring the expanded group to the point where Daniel, Lydia and I had suspended our conversation.

I expressed my fear of creating a more dangerous security issue for Daniel and Lydia, for the people gathered in that room, and for their entire house-church movement. I admitted that I was putting them in danger just by being there. I mentioned that I had questioned Daniel and Lydia's decision to let me come—and that they had told me that they would never refuse a guest. I again made the point about the difference between being persecuted for my sake and suffering persecution for Jesus' sake.

I suggested that the next time an outsider inquired about visiting them or their house churches at a difficult, dangerous, or especially inconvenient time, there might be a simple and straightforward strategy. They could graciously let the person know they that they were welcome—and that they would look forward to a time to meet and host them. But then they could also honestly explain why it was not the best or most convenient time for such a visit. Finally, they could suggest that their inquirer check back at a later time when it might be a better time for a visit. When that time came, they could assure the visitor that they would do everything to make the visit meaningful and productive. In the meantime, they could pray that God would lead everyone involved in working out the timing and details of the plan.

That approach honored their cultural and Christian value system by allowing them to maintain a genuine welcoming spirit of hospitality. They would be presenting a practical and sensible plan that would never offend any reasonable, would-be visitor. And they would be able to do so without compromising their own security or unnecessarily endangering any of their congregations or members. They would never have to say "No" to an outsider; they could simply say, "Not today!"

Over the next three days, I was even more encouraged by what these house-church members were able to teach me. I heard wonderful stories of how these individuals had come to know Christ and other reports about what God was doing through their house-church movement.

What I appreciated most was their description of life for believers in communist China. Several of the people I interviewed assured me that the communist government actually didn't care what its citizens *believed*. They claimed that the government's long and brutal opposition to religion had not been about *faith*, but about *control*.

I knew, of course, about China's "one-child policy." My new friends explained that the enforcement of that law through involuntary abortions was merely one of countless ways the government determined to control every aspect of an individual's life. The government mandated where people could live and whether or not they could ever relocate to another part of the country. The government determined where children could go to school. School authorities determined if and where each student could continue his or her education. The government would decide each person's career, where a person would work, and even what the salary would be.

Before young people could marry, they would have to get permission from their supervisor. Applying for a marriage license, they would wait for government approval. If a couple wanted to start a family, they were required to seek permission from authorities at their place of work and in the local government.

All pregnancies had to be reported and were supposed to be preapproved. Unexpected or unplanned pregnancies, even when it was a couple's first, would sometimes be aborted. Once a woman had given birth to her one allotted baby, any subsequent pregnancies would be automatically terminated by an involuntary, government-ordered abortion. Many work places required regular pregnancy tests for all female employees of child-bearing age in order to catch unapproved pregnancies early.

Women seeking government permission and paperwork to travel from one province of China to another would first be required to pay for a pregnancy test to make sure that they weren't going somewhere to secretly give birth to an unapproved child. The personal cost for an elective pregnancy test could be more than one-month's salary.

Any woman who somehow managed to escape the notice of the pregnancy police, or any family that refused to abide by the government's *one child policy,* would pay a terrible price. Because the government issued only one child identity card per family, no additional child could ever have an official identity. As far as the government was concerned, that additional child did not exist. That child could never attend school and that child could never get a job.

Clearly, any government that intent on total control over its citizens would be unable to acknowledge the power of an omnipotent God! Any religion that called for obedience and commitment to Someone (seen or unseen) who was above and beyond the government would be calling the power of the government into question. Such a threat could not, and would not, be tolerated.

I suddenly realized how dangerous it would be simply to speak the words: "Jesus is Lord." The faith of believers would strike at the very heart of the government's power.

I began to absorb another instructive lesson from another interview.

When the authorities arrested and imprisoned a house-church pastor and father of seven children, they also placed his wife under house-arrest. The pastor's wife was told that she was allowed to leave her home only to shop at the local market. That didn't seem to matter much to her; she had no money to purchase food at the market anyway. She had to rely on faithful fellow house-church members for food. As it turns out, they provided for her well.

She would wear a baggy smock with large pockets over her other clothes when she went to her village's open-air market. Walking slowly through the crowd as she wandered in and out among the stalls, she would notice a nudge here and a tug there until she had walked through the entire market. By the time she reached home, her pockets would be filled with tomatoes and onions and other items. Sometimes there was money in a pocket. She always seemed to come home with just enough food to feed her family of eight for another day.

Occasionally, when those seven children got really hungry, the mother would be surprised to find a chicken on her front steps. One day her oldest son was offered a job in a nearby city—and there *just happened* to be a bicycle leaning up against their front door. Seemingly out of the blue, the boy had transportation to and from work.

The network of house churches did not have, or want, church buildings to gather in, or sanctuaries with rows of pews where people could sit and worship on Sunday mornings. But they certainly knew what it meant to love and look after the concerns and needs of their members.

They knew what it meant to *be* church for one another.

I believed that their example could serve as an inspiration and challenge to other believers. And indeed it did—much sooner than I ever expected.

25

One Extra Pair of Underwear

From southern China, I flew to a major city in another province where two of David's friends met me at the airport. As I slipped into the back seat of their car and out of public sight, one of the men pulled out his cell phone to make a short call: "Our visitor has arrived. We will bring him to location number four at time number seven."

After he hung up, he explained that for security reasons their house-church movement had developed a system of frequently changed numerical codes that they used when they needed to discuss logistical arrangements over the phone. They never used names of people or places unless it was absolutely necessary. Even if the authorities happened to be listening to his phone conversations that day, they couldn't discern our plans. Because the friend on the other end of the line was working with the same list of codes, he knew exactly where and when we were to arrive at our destination.

Once we merged into heavy, late afternoon traffic on a major thoroughfare, my driver slowed down and lost all sense of urgency. I had plenty of time to get acquainted with my hosts as we drove what seemed to be a series of aimless, meandering, irregular circles around and through the city until the dead of night. We finally stopped on the perimeter of a sprawling inner-city government housing complex—acres and acres of fifteen-story concrete-gray rectangles looming up into the starlit sky.

I stayed right on the heels of my guides as they hurried through the night shadows and darted around to the backside of an apartment building. They hurried me through a rear exit door and then rushed me up the back stairs and into a hallway where they proceeded to knock softly on one of the apartment doors.

When the door opened, I was welcomed into the presence of seven house-church pastors and evangelists, four of whom I quickly learned had been recently imprisoned for their faith. They had just been released from prison and had stayed in the city an extra few days to talk with me. After our meeting, they would finally go home to be reunited with their families. One of the men spoke passable English, so he would do the translating as I interviewed the others over the next few days.

Because this part of the city was restricted to Chinese only, I was confined to the apartment for the next four days. My Chinese companions, on the other hand, were free to come and go as they wished. They took strolls in the fresh air. They walked to the nearby grocery to purchase ingredients for the simple meals that they prepared on a single-burner butane stove.

The four men who had just been released from prison clearly relished their freedom. Their stories were remarkable.

I was especially intrigued by Pastor Chang. He was eighty-three years old and had been out of prison for three days. Pastor Chang had spent his entire adult life preaching and teaching the gospel—and paying a high price for the privilege. He was old enough to remember the early days of communism when Chairman Mao's new government attempted to purge the country of Christian (and western) influence.

Missionaries from other countries had been banished from China overnight. Church buildings were boarded up or turned into brothels and drinking establishments. Thousands of believers and church planters like Pastor Chang were arrested and subjected to brutal labor camps and re-education programs.

In fact, Pastor Chang had been sent to prison three different times. He first went to prison when he became a believer. A second time he went to prison for leading others to faith in Jesus and for planting a church. He was arrested and sentenced to prison a third time for leading a house-church movement.

That kind of mistreatment was common in China. In fact, imprisonment was so common for believers that they would typically find themselves in prison with other believers. Small groups of believers, in prison, would band together for fellowship and study. They encouraged each other to share their faith, to win converts among their fellow prisoners, and to plant other small churches in various parts of the prison. Amazingly, there was a huge church-planting movement *within* China's prisons!

In prison, countless new converts were discipled. Eventually they were released to return to home communities scattered throughout every region and province of the country. Returning home, they would either join the local house church or help start a new one. These house churches spread like wildfire across China.

David Chen had already given me an excellent overview of Christianity's history and impact in China. And I had done additional research on my own. I felt that I had a good grasp of the major historical trends and milestones. Hearing the story fleshed out in the first-person narrative of an active participant in the fastest expansion of Christianity in the history of the world, however, was a remarkable privilege for me.

Pastor Chang had not only survived his government's relentless campaign to wipe out the gospel's gains, he had also watched the number of Chinese believers multiply dramatically during his ministry. At a certain point, when there were too many pastors to imprison, the communist party changed its strategy and created the officially recognized and approved "Three-Self Church" as a means of regulating and limiting the spread of what they called this "foreign religion."

That strategy proved to be too little and too late. By the early 1960's, illegal house-church movements had spread so far and so fast that there was no containing the Holy Spirit. Even the re-arrest and re-imprisonment of the most influential leaders, like Pastor Chang, failed to quench the quickening flames of faith.

When Christianity was first outlawed following World War II, the number of Chinese believers was estimated to be in the hundreds of thousands. (This was the fruit of nearly a century of labor by western workers who had not been allowed into China until the last half of the nineteenth century.) By the time of Mao's Cultural Revolution, after more than twenty-five years of communist persecution, there were millions of Chinese believers worshipping secretly in house churches throughout the land. (By 1983, estimates suggested that there were ten million believers in China.)

By the time of my visit in 1998, after fifty years of governmental opposition to Christianity, no one knew for sure how many Chinese believers there really were. Many experts estimated that the number might be higher than one hundred million—and increasing daily.

Before I would leave China, I was scheduled to meet personally with leaders of four different house-church groups. Each group claimed more than ten million members. The seven men that I met in that apartment were all evangelists/church planters in one of those movements.

It seemed that Pastor Chang had lived through it all. Like the apostle Paul, he had learned to be content regardless of his circumstances. Inside prison or outside of prison, he preached the same gospel message and he discipled anyone interested in becoming a follower of Jesus Christ. Pastor Chang was like the apostle Paul in another way too. He devoted his life to mentoring and training younger believers—just as the apostle Paul had done with young Timothy.

Indeed, the six other men in the apartment with us, ranging in age from their twenties to their forties, were Pastor Chang's "Timothys"—men he had led to Christ and mentored over the years. Pastor Chang's joy was obvious as he talked about his own faith journey and celebrated the way that his life had intersected with the lives of these other men. For two days, I listened as Pastor Chang quietly recounted story after story of God's faithfulness, protection and provision over the many years of his spiritual pilgrimage.

What struck me most about Pastor Chang, even more than the details of his remarkable life, was his demeanor over the following days as he listened to me interview his spiritual protégés. As the younger men shared their testimonies, the old man squatted in a corner of the room. He closed his eyes and listened. From time to time I noticed that he was humming what sounded like praise songs. Even then, I could tell that he was still listening intently to what the others were sharing. Over and over again, he smiled in satisfaction and nodded with pride and approval at appropriate points in his young friends' stories.

I felt as if I were watching something akin to the passing of the mantle from the Old Testament prophet Elijah to his young replacement Elisha. This old man—only days out of prison, without a penny to his name—owned nothing but the clothes on his back and one extra pair of underwear. He had no home to return to and no surviving family to take him in. He planned to live out the remainder of his days much like a New Testament apostle, traveling the land and visiting one house church after another. He would encourage believers in their faith, while trusting the Lord and local bodies of Christ for His provision. He would do that unless, or until, he was arrested and thrown in prison again.

By any standard, Pastor Chang had lived a hard life. He had nothing tangible to show for all of his labor. Even so, he seemed more content, more filled with a spirit of peace, and more aware of the joy of living than anyone I had ever met.

The two men who had met me at the airport and made arrangements for these interviews stopped by the flat every day to check on us. Each time they showed up, I thanked them profusely for setting up this opportunity for me. I tried to convey the excitement that I felt about what I was hearing and learning.

For four days, I was able to talk at length with Pastor Chang and three of his spiritual protégés. It had been a mountaintop experience. I think that my Chinese friends, however, sensed that our cramped quarters and my own confinement were wearing me down. I couldn't deny that; four nights of little or no sleep had left me feeling that I had nearly reached the end of my rope.

David Chen's two friends assured me: "We still want you to interview these other three men who just got out of prison. Instead of doing that here, however, we are going to check you into one of the tourist hotels downtown. We will let you do the next interviews there." I was grateful for the change in scenery and for the prospect of getting a good night's sleep.

Checking in to the tourist hotel, I noticed a vigilant employee behind the tourist registration desk. It seemed that his sole responsibility was to take notice of everyone who came through the front door. He seemed especially interested in Chinese individuals who spoke with any of the hotel's foreign guests.

I asked my local hosts if it would be safe for these recent parolees to come to my room the next day for interviews. They assured me that no one else in that entire city knew or could identify any of these men. They would be leaving for their homes throughout the province shortly and they wouldn't be around long enough to raise any serious concern with the local authorities. Their response to my concern was strong and unequivocal: we would be "safe enough" for the next couple of days. I was glad that they thought so, because my new accommodations suited me much better than the previous ones.

I had expected that there would be three more individual interviews. Instead, the interview lasted for two days and included all three of the believers at once.

This trio of thirty-something evangelists decided to do the interview together because they had shared many of the same experiences. In fact, one of the things that they were most grateful for was that they had all been arrested at the same time. They had also received the same sentence, and they had even been sent to the same prison. They claimed that being imprisoned together had turned out to be a marvelous blessing from God. They also had been released at the same time, less than a week before I met them.

When I asked one of them a question, the other two would follow up his answer with thoughts of their own. Sometimes, they completed each other's sentences. And they felt free to tease one another, correct mistaken recollections, and laugh at each other's memories.

Their stories reminded me of something that I had seen in Somalia and had confirmed again in some of the interviews that I had already done in Russia and other former Iron Curtain countries in Eastern Europe: the psychological aspects of persecution often cause deeper wounds and leave greater scars than physical mistreatment.

These men acknowledged that they had suffered both psychological pain and physical mistreatment. Somehow, they had survived unbroken, in large part due to the shared strength of their bond of friendship. Before being arrested, they had served together as house-church planters. Then, after their arrest, they had together endured years of imprisonment and cruel treatment because of their faith. In prison, they had together led hundreds of fellow prisoners to Christ. And now, less than a week out of prison, they sat in my hotel room and together actually re-enacted for me some of the torture that they had received in prison. At the time, their antics were light-hearted and even humorous. In fact, they explained that a good sense of humor was an effective tool for dealing with physical mistreatment. All the same, it was clear that there was deep pain behind their now-smiling faces.

For their most memorable skit, they asked me to imagine an Asian toilet in the middle of my hotel room floor. (Given my recent experience, that wasn't hard for me to do.) Then two of the men roughly grabbed the other one by his wrists and elbows, twisted his arms back and hiked them up. They forced their victim to bend over with his face down closer and closer to the imaginary "toilet." They turned and twisted the man's arms as if they were adjusting rabbit-ears antennae on the top of an old television set.

"Let's see what kind of reception you can get today," they taunted. They mimicked their former guards as they again twisted the arms of their "prisoner" and forced his face lower and lower toward the "toilet" recessed in the floor. If there was waste in the toilet bowl, the guards would sarcastically exclaim, "This is your lucky day, reception is good—we have *color* television today!"

If the toilet had nothing in it but urine, the guards would laugh and say, "Too bad, only black and white television for you!" Then they would make more wisecracks as they further adjusted the "antennae" until their "prisoner" finally collapsed to his knees where they could force his head down into the toilet.

What they were describing and acting out to me was horrifying. I could barely imagine the treatment that they had experienced. The fact that they were laughing about it now—especially since they had only been out of prison a short time—was actually reassuring. It may seem odd to be talking about humor in the midst of this kind of horror. But humor is a powerful indicator of psychological health.

One of the clearest warning signs of undue psychological stress that we watched for among our relief staff in Somalia was the loss of an appropriate sense of humor. When our workers found it impossible to see and respond to humor, it was clear that they were in serious need of emotional relief and healing. When that happened, it was time to retreat and recover.

It dawned on me that, despite the horrible suffering that these men had endured for years, there was never an opportunity for them to step away to retreat and recover. Their abuse was constant. They endured three long years of persecution and horrible mistreatment with no relief. Still, somehow, when given the opportunity to share their ordeal, they were able to do that with healthy and healing humor. Clearly, the persecution that had been designed to break their spirits had failed to do that. The persecution that had been designed to intimidate these men of faith into silence had failed to do that. Having now been released from prison, their spirits were strong and their faith was vibrant.

After years of cruel emotional and physical mistreatment, these three friends had walked out into freedom with an obvious and contagious sense of joy. Their testimony was one of humor and hope. Their lives were evidence to the strength that can be found in community and fellowship and faith.

26

The Power of Prison

I left that province and flew to my next destination—another large city and regional capital. It was clear at the outset of my trip that I would need to trust my Chinese contacts (and the Lord) to take care of any and all security precautions wherever I went. I was completely unfamiliar with the culture. I determined that the best way—and perhaps the only way—to avoid making unwitting dangerous blunders would be to trust the people who were helping me. My greatest fear was to unintentionally cause trouble for local believers; I could not bear the thought of persecution that might happen because of my mistakes. Still, it was sometimes a challenge to trust other people.

In light of all that had happened so far in China, I was surprised when my contact in this next city phoned my hotel room and instructed me to join him and a number of his believer friends at a restaurant a few blocks from my tourist hotel. Not once in China, to this point, had I been part of a public gathering. In fact, I had been hidden since my arrival.

After a short walk, I arrived at the appointed place. When I mentioned my name to the greeter at the restaurant, I was immediately led up a nearby set of stairs, down a short hall, to the open double-doors of what was evidently a private dining room. It was already occupied by ten or twelve people. They were standing and casually chatting in two or three clusters.

When I entered the room, I was welcomed by a man who I assumed was my host. He explained that he had planned the evening as my introduction to a small gathering of evangelists and church planters from another regional affiliation of house churches. He asked me to share a little about myself and explain the reasons for my visit. He explained that then there would be time for me to ask questions that I might have for the whole group. And, then, before we left, there would be an opportunity for me to make appointments for individual interviews with anyone willing and able to talk with me. Our time was short, however, because I would be leaving for Beijing in less than forty-eight hours.

His plan sounded fine to me. He ushered me around the room and made individual introductions before we sat down for dinner. One of the younger men in the room, perhaps twenty-five years old, was already anxious to set a time for an individual interview appointment. He and I set a time for later that night.

After we were out of earshot from that young house-church leader, my host leaned toward me and whispered: "He's going to be someone God can use in a powerful way someday. But you cannot trust what he says now; he hasn't been to prison yet." This was an attitude that I would encounter often in China. Personal trust and respect for spiritual maturity were often in direct proportion to the amount of suffering that had been endured for the faith. If someone had not yet experienced personal persecution and suffering, trust was withheld until that happened. What was perhaps most remarkable about that was the underlying assumption that the suffering and persecution would inevitably happen!

Our host spoke a few words of welcome. He thanked everyone for coming and briefly described the agenda for the evening. That led to a twenty-minute discussion about whether or not the group should bless the meal out loud. One middle-aged man insisted strongly that we do so. We all bowed our heads and closed our eyes as he stood, raised his face toward heaven, and lifted his voice a few decibels—as if perhaps he thought that God was a little hard of hearing—and proceeded to *preach* a blessing.

Two or three sentences into his prayer, I heard some commotion and glanced up to see our waiter disappear into the hall. From the sound of his steps, he picked up the pace to a near-sprint as he made his way down the hall. Moments later, I heard someone rush toward our dining room at a more dignified, yet rapid rate.

Meanwhile, the prayer was continuing. The man who was praying was quite passionate—and it was also clear that he was not finished. Suddenly, the approaching footsteps stopped. I took another quick peek to see a professional man—most certainly the restaurant owner—standing in the open doorway, looking and listening, his face full of surprise and concern. Before we ever neared an ending to the prayer, he closed the double-doors to the hallway, and left behind a guard. Those doors remained closed for the remainder of the evening except when our waiters were coming and going.

For the next thirty minutes, the gathering entered into spirited discussion about whether or not believers should always pray a blessing over their food in private **and** in public. At this point, I began to fear that this particular house-church movement was on the verge of a split over the blessing of our meal. Finally, my dinner companions turned to me for input. "What did I think?" they wondered.

I asked them if persecution might come because of praying out loud in a public restaurant. I then asked if that kind of resulting persecution would actually be for Jesus' sake (because of who Jesus is) or if it would be happening simply because of a loud prayer spoken in a public place. They continued a lengthy discussion in Chinese about this, but eventually a sense of peace seemed to settle on the group. The discussion grew less and less heated. I assumed that they had finally agreed on their approach to praying out loud in public over their food.

Unfortunately, they never told me what conclusion they had reached!

After our meal, it was time for me to say a few words to the group about myself. I gave them a brief version of my personal and spiritual journey.

As I always did to orient and establish a little foundational rapport with potential interviewees, I also summarized my experience in Somalia. I talked briefly about the frustration and the questions that I was struggling with. I explained how my experience in Somalia had led me to places like this and why I wanted to meet with them. I was seeking wisdom that would help encourage believers around the world who were dealing with persecution. To illustrate the kind of things that I had already heard and learned thus far on my pilgrimage, I shared a small sampling of the stories that I had gathered.

Then, I gave them each a couple of minutes to sum up their own life story for me. We then opened the floor for questions. I invited them to ask anything that they might want to ask.

We had a very lively and productive exchange. Several specific topics stood out to me.

From the introductions that I had just heard, it seemed that most of the house-church leaders in the room had served at least one three-year prison term for their faith. I had observed the same thing at both of my earlier stops in China. Surprisingly, none of the people who reported on their time in prison seemed particularly resentful about the experience. At the same time, the believers who had not yet been to prison did not seem to be especially fearful about the possibility of someday having to go themselves.

It was clear that these Chinese believers were not seeking persecution. However, their attitude about the likelihood of persecution seemed to be an attitude of calm acceptance. The attitude was not so much "if it comes." The more common attitude was "when it comes." I was reminded of what the old Russian pastor had said to me earlier. Here, too, it seemed, that "persecution was like the sun coming up in the east."

Virtually every believer who I had met in China had either been to prison for the faith—or they knew someone who had. They were personally aware of many of their spiritual brothers and sisters who had endured persecution and had come out of it with deeper spiritual roots, a more mature faith, and a greater appreciation for fellowship with other believers. They had also come out of the experience with a much stronger relationship with the Lord. One of the house-church leaders actually asked me, *"Do you know what prison is for us? It is how we get our theological education. Prison in China is for us like seminary is for training church leaders in your country."*

What an insight that was! And it certainly explained a lot about the wisdom that I had seen in Pastor Chang. He had graduated with honors from three of these "seminaries."

I couldn't help thinking about my own education and training—and how that compared to what was being described to me now.

Another very interesting discussion happened that evening. As a matter of course, I posed a question that turned out to be an effective discussion starter on many points in my trip. I asked the question this evening: "If I were to visit your home communities and talk with the nonbelieving families, friends, and neighbors of the members of your house churches—and if I would point out your church members and ask, 'Who are those people? What can you tell me about them?'—what answer would I get?"

Many people started to answer at once. The response that jumped out at me, though, was the answer of a man who told me that his church's neighbors would probably say, "Those are the people who raise the dead!"

"REALLY!" I blurted out involuntarily.

Several of the men in the room, especially the older men, smiled and nodded.

I was stunned.

Then, as if to validate the claim, people around the table began recounting story after story from their own churches—stories of healings, stories of miraculous answers to prayer, stories of supernatural occurrences, stories that could be explained only by the activity of God. These miraculous events seemed to be milepost markers in their personal faith journeys. These were the happenings that had forever proven God's power in their minds. These were the stories that had drawn unbelievers into Christ's Kingdom.

In addition to reminding me of who God really is, these amazing narratives helped me connect a few more dots. What I had just heard in China was additional persuasive evidence in support of what started as a *hypothesis* in the former USSR. This hypothesis was quickly becoming a conviction:

> God seemed to be demonstrating His power on earth today in places like Russia and China. It seemed that He was using the same miraculous and supernatural means that He used in the first-century church of the New Testament.

Believers in persecution were teaching me that. And I realized that I wasn't yet finished with my learning. I just never imagined how far I still had to go.

27

The Chinese Road Trip

Arriving in the next city, I noticed a man who motioned to me. At least I thought that he had motioned to me. His movements were so subtle that I couldn't be sure. He glanced my way a couple of times and seemed to be marking my progress as I walked down a row of parked vehicles. Other than his slight attention to my presence, he showed no signs of welcome or recognition. None of the other men standing around him even turned their heads in my direction. I concluded that maybe they were waiting for someone else.

Now I wasn't so sure that the man had motioned to me at all.

There in the airport, I didn't feel that I was in danger. All of a sudden, however, I felt unsettled and wondered if there would be a problem finding my contact.

I had just landed in another major Chinese city with a name that I couldn't begin to pronounce or spell. I likely wouldn't recognize the name of the city on a map today. I didn't know a single person there, and I didn't even know who had been sent to find me. It dawned on me then that no one in the world knew where I was at that particular moment. And I am not sure that I even knew.

Even worse, I didn't even know how to make contact with Ruth or anyone else in the States. I guessed that I would have been welcome in a local house church, but a local house church would have been difficult to find. On the other hand, I realized that in a country of 1.3 billion people, I was unlikely to be alone for long.

I worked up the courage to approach the men clustered beside the van. I wasn't exactly wary, but I was certainly curious and filled with anticipation.

The man that I had first noticed finally turned to acknowledge my presence. "Dr. Ripken?" he asked quietly. The other men slipped around to the side of the van, opened its doors, and began to climb in. I thought, "Surely this must be the contact that David arranged. Who else could possibly know my name?" I decided not to press the matter any further. At this point, there was no turning back.

I nodded and offered my hand. The man nodded and gave me a polite smile. We shook hands briefly as he introduced himself. He did a quick visual survey of the parking lot, and then reached for my bag. "I will hand this back to you after you get in," he told me as he gestured toward the still-open side door of the van. "The rear seat will be yours."

The other passengers now smiled a warm welcome as I stepped up into the van. We all shook hands and introduced ourselves as I slowly wedged my way past them toward the rear bench seat of a twelve-passenger van. The men seemed friendly enough now. I was still hoping that they weren't secret police.

My bag got back to me about the same time I found my seat. Even then, I still wasn't sure whether or not I was among friends. I felt much better seconds later when the leader of the group slid into the driver's seat holding a cell phone to his ear. I heard him say, "Our visitor has arrived. I picked up all the others first. We are pulling out of location number two now and should arrive at location number eleven at time number seven." It was the same basic house-church security protocol that I had encountered before. I began to breathe a little easier.

My sense of calm did not last long, however. The driver turned back toward me and, in a rather apologetic tone, said: "We have an eighteen-hour drive before we reach our destination tomorrow. You will need to lie down and stay out of sight. We cannot afford to have the authorities see you. While we travel, you can rest and even sleep if you like."

"Okay," I responded as cheerily as possible. I tried to nestle down into the least uncomfortable position I could find as we pulled out of the parking lot. I couldn't help thinking, "Good grief! Eighteen hours slumped down in the back seat through a lot of China that I'm not going to see sounds like a miserable road trip!"

When I had last talked with David Chen, he had promised that he would be waiting for me at my next destination. He had also told me that my next destination would be very different from the big cities where I had already been. He had said that it would be "very rural, but also a very scenic part of China."

It looks like I'll have to take David's word on that, I thought. Crammed into the back seat, I managed to see only the sky and the tops of the buildings, light poles and trees that we passed. Those partial clues, combined with the feel of the pavement beneath us, the blare of horns and other traffic sounds outside, plus our plodding, stop-and-go pace, told me we were still in the city. But that was about all I knew.

Ordinarily I would have used this travel time to get to know some of my fellow passengers. Under the circumstances, however, any substantive conversation was obviously going to have to wait. Mostly, I spent the time thinking.

I thought about the places that I had been in China. I tried to picture in my mind the face of every believer I had met and interviewed. Already, there were too many to remember.

My China trip had already been the most grueling travel experience of my life. And I had come to a few new and unanticipated conclusions regarding culture shock. Perhaps these truths should have already been obvious, but I was learning them day by day. First, the greater the differences between cultures, the more culture shock a traveler must endure. And, second, the greater the culture shock, the greater the energy that is required just to make it through each day.

Again, those conclusions might seem obvious. But in all my travels I had never experienced the culture shock that I experienced in China. I had spent time in Western Europe, Eastern Europe, Africa, and many other places—but China seemed like a different world to me.

Even with my experience and aptitude for languages, I could seldom pick out and understand any spoken words. The words and symbols of directional signs, advertisements on buildings, newspaper headlines, and even menus were indecipherable to me. I had always enjoyed a wide variety of ethnic foods. On this trip, however, I had eaten foods that I couldn't recognize by sight, smell, taste, or texture.

So many personal adjustments had to be made—and the need for adjustment seemed so constant—that each day seemed to last forever. The physical toll was immense. At the same time, I was so overwhelmed and excited by what I was seeing and hearing that each day I went back and forth between emotional/spiritual exhilaration and physical exhaustion. Some days I survived on pure adrenalin. By evening, I often felt like my internal engine had drained its gas tank and I was barely chugging on fumes.

In biblical terms, my spirit was willing, but my flesh was weak.

Now, relegated to the rear seat of a van full of strangers at the start of an eighteen-hour drive, I realized that the failure to anticipate the amount of stress created by the culture shock was just one of the miscalculations that we had made in planning this trip. In pursuit of efficiency and frugality, we had sorely overestimated where I could go, who I could meet with, and what I could get done in one trip. We had underestimated the distances, the climate, the terrain differences, and the host of other logistical and physical challenges to be encountered traveling in China.

It had been easy to draw lines on a map. It had been relatively easy to reserve bus, train, and plane tickets. Doing that, we had failed to realize that China is almost exactly the same size as the entire United States.

The friendly banter and frequent laughter among my fellow passengers told me that they were already well-acquainted. Evidently, they were also happy about this opportunity to fellowship together. They were enjoying themselves on our trip. Clearly, I was an outsider and, at this point, could not experience the joy of their camaraderie.

In that moment, I sensed again the aloneness and loneliness of being an alien in a strange land. I had felt this when I first entered China—and that feeling had stayed with me. I had been unable to shake the feeling of being constantly watched by someone whatever I did or wherever I went. More likely, it wasn't someone who was watching me—it was everyone! There was also that subtle, but unrelenting, stress that came from the realization that if any of my meetings were somehow compromised, my hosts would go to prison simply for being with me. I wasn't terribly worried about my own safety; I would simply be escorted to the nearest airport and told to go home. But I carried the weight of their safety like a heavy burden.

We finally picked up speed and I began seeing only treetops. Now, there were few buildings or streetlights. I knew that we had left the city. Certain that no one could be expected to lie down and out of sight for eighteen hours, I slowly sat up to see more of where we were. If our driver ever looked in his mirror to see me sitting up, he wasn't concerned enough to say anything. And I thought I knew why.

He had been extremely cautious driving at slow speeds through the heavily populated city. Here, driving much faster in the bright daylight, it was unlikely that anyone could have seen through the tinted windows and discern my ethnicity. I stayed alert and was ready to hide at a moment's notice. But I was finally able to relax a little. My emotional health improved immensely at the simple thought of being able to sit up and actually see what was happening outside (and inside) the van.

Unfortunately, that wasn't as comforting as I had anticipated. Looking out of the window, I discovered a rather disturbing cultural distinctive. It seemed that the Chinese concept of personal space is pretty much the same on the country's highways as it is on the pedestrian-packed sidewalks and in the crush of the crowds in the markets. As long as they weren't being physically jostled or touching someone else, Chinese people seemed to believe that they had more than enough space.

The same thing proved to be true on the roads. I hadn't realized it before, but we were driving down a two-lane road with a steady stream of traffic going both directions over one hundred kilometers per hour. Every time we met another van or truck, the mirrors on the side of those vehicles came within centimeters of ours. My companions, including the driver, kept laughing and chatting. They seemed to pay no attention at all to what was for me the most terrifying road experience in my life. Lying back down out of sight suddenly seemed to be much safer. It probably wasn't any safer—but it felt safer.

A little later, I felt our vehicle accelerating. I raised my head to peek over the back of the seat to see that we were now on what looked like a four-lane American interstate. We were traveling at least one hundred and forty kilometers an hour. The road looked new, smooth and safe. I settled back down thinking that maybe I could fall asleep for a while. Before I could drift off, however, we suddenly swerved so violently that I had to grab the back of the seat in front of me to keep from being rolled off of my bench onto the floor. This time I didn't even peek. I assumed that maybe it would be better not to know.

When we swerved again a minute or so later, I sat up far enough to look out of the back of the van to see that we had just dodged a two-wheeled donkey-cart piled high with produce of some kind, driven by a farmer dressed in traditional Chinese peasant garb.

Our driver laughed and talked as fast as he drove. He seemed to be driving as fast as the house churches were growing.

Eventually, we exited the "expressway" onto smaller country roads. After dark, we drove several miles on dirt roads until we turned down a long dirt driveway and pulled to a stop behind a two-story farmhouse out of sight from the road. Our driver explained, "Friends are letting us stay here tonight. We will continue the trip tomorrow morning and we should reach our destination before dark tomorrow night."

A middle-aged woman who seemed to be expecting company opened the door, welcomed us into her home, and served us cups of tea. Then she led us upstairs in what was the nicest, and by far biggest, home that I had visited since I had arrived in China.

Slipping out of bed just before dawn the next morning, I quietly and quickly washed and dressed for the day. I was hoping to be out of the way when the others awakened. I tiptoed down the stairs and into the kitchen. There was just enough daylight to see a uniformed man across the room. We both froze. I had no idea what kind of uniform he was wearing, but his bearing was one of great authority. I stood and stared right at him. His eyes seemed to be looking right through me, focused on something behind me. It was as if I wasn't even there. I certainly wished that I wasn't.

Neither one of us said a word or acknowledged each other. He turned abruptly on his heel, took something off of the counter behind him and disappeared out the kitchen door. My heart was pounding and my knees were trembling long after I heard the start of an engine, followed by the crunch of gravel as a heavy vehicle slowly rolled onto the road at the front of the property.

When our driver came into the kitchen a few minutes later, I told him what had just happened and I asked if he knew who the man was. Instead of answering my question, he told me that they should have warned me not to come downstairs by myself early in the morning. I apologized. I told him that I had not intended to do anything to endanger him or the others. He, however, seemed more concerned for the man that I had encountered.

He went on to explain why the officer had chosen not to speak to me or even to acknowledge my presence by looking right at me. If the question ever came up, he could honestly say that he had never met, spoken to, or seen anyone like me at his house that morning. "He is a very good friend and a supporter of our house-church movement," the driver said. "We know that we are safe when we stop here because the government would never think that such a high-ranking military official is a believer. But he and his family allow us to use their home as a safe house at great risk to themselves."

The second day of our journey was much like the first. The only difference was that when we passed through a big city in the middle of the day, we saw enough foreign tourists on the sidewalks that my companions decided that it would be safe for me to go into a restaurant with them to eat lunch.

I was so exhausted that I actually fell sound asleep sometime in the afternoon. I didn't awaken until it was almost dusk when I felt the motion of the van change. I sat up and looked out to discover that we were driving down a long two-track dirt road. Lush green trees were close at both sides; their branches sometimes formed a canopy overhead that nearly blocked out the sky.

After four or five miles of nothing but trees, we suddenly emerged into small clearings of farmland divided into dozens of fields clustered around a farm compound. The compound was surrounded by a ten-foot, whitewashed fence.

Our van followed the two-track between the fields. As we approached the structure, an old rusty gate swung open and our driver pulled into a typical rural dwelling for that part of China. It was not a farm*house* exactly, but a residence of individual "rooms" built along and around the inside walls of the compound. On closer inspection, the walls seemed to be crude, but effective, protective barriers constructed out of rock and stone. Every few feet, long, upright wooden poles were sunk into the ground to help anchor the fence, and the entire structure was then whitewashed. This place had none of the forbidding, high-security feel of a walled compound in Somalia. This felt more like a safe place of welcome. It felt like someone's home.

Sure enough, David Chen was already there to greet me. He was there to greet me along with about one hundred and seventy of his closest house-church friends! They were sitting or standing in small groups all around the farmyard, chatting and curiously noting our arrival.

After introducing me to a couple of the leaders of the movement, David accompanied us to interpret the brief guided tour that the local hosts wanted to give me. The enclosed compound covered maybe a quarter of an acre of packed dirt and trampled-down grass. An open kitchen and several other individual rooms were built right up against the outer wall. Since the rooms weren't connected, it was necessary to come out into the farmyard to get from one room to another.

I looked at the size of the little rooms and quickly surveyed the courtyard full of people. I asked, "Where are all these folks going to sleep?" One of the guides replied, as David translated: "Right out here, where they are sitting and standing now."

My hosts must have noticed the surprise on my face because they quickly assured me, "But you will sleep over here in this room—and while we are meeting and training the people out here in the yard, you can do your interviews in the same room." They led me over to one of the enclosed rooms to show me my accommodations. It was a tiny room, but I would be able to be comfortable there. "Now, come with us" they said "and we'll introduce you to the three of our senior leaders who will share the room with you." I was just glad that it was only three.

David Chen had told me that this particular house-church movement was one of biggest and most diverse in the entire country. Many of its congregations and their leaders, like those who rode in the van with me, were urban, educated and comparatively sophisticated in the modern ways of the world—or at least in the modern ways of China.

At the same time, a significant percentage of this regional movement had sprung up and spread among people in places so provincial and so remote that much of the twentieth century had passed them by. Some of the church leaders from the most rural areas had little knowledge of the outside world.

In light of what David had told me, I was somewhat prepared for the curious stares during supper that night. But I was profoundly surprised after supper when I was formally introduced to the group. One of the local pastors raised his hand to ask a question. What he wanted to know was this: "Do the people in other countries also know about Jesus—or is He still known only in China?"

I had never been asked that question before—or even considered that point of view. For several long seconds I gathered my thoughts, trying to figure out where exactly to begin my answer. Then, with David interpreting for me, I told the group that millions of Americans and even more people in different countries around the world knew about and followed Jesus. I then told the group that believers in other parts of the world also knew about them—the Chinese believers in house churches. I told them that believers in many parts of the world prayed for them and their churches.

"Wait, wait!" people cried out. They could hardly believe what I was saying. One man responded this way: "Do you mean that people in your country know that we believe in Jesus? Do you mean that they know that some of us are suffering for our faith? Do you mean that they haven't forgotten us and that they pray for us?"

I assured them: "Why yes, we have always loved you. And we have never forgotten you. For a long time, we have prayed for you." It was a holy moment as these believers realized that they were recognized, remembered and prayed for by fellow believers around the world.

One of the younger women in the group asked, "Since Jesus is known in other countries, are the believers there persecuted like we are?"

I told them about the experience of believers in two very oppressive Islamic counties. The entire gathering of house-church leaders in the farmyard became strangely still. Just minutes before, they had been clapping and shouting and asking questions. Now they were completely silent and still. They sat expressionless.

I attempted to enliven the group by sharing about Muslim-background believers we were close to—people who had exhibited inspiring faith under the most oppressive circumstances. But there was still no movement and no questions. When I had told a number of such stories, I felt half-dead myself.

I lowered my voice and I said to David, "That's it. I'm done. I'm drained. I have nothing more to say tonight!" I stepped off the little stage in the middle of the compound and headed for the room where I was to sleep.

At 6:00 the next morning I was awakened by screaming and shouting outside in the compound. My first thought was that the security police had come.

As my eyes adjusted to the daylight, I saw that there were no security police swarming into the compound. What I saw were those Chinese house-church leaders and evangelists scattered around the farmyard, either lying or sitting on the ground, crying, screaming and yelling hysterically (or so it seemed to me). Many of them were pulling their hair or clutching at their clothes.

I spotted my friend David across the way and I rushed over to him. I demanded to know: "What in the world is going on?"

He told me to be quiet and to listen.

"You know that I don't know a word of Chinese," I told him. "What do you mean 'just listen'"?

Again he insisted, "Just be quiet, Nik!" Before I could protest again, he took me by the arm and began to walk me among these people who were crying and screaming. Because I was now silent, I actually began to hear and recognize the names of the two Muslim countries that I had told them about the night before. The names of those two countries were being repeated again and again in passionate and anguished prayer.

When David stopped and turned to look at me, there were tears streaming down his face. He said, "They were so moved by what you shared last night about believers who were *truly* persecuted, that they have vowed before God that they will get up an hour earlier every morning to pray for those Muslim-background believers that you told them about in ________________ and ______________ (and he named the two nations*) until Jesus is known throughout their countries."

In that instant, I could see why the number of Chinese believers had gone from a few hundred thousand to perhaps hundreds of millions!

*Even today, more than a decade later, security concerns prevent me from naming these specific countries. If the normal security apparatus were to read this, let alone Al Qaeda or other jihadists, they would search out believers in those countries or use my mention of them here as an excuse to kill people they oppose.

28

Preparing for Persecution

Most of my encounters with believers and most of the interviews I had done in China were one on one. Knowing the communist government's policy and practice of relentless and brutal persecution of the faithful, and recognizing the security challenges that I would face on this trip, I never in my wildest dreams imagined that I would have an opportunity like this.

More than one hundred and seventy house-church leaders were together in one place. And all of them are willing to sit down and talk with me. I was thrilled!

Oddly, the opportunities provided by this gathering were perhaps even more exciting for the other attendees than for me. In planning for this trip, David Chen had explained that believers in house churches around the country had several strict rules when it came to security. Through decades of oppression, they had learned that they could usually avoid attention if they never met in groups of more than thirty or so—and if they never met for more than three days at a time. That explained why local congregations met regularly but at different times throughout the week. And that also explained why a local body would subdivide into groups of fifteen when the total group grew to include thirty people or so. The "thirty people and three day" limits were observed as strictly as possible. Larger groups or longer gatherings presented a much greater risk of discovery.

Of course, I had assured David that I would gladly abide by the security parameters that he and his national contacts felt necessary. That's when he told me that he was already scheduled to help lead a conference for house-church leaders. He suggested that this might be my best and safest chance to be with a larger group of believers together in one place at one time. The opportunity sounded so promising that I had told him that I was willing to contribute much of my task force funding toward the cost of food and transportation for the conference.

What I didn't learn until later was that the unexpected prospect of those additional resources had prompted the conference organizers to plan a bigger week-long event. They would naturally follow the most stringent security precautions (such as meeting at a secluded farm location). But they also decided that this would be an unprecedented opportunity for training, teaching, and encouragement. They concluded that it was worth the risk. According to David, never before had that many leaders gathered for training, worship and fellowship in the history of that house-church movement. I felt privileged just to be a part of it. I could hardly wait to get started with the interviews on my first full day at the conference.

When the large-group training session started in the farmyard later that morning, I retreated to "my bedroom" with eight of the movement's leaders. They knew that I would be interviewing one person at a time, but the others wanted to sit in and listen. That was fine with me.

The first three life and faith stories that I heard in the room that morning energized me. The researcher in me came to life. And I was as inspired personally and spiritually as I had been in any interviews thus far. Each of these three men had been sentenced to prison at least once. They had each faced and overcome serious challenges while suffering great hardship for their faith. Yet all three were much more interested in recounting for me the ways in which they had seen God's power at work in their own house-church movement. God had granted spectacular growth in their movement, and that is what they wanted to talk about most. The number of believers had gone from hundreds to millions.

As I listened that morning, I sensed the spiritual significance of what was happening in China. The story was hardly known to Christians around the world, but it represented something unprecedented. These leaders had been born into an environment of oppression. They had lived their lives under that oppression. Even so, these leaders and their colleagues outside in the farmyard had witnessed the greatest spiritual awakening that the world has ever known. And they had played a part in it. God was using these faithful and courageous followers of Jesus, and countless more just like them, to spread the good news of the gospel further, faster, and to more people than had ever happened before in human history. The growth of the church during fifty years of communist rule in China was even greater than the growth experienced in the church over the first few centuries after Christ.

For some of us, this amazing movement of the Spirit in China had happened during our lifetime—and, likely, we were not even aware of it.

Each interview was exciting, revealing, and instructive. Each interview lasted about three hours apiece—and that was not nearly long enough. I hated to draw the interviews to a close. At the same time, I could hardly wait to see what the next person would tell me. The stories were amazing and almost beyond belief.

As had happened in the former USSR, it was as if the pages of the Bible had opened and the saints of old were once again walking the earth. And I had suddenly found myself among them.

As engrossed as I was in their stories, I couldn't help asking myself: "What will I do after hearing such amazing witness to the power of God?" My heart broke for Somalia. "This is what Somalia needs," I silently prayed. "How Somaliland needs an on-fire faith like this! *Oh, Somalia, Somalia—how God wants to gather you as a mother hen gathers her chicks!*"

I was shocked near the end of that first day. There had been nine long hours of interviews—three incredible interviews. The leaders who had listened to those first interviews consulted with each other. One of them informed me in broken English: "We are very sorry, Dr. Ripken. But we have talked and we have decided that we will do no more interviews like this."

My heart nearly stopped. I was distraught. "But," I started to protest, "you can't do this . . . I am learning so much from you."

Words failed me. I tried to think what I might have done or said to offend them, what cultural gaffe I might have committed. "I'm sorry," I said, thinking it wise to apologize in preface to arguing. "But the stories that we have just heard are so encouraging and so important. Surely there are others here at this conference I can talk with." I wasn't going to accept their decision easily. I simply could not let this opportunity pass.

The Chinese spokesman smiled and turned to address David Chen, who had been translating for me during the interviews. David smiled back at him and then at me as he translated: "He says, 'You don't understand.'"

"He says, 'They think that these interviews are a very good thing.'"

"He says that you are pulling so much out of them, so many

details and experiences from these stories that they have never heard before. They think that there is so much they can benefit from that they want you to do the rest of your interviews out in the compound in front of the whole group. If we do them that way, everyone can listen."

They ushered me outside and had me sit on a little platform. One of the leaders explained to the group a little more about the purpose of my trip, and he told them how the interviews that we had been doing all day had been so inspiring and informative. He told them that they had decided that everyone at the conference should hear the rest of my interviews. (David whispered the translation to me.)

For my first public interview, the leader called up two brothers who had recently been appointed to leadership positions upon their release from the standard three-year prison sentence for "religious crimes."

Back in that quiet room, I had just finished three amazing interviews that had each reminded me of something right out of the book of Acts. Now in front of one hundred and seventy witnesses, I found myself talking to two men who were difficult to figure out. So far, I had been impressed with the wisdom and maturity of the people that I had talked to. But my first impression of these two men was less than positive. They didn't seem to be spiritually mature. They seemed to be about the most shallow believers that I had met in China.

I am embarrassed to admit it now, but I reached the conclusion quickly that they were spiritual misfits. They seemed to barely know who Jesus was. After talking with these men for about ten minutes, I was looking for a way to end the interview. The fact that this was being done in public was even worse. It was turning out to be a humiliating experience. Finally, after a few more pointless questions, I ushered the men off the stage. They wandered back through the crowd to sit down together under a tree in the far corner of the compound.

I was then given a brother and sister (he was a pastor and she was an evangelist) to interview next. Thankfully, that went much better, but their interview still didn't quite measure up to any of the ones that I had conducted back in the little private room. I was not happy about the way things were working out.

It had been an exhausting fifteen-hour day. When I finished with this brother and sister, I was ready to quit for the day. I simply needed to rest. I gave a conclusive "thank-you" and started to step down from the platform. As I moved toward my room, one of the leaders jumped up and asked, "Where are you going, Dr. Ripken?" I looked at the translator uncertainly, and I said, "Well, uh, I guess I'm not going anywhere yet."

The man who had stopped me went on to say, "You've gotten so much information out of us already. Now, it's your turn. We want *you* to teach *us*!"

"What is it that I am to teach you?" I asked.

The man said, "Well, you have been to seminary, right?"

I nodded.

He continued: "And you are travelling all around the world to talk to people about persecution."

Again, I nodded.

"Well, maybe you could teach us this," the man continued. "We have one hundred and seventy leaders here. They are mostly evangelists and church planters. There are also a few local church pastors. Only about forty percent of us have already been arrested and put in jail for our faith. That means sixty percent of us have yet to go to jail. Would you please share with us how to prepare for prison? What do we need to do to get ready to go to jail for our faith?"

I have always considered myself a well-educated person. I have studied for years and I am fairly well-read. But I have never had a course on how to prepare for prison. In fact, I have never heard of such a course. I silently offered a rather desperate prayer: *Lord, just a few minutes ago, I was irritated about how the interviews were going. Please forgive me for that. Now, I really need for you to show up. Lord, I have nothing to teach these people about this subject—unless you can give me some words to speak.*

I moved back to the platform and simply began to tell the assembly of house-church leaders the stories that the Lord brought to mind in that moment—a sampling of testimonies from believers who I had met in Russia, in the Ukraine, throughout Eastern Europe, and in other parts of China. I told them the story of another secret gathering—that historic youth conference in Moscow back in the 1950's—and I told them what I had learned about believers who had hidden the Word of God in their hearts. I told them about Dmitri and his seventeen years in prison; I told them how he would write out all the Scripture he had memorized as an offering to Jesus, and how he had sung HeartSongs to the Lord in praise and worship every morning.

As I retold those stories, I watched the faces of the house-church leaders. They were listening in rapt attention. I felt that the Holy Spirit was moving and working in that farmyard. I could sense that these leaders were pulling real biblical principles out of the stories.

Then, in the middle of the final story that I was going to tell, I heard a noise, a disturbance. I looked around and, in the back corner, I saw movement.

It was those two brothers that I had tried to interview a little earlier. They were standing up and waving their arms. I couldn't imagine what they were doing. I tried to ignore them, hoping that no one would notice the commotion.

But they rushed forward. Weaving their way through the crowd, they made their way toward the platform. I tried in vain to figure out some way to keep them from coming up on the stage. As they drew closer, though, I could tell that they were crying. Instinctively, I moved back and gave way. By the time they stepped up on the platform, they were shaking and sobbing. They said to the assembled group: "Listen to this man! Listen to this man! The stories he tells are true! You can only grow in persecution what you go into persecution with."

Then they opened their hearts to their Christian brothers and sisters seated before them. What they said sounded like a confession: "You have honored us and you have made us leaders just because the authorities arrested us and we went to jail for three years. But you never, ever asked us our story."

"We know that when most of you went to prison, you shared your faith, you preached the word of God, and you brought hundreds if not thousands of people to Jesus. You started dozens of churches, and you began a movement that has grown out of the prisons. The Lord used you in a mighty way."

"But when we were arrested, we barely knew who Jesus was! We did not know how to pray! We did not know the Bible! We did not know many songs of faith. We have to confess this to you today and beg your forgiveness. For three years in prison, we did not share our faith with one person. We hid our faith. And yet, when we came out of prison, you made us leaders just because we had been put in jail. The truth is, we failed Jesus in prison. Would you please forgive us?"

"You must listen to this man! Listen to this man! What he is teaching is true: You can only grow in jail what you take to jail with you. You can only grow in persecution what you take into it."

There seemed to be nothing more that I could add to that. I silently asked for God's forgiveness. I had been upset about my interview with these two brothers. Evidently, God had a purpose in bringing them to the front.

While feeling spiritually uplifted and radically changed by all that I was experiencing and learning, my human shell was exhausted from four grueling weeks crisscrossing China before I had arrived at that conference. I had been on planes, trains, buses, and clandestine automobile rides. I had been smuggled over provincial borders and hidden in safe-houses. Many days, I had risen before dawn and stayed up past midnight doing interviews.

By this point, I was exhausted. Still, I knew that this was a holy opportunity. Somehow, I made it through several good, solid interviews before suppertime on the next day. At that point, the conference leaders told me that, since they were now spending all day doing the interviews with me, they needed to do their originally planned training later at night. They asked David and me if we could both lead Bible studies on the remaining nights of the conference. David took Paul's letter to the Romans; I chose the Gospel of Luke.

It was a sobering honor to teach Gospel stories and lessons from God's Word to those courageous and faithful house-church leaders. Their lives and ministries were already inspiring and teaching me so much. But even more sobering and moving for me was a scene that I would witness later that week.

Early one morning I was surprised to come out of my room and see a small group of men walking among the entire assembly of house-church leaders filling the courtyard. From a distance I could see that they were tearing some books into shreds and handing loose pages to those sitting on the ground. As I walked closer, I was shocked to realize they were tearing a Bible into pieces.

Noting my reaction, David Chen hurried over to explain: "Only seven of the house church leaders at this conference own their own copy of the Bible. Some of us met last night and we decided that when the conference ended each leader would go home to his city, village, or farm with at least one book of the Bible. So that is what we are doing. We are asking each leader what books of the Bible they have not yet been able to teach, and we are giving them each at least one new book."

I could only imagine what a joy it would have been for those whose portion of Scripture was the book of Genesis, the Psalms, or the Gospel of John. But I felt a little bad for the church leader who was handed a smaller portion like Philemon.

I had been not only inspired but also deeply convicted by the faith and the life examples of these Chinese church leaders. Even today, looking back fifteen years later, I view that whole trip, and especially that week, as one of the most significant turning points in my spiritual, personal, and professional life.

At the time I sensed that our conference that week would change my life and my work forever. Yet, neither the conference nor my China adventures were over yet.

29

Rebuked by God

About ten percent of those attending the house-church conference were women. I was intrigued by them. I realized that any church-house leader was taking a huge risk—but I wondered about the women who were willing to take that risk. And, even further, how had they become leaders of groups? I was looking forward to the opportunity to hear some of their stories. How had they come to know Jesus? How had they come to take on leadership roles?

My large-group interviews had continued. Amazing stories were being heard by the entire gathering. Between our large-group gatherings, however, I made a point of spending time with smaller groups that huddled together during meal times and breaks. It didn't take me long to discover that all of these leaders were strong individuals. I found them to be spiritually mature and exceptionally articulate about their faith. The women, in particular, were passionate evangelists. They had spiritual fire in their bones. I sensed that they could have witnessed about Jesus for three hours straight without stopping to take a breath. Their passion and their enthusiasm were astonishing.

I learned that the women at this conference had planted churches all over that province and neighboring provinces. When I asked them about the biggest challenges facing house-church leaders and pastors, they explained to me that they did not have those titles. "All the women here at this conference," they explained, "are evangelists and church planters." I was beginning to learn a lot more about what those titles meant. To this point, I had assumed that being a leader or a pastor of a house church was the most dangerous position. After listening to these women, however, I began to wonder.

Based on their stories, being an evangelist or a church planter was perhaps an even more dangerous responsibility in a house-church movement than leading a local congregation. Fulfilling the role of an evangelist or church planter required witnessing to non-believers. It was a constant danger to interact with people and to decide whether or not those people could be trusted. These evangelists relied on the leadership of God's Spirit when it came to the matter of trusting people. They were passionate about sharing their faith, but they knew how much risk was involved.

I asked them how they had become evangelists and church planters.

They told me, "Oh, it is just common sense!"

"What do you mean?" I asked.

"Once churches are planted, the leaders are often imprisoned," they explained. "When those leaders are away, other people begin to lead. Sometimes, those leaders are taken to prison too. Every time, though, others rise up to take their place. We simply do what we have been trained to do; we take God's Word and we share it. When people receive the message, new churches are started. That seems to be the way that God grows His church."

I was astounded by the clarity and simplicity of the strategy—and by their commitment to it. These women seemed completely uninterested in titles, positions, and formal structure. They were committed to sharing the story of Jesus; nothing else seemed to matter to them.

In that moment, I thought of so many American denominations that are engaged in conflict over matters of authority and leadership. These believers seemed to understand that the only thing that mattered was sharing Jesus. I was certain that if there was ever disagreement about leadership roles in the house churches in China, the argument would be over who would most quickly and most passionately venture out into a hostile world to share the gospel with the lost and win people for Jesus. These women, in particular, didn't seem to have the time or the inclination to debate responsibilities or titles within the church.

At the end of that week, as I finished my last session of interviews and storytelling in front of the conference crowd, I felt a surge of gratitude for all that I had heard and learned from these house-church leaders. As different as our cultures and our faith journeys may have been, I had developed a deep sense of spiritual unity and oneness with these brothers and sisters. I wanted to open my heart to them in a way that would demonstrate my respect and appreciation for them.

What I wanted to say to the house-church leaders gathered there was something like, "How can we partner together? How might we continue to learn from each other? How can I, and others in the western church, come alongside you and maybe even do ministry and mission together?"

That's what I wanted to ask. That's what I should have asked. That's what I meant to ask. However . . .

Sick and sleep-deprived, I was by this time exhausted. What I ended up saying was this: "How can I help you?"

I knew the moment those words crossed my lips how they would be heard. I knew what kind of response those words would elicit. My listeners heard my question as an offer of financial support. And, naturally, one of the house-church leaders had a suggestion for how they could use the money that they thought I was offering.

"Dr. Ripken," this man said. "Right now four hundred of our leaders are in prison. Their families are suffering. Many of them have no financial resources for school fees, rent, food, or clothing. They have nothing. Now that you have heard our stories, perhaps you can go back to your country and tell people about us. When you do that, maybe you can gather an offering to help us take care of those poor families who are suffering while their husbands and fathers are in prison."

It was a sobering request. After all that I had heard and seen, I felt inspired to tell them that I was ready to make this my life's work. I would vow to tell the stories of these committed house-church leaders wherever I went. Surely there were no more needy and deserving people in the world. Surely there was no nobler cause than to rally the western church to support these churches in persecution. Of course, I would commit to help them care for the struggling families of these Chinese believers who have sacrificed so much for the Lord.

I looked out over the gathering of courageous believers, fully prepared to promise them that, when I returned to America, I would indeed tell their stories.

But when I opened my mouth, no words came out.

A second time, I started to speak, intending to assure them that I would do everything in my power to make their cause my cause.

But when I opened my mouth to say that, nothing came out.

A third time I attempted to speak. Again, I had no words.

For some reason, I was suddenly unable to speak. Nothing like this had ever happened to me before. I had been rendered speechless by the Holy Spirit.

In that moment, I prayed a silent prayer: *Lord, speak. Your servant wants to hear.*

And God gave me a message to share with these house-church leaders.

I recognized God's voice because this wasn't the first time that I had heard it. Sensing the message that I should share, I silently argued with God. I tried to tell God why this particular message would be wrong. At the same time, I felt commanded to speak this word.

Looking at these leaders who had, by now, become dear friends, I asked, "How many believers do you have in this house-church movement?" It was an odd thing to ask. We had gone over that figure time and time again. Patiently, one of the leaders answered, "As we have told you, there are ten million of us."

"We have only been together a short time here," I said slowly. "You don't *really* know me! And I realize that I don't have any authority over your lives or your churches! I am not your pastor. I am not one of your leaders . . ."

". . . I know I have no right . . . no real authority to say this," I continued. "But I feel that God has spoken to my heart just now . . . to keep me from saying what I was planning to say to you. I feel now that God would have me say something different. If I am correct in what I am feeling—and if this is, in fact, a word from God—then we should be careful to hear it."

I paused, took a deep breath for resolve, and I plowed ahead: **"If ten million believers in your movement cannot take care of four hundred families, do you have the right to call yourselves the Body of Christ, the Church, or even followers of Jesus?"**

The words brought no reaction. I looked and I saw one hundred and seventy faces staring at me with an icy silence.

I had nothing more to say. And I was hoping that God would put no further word on my heart.

I didn't know what else to do, so I retreated to the back of the little platform. I feared that I had offended people who I had already grown to love.

I plopped down on the bench and sat there all alone. A few minutes passed. My sympathetic friend David offered his moral support by coming over and sitting down beside me.

I have no idea how many minutes passed. It felt like an eternity to me. Then I noticed that a woman had started crying. Then several people were crying. Eventually, the entire group seemed to be crying. This went on for maybe thirty minutes. Finally, one of the leaders rose to his feet. He wiped tears from his face.

Walking up to me and standing right in front of me on the platform, this leader addressed me. "Dr. Ripken, you are right. When you go home, you and your wife should continue doing what God has called you to do. And, here, we will continue doing what God has called us to do. You were right when you said, 'If ten million of us cannot take care of four hundred families, then we have no right to call ourselves followers of Jesus or His church.' You were right. And we take that word as a word from God. Now, you go home and do your job, and we will stay here and do ours. We **will** take care of these four hundred families!"

It was a gracious conclusion. The house-church leaders rejected neither the messenger nor his message. They took my hard words as a message from God. Responding to the challenge, they recommitted themselves to care for those among their number who were suffering so greatly.

My time in China, like my time in Eastern Europe, had provided little opportunity for reflection on what was happening day by day. I had little time to think about what I was learning or experiencing. Most days, it was enough simply to survive. I wondered how I would make sense of what I was seeing—or if that would ever happen.

Anticipating that struggle to a small degree, we had reserved a few extra hours in our planning for a short layover in a city boasting one of China's most popular tourist attractions and something that I had always wanted to see. By the time I actually arrived there, though, I was too exhausted to explore. I simply wanted to rest.

That down-time allowed me to sit still long enough to begin fleshing out all the cryptic notes that I had taken since my time in Hong Kong. It was a gift to have a brief time to process my experiences, to look for underlying patterns, to re-examine my initial observations, and then to begin to see and connect the dots between different people and places that I had come across on my journey.

I had noticed a number of significant cultural differences—some small and others huge—between believers and churches in Eastern Europe and those I had visited in China. I had actually expected that. Beyond the obvious differences, though, I sensed an intangible difference in attitude that I couldn't quite identify or articulate. Something was there that I couldn't quite put my finger on.

I had been inspired by the steadfast faithfulness of the believers who had endured decades of oppression in the former USSR. The suffering under communist rule still weighed heavily on many of the survivors. Even many years later, they remained wary, wearied and deeply wounded. The pain of suffering was still very real even ten years after the fall of communism. In contrast, the Chinese believers who I had met later that same year of 1998 had a surprisingly relaxed, upbeat, and almost buoyant air about them.

These Chinese believers still lived under the very real threat of arrest and imprisonment for the practice of their faith. That threat required constant vigilance and painstaking attention to security precautions. Every time the believers gathered for worship or met with a foreign fellow-believer like me, they were in a situation of great danger. Even so, the believers in China exhibited a constant *joyfulness* in the midst of harsh circumstances. I never heard them deny or down-play the danger. They never made light of it. They were painfully aware of the reality of their lives. Still, they exhibited an undeniable, irrepressible joy.

I had seen it on the face of old Pastor Chang crouched in the corner, humming and smiling as he listened to me interview the young men who he had mentored. I had sensed it in the spirit of enthusiasm and vitality of the young university students who I had met in Beijing. Those students didn't merely *accept* the potential cost of their commitment to Christ, they *embraced* what they considered the *adventure* of following Jesus. I heard it in the voices of the women evangelists who expressed gratitude to God for their call and ministry. I watched it acted out by the three pastor friends who could laugh and make me laugh over the torture that they had endured.

I remembered how my very first Chinese contacts back in southern China had explained the government's primary motivation for persecuting believers. It was not that the communists opposed or even cared about what Jesus taught His followers. The communists were not concerned with what Christians believed. Their concern was something quite different. Any commitment to something or Someone other than the State was considered a serious threat to government authority and control. What they cared most about was political allegiance. And they understood clearly the threat from those who declared the Lordship of Christ, a Lordship that would not be shared with the State or with any other power.

By the end of my time in China, my understanding had grown. And my understanding would grow even more after I met and interviewed yet another group of leaders (representing another major house-church movement) at my very last stop in China.

I asked whether, when and how the oppressed could truly threaten a totalitarian oppressor. They offered this scenario in response:

> The security police regularly harass a believer who owns the property where a house-church meets. The police say, "You have got to stop these meetings! If you do not stop these meetings, we will confiscate your house, and we will throw you out into the street."

Then the property owner will probably respond, "Do you want my house? Do you want my farm? Well, if you do, then you need to talk to Jesus because I gave this property to Him."

The security police will not know what to make of that answer. So they will say, "We don't have any way to get to Jesus, but we can certainly get to you! When we take your property, you and your family will have nowhere to live!"

And the house-church believers will declare, "Then we will be free to trust God for shelter as well as for our daily bread."

"If you keep this up, we will beat you!" the persecutors will tell them.

"Then we will be free to trust Jesus for healing," the believers will respond.

"And then we will put you in prison!" the police will threaten.

By now, the believers' response is almost predictable: "Then we will be free to preach the good news of Jesus to the captives, to set them free. We will be free to plant churches in prison."

"If you try to do that, we will kill you!" the frustrated authorities will vow.

And, with utter consistency, the house-church believers will reply, "Then we will be free to go to heaven and be with Jesus forever."

I had flown home from my Eastern Europe trip asking myself: *Is the resurrection power that the New Testament describes still real and available to believers in our world today?*

I left China convinced that it was! I had learned of millions of Chinese believers who had found it and were living it. I had heard resurrection power in their words, I had sensed it in their spirits, and I had seen overwhelming evidence of it in the lives and ministries of so many people still enduring persecution all over that country.

Professionally, I wanted to better understand that resurrection power. Personally, I wanted to experience it for myself.

30

Dreams and Visions

With the counsel of our Persecution Task Force team and based on research, Ruth and I had developed a target list of forty-five countries where we thought we would find significant oppression of believers. By the time we finished putting together an itinerary for my first two trips that summer and early fall of 1998, we had sketched out what seemed like a logical plan for covering the rest of the world.

After trips to Russia, Eastern Europe, and China, the plan was to travel to Southeast Asia, then to the Indian subcontinent and its neighboring countries, then to Central Asia, and then finally to return to where it all started for us in the places dominated by Islam—the Persian Gulf, the Middle East, the Horn and across Northern Africa.

When conditions were right and contacts fell into place for me to schedule one last stop on my trip home from China, I took the opportunity to spend a few days in a large, very strict Islamic nation. Our original plan would bring us to Muslim countries the following year, but this opportunity presented itself and we saw that as an open door.

During my time there, a forty-three-year-old Muslim-background believer somehow heard through the oral grapevine that a Westerner had come to his country wanting to discover how Muslims were finding Jesus and what challenges these converts were experiencing as they lived out their faith in hostile environments. I still have no idea how he learned that I was coming or where I would be.

It turns out that Pramana traveled twenty-nine hours to find me. He had lived his entire life in a remote, tropical, and rural region of his third-world country. He had never before been on a bus. He had not even traveled on a paved highway. Yet, somehow, he found me in one of his country's major cities. Upon his arrival, he matter-of-factly announced: "I have heard about what you are doing. You need to hear my story also."

This man had been born into a people group with a population of twenty-four million. In his people group, there were only three known followers of Jesus, and no church. The only religion that he had ever practiced or known while growing up had been a sort of folk Islam. Pramana knew the Quran by rote. He couldn't actually speak Arabic, so (as an oral communicator from an oral culture) he simply memorized the words of the book as if they were part of some sort of magic formula. He knew the story of Mohammad, of course. But he had never heard of anybody called Jesus, he had never met a believer, and he had no idea what a Bible was.

"Five years ago," he told me, "my life was in ruins. My wife and I were always fighting; I was ready to divorce the woman. My children were disrespectful. My animals were not growing or multiplying. My crops were dying in the fields.

"So I went to the imam of the nearest mosque for help," Pramana continued.

The imam, who also functioned as the local spiritualist, told him, "Okay, son, here is what you need to do. Go buy a white chicken. Bring it to me and I will sacrifice it on your behalf. Then, go back to your village to meditate and fast for three days and three nights.

On the third day, you will receive the answer to all the problems that you are having with your wife, your children, your animals, and your crops."

Pramana did exactly as he was told. He went back to his village. He meditated, he fasted, and he waited. Then, as he explained it: "I'll never forget, on that third night, a voice without a body came to me after midnight. That voice said, 'Find Jesus, find the gospel.'"

This Muslim man had no clue what that even meant. He didn't know if *Jesus* might be a fruit or a rock or a tree. Pramana told me that the voice without a body also said, "Get out of bed, go over the mountain, and walk down the coast to ________________ (a city where he had never been). When you get to that city at daybreak, you will see two men. When you see those men, ask them where _____________ street is. They will show you the way. Walk up and down that street and look for this number. When you find the number, knock on the door. When the door opens, tell the person why you have come."

Pramana did not know that it was an option to be disobedient to the Holy Spirit. He simply assumed that he was required to obey what he had been instructed to do. So he went. He didn't even tell his wife that he was leaving, let alone where he was going. It turns out that he would be gone for two full weeks. During that time, his family had no idea where he was.

Pramana simply got out of bed, hiked over the mountain, trekked down the coast, and arrived in the specified city the next morning at daylight. He saw two men who told him where to find the street he wanted. He walked up and down that street until he found a building with the right number on it. He knocked on the door. A moment later, an older gentleman opened the door and asked, "Can I help you?"

The younger man declared: "I have come to find Jesus; I have come to find the gospel!" In a flash, the old man's hand shot out from the darkened doorway. He grabbed Pramana by the shirt, dragged him into the apartment, and slammed the door behind him. The old man released his grip and exclaimed, "You Muslims must think I am a fool to fall for a trap as transparent as this!"

The very startled and confused traveler replied, "I don't know if you are a fool or not, sir. I just met you. But here is why I've come." Then Pramana told the older man the story of how he had come to be there that day.

The Holy Spirit of the Living God had led this young Muslim man through his dream and vision and his obedience to the home of one of the three believers in his twenty-four million people group. Stunned, the older man explained the gospel to this young Muslim man and led him to Christ. For the next two weeks, the old man discipled this new convert in the faith.

That had been five years ago. Now, Pramana had made another journey. This journey was to find me and to tell me his remarkable story. He had traveled twenty-nine hours to share how his life had changed since he had found Jesus. There had been blessings and trials and tribulations during the last five years, but his life had clearly been changed in startling ways.

I rented a room for him in the large hotel where I was staying. We spent the next three days conducting one of the most memorable interviews I have ever had. We tried to encourage him, and he certainly encouraged us. We were deeply touched by his genuine and growing faith. We marveled that his faith had grown in this hostile world where there had been almost no opportunity for fellowship with other followers of Jesus.

Even before my time with Pramana and a few believers from other people groups in his country, I had already felt overwhelmed by the sheer mass of raw data that I had collected in China. There were names, places, dates, memories, images, stories, tapes, notes, information, photographs, thoughts, details, and observations—not to mention all the feelings that I carried in my heart. Now, as I flew home, I wondered how I would ever be able to sift through it all and to make sense of all that I had seen and heard thus far.

Even at that point (the fall of 1998) I sensed a growing conviction that the most important lessons to be learned from my ongoing pilgrimage would come not from the facts and details, but from the stories. I sensed that I would be hearing powerful stories in my upcoming trips, and I knew that I had already heard so many stories that had changed me deeply.

To this point, the stories had been personal enough to speak to me. And the stories had been powerful enough to begin to restore hope to a weary soul worn down by years of living like a sheep in a world of wolves, a world marked by death, destruction, deceit and doubt.

Returning home, I once again huddled with Ruth and the college students. Together, we debriefed and tried to make sense of all that I had seen. We had now been with the college students for over a year. They had become a part of our family.

Our local church, the college community, and our own families were the tools and the blessings that God used to slowly heal the wounds that we had suffered after Somalia and Tim's death. Even more, the way that the college students welcomed us into their lives, embraced us, adopted us, loved us, and became "church" for us saved our lives.

The richest times were when we simply gathered together to share our hearts with one another. We would talk about our lives and we would pray. We shared our stories, and we invited the students to share theirs. Week by week, the students gave us the privilege of talking honestly about what the Lord was doing in our lives. And we loved hearing about what He was doing in their lives.

During our first school year on campus, we had shared a lot of stories and answered a lot of questions regarding our years in Africa. We talked about the spiritual hunger that we had found among the people in Malawi. We talked about the challenges that we faced working under apartheid in South Africa. We also, of course, talked about the suffering that we had witnessed in the drought, famine, and violence of Somalia's civil war. We shared honestly and openly about our own pain in the wake of Tim's death.

Because of the depth of our relationships, it seemed only natural, during our second year there, to share my experiences and to tell the stories of the believers that I was encountering on my trips around the world.

Sharing stories with such a caring audience gave me the chance to debrief and cement in my mind the memories that I had made. More than that, though, my storytelling with the college students actually helped me process and analyze the experiences. As I talked with the students and tried to articulate what I had seen and heard, I was able to find deeper meaning in the stories. I was also convinced of the potential impact that these stories could have on others.

Word of our weekly gathering time soon spread across the campus. Students began to invite their friends. Eventually, as many as ninety students were gathering. We moved the furniture out of the large living room, and filled every inch of the floor with people. I told the stories and, then, together, we would talk about implications and applications.

I told the students about different Chinese believers who I had met. I explained the unprecedented growth of the house-church movement in China where the body of Christ had grown faster and spread further in a couple of generations under communist oppression than it had for centuries after Jesus' death and resurrection.

I shared Pramana's story about the voice of the Holy Spirit telling him to "find Jesus, find the gospel." As I told the students how he obeyed the voice instructing him to go to a certain city, a particular street, and a specific number on that street—and, then, how he had found the one man who would disciple him—many of my listeners quickly noted that the story sounded a lot like the story of Saul of Tarsus finding Ananias to instruct him in the teachings of Jesus (Acts 9).

That connection gave me the chance to confess something to the students. I reflected on a recurring theme in my life. It had surfaced when I had been a student on this very campus. I sensed it again when I was in seminary. The same thought was there when I served as a pastor. And it was still there when I was privileged to go out on mission to take Jesus' love and teachings around the world. In all those settings, I had studied and taught Scripture. And I certainly had believed the Bible stories about God speaking to people in dreams and visions. I knew that God had done miraculous things such as healing sick people and raising the dead. I believed that those things had happened. In fact, I was certain of it. *The problem was—I had always seen God's Word, especially the Old Testament, as a holy history book. For me, it was an ancient record of what God had done in the past.*

I suppose that's why these recent interviews were affecting me so deeply. The life experiences of these believers in persecution were convicting me profoundly. In light of all that I had heard, there was no way to avoid the conclusion: God, evidently, was doing today everything that He had done in the Bible! The evidence was compelling. At least among people who were faithfully following Him in the world's toughest places, God was still doing what He had done from the beginning.

Interestingly, the places that I had visited were often very much like "Old Testament places." In these places, many people knew nothing of Jesus. Many people had never heard His gospel message of love and grace. Many people in these places had not ever had the opportunity to see or experience the Body of Christ at work in their midst.

Yet, somehow, God could still manage to make Himself known to people like Pramana who were searching for Him! The explosive growth of the believing community described in the New Testament was mirrored in China and in so many other hostile environments.

I honestly admitted to our mission fellowship that, after witnessing the horror of so much evil in Somalia, I had sometimes wondered if God actually understood the true nature of human pain today. I wondered if God was aware of that pain. I wondered if God could do anything about that pain. I wondered if the Bible stories that I loved were only history.

Especially then, I needed to be reassured that God knew about the Somalis of our world. I needed to know that He cared about the Somalis of our world. I wanted to believe that He could do something about the pain of Somalia. I was desperate to be sure that He was not just a past-tense God who lived and acted there and then, but that He is still showing His power and His love here and now.

The stories that I was hearing saved my life. God is indeed still present in this broken world. He is working. He is doing what He has always done. And, through the stories, my hope and my faith were being rekindled.

Another important insight that we grappled with in our mission fellowship had to do with persecution. It was obvious to me, by now, that believers in different settings view persecution very differently. For example, the way American believers see persecution is starkly different from the way that believers in Chinese house-church settings see persecution. The suggestion that imprisonment for the faith is equivalent to seminary training, for example, is a startling thought for most American believers. But that startling view is based on a crucial truth. Chinese believers had learned something that Jesus plainly taught: that persecution can actually change a person's faith. Before persecution, a person's faith might look a certain way. After persecution and suffering, however, that faith might look very different. In fact, after persecution, the believer might not even look like the same person. And, interestingly, the change might be cause for celebration.

That should come as no surprise to us. Recalling the New Testament stories of the disciples, we see the transition of their lives and faith. At one point, they are a fearful, quivering group ready to run and hide. At Pentecost, though, we find a very different group. Suddenly, they are filled with courage, willing to take a public stand, and eager to suffer for the sake of His name. *The turning point between that crippling fear and this new-found courageous freedom is the resurrection of Jesus.* In one sense, the change happened very quickly. In a short time, these early followers of Jesus became completely different people.

What I was hearing in the stories was this very same first century account of faith. Believers who experienced and endured persecution found their faith strengthened, deepened, and matured. They were being changed.

I didn't know it at the time, but I would soon discover even more evidence to support that truth.

The next leg of my pilgrimage was a carefully planned trip to Southeast Asia.

I will always remember, during the first stop on my itinerary, walking and talking with a national believer along the streets of a major city in his country. As had already happened to me numerous times, I found myself so overwhelmed by the inspiring story that I was hearing that I simply zoned out as I tried to absorb it all.

After a time, I realized that my companion was still talking and I had no idea what he was talking about. I apologized and confessed to my new friend that I hadn't been paying attention.

He said, "That's all right, Nik, I realized that. But I wasn't talking to you. I was talking with the Lord to see where we were, and what we should do today."

I decided then and there that I wanted to know Jesus that way. I decided then and there that I wanted to walk with Jesus that way.

On my last morning in this Southeast Asian nation, I received a call from the next person I was scheduled to interview. He said, "I think I'm being followed, so I won't be able to meet with you today."

In light of that missed opportunity, my hosts suggested they we go to the international airport a few hours early. We drove across the city toward the airport. Suddenly, our driver began driving much more aggressively, weaving through a maze of narrow alley-ways.

I was terrified. I had no idea what was happening.

Eventually, the driver explained, "I'm sorry, Dr. Ripken, but I heard early this morning that one of our church's leaders, a man who has much experience making Jesus known in persecution, may have returned earlier than planned from a trip among the tribal people in the hill country. I just realized that we are not far from where he lives, so I decided to swing by his apartment so you can meet him—if he is there."

We soon stopped, got out of the car and climbed some rickety stairs to a fourth-story apartment in a dilapidated old building. Before we could knock on the door, it opened, and there stood the man that we had come to see.

He greeted us by saying, "The Holy Spirit told me that you were coming this morning." And sure enough, as he motioned us into his tiny home, we could see that he already had his table set with four places. We sat down and shared breakfast together.

I cannot begin to number the stories about times when that sort of thing happened. How did that man know that there would be four people at breakfast? If you had asked him—and I did—he would have answered quite simply: "The Lord told me."

Evidently, God is still very much at work in His world. And, evidently, He still speaks to those who walk with Him. The man was certain that we would come; God had made that clear to him. In response, he had already prepared breakfast for four.

I hungered for that kind of intimate relationship with God. I hungered to pray like that.

31

The Toughest Man I Ever Met

Before I had even arrived at the first stop on my planned Southeast Asia tour, I received an e-mail from a European doctor living and working on the border of two Central Asia countries that were experiencing a great deal of violence and unrest. The words of his e-mail were guarded and carefully worded. The message read: "Dr. Ripken, I have heard about the research that you are doing from a friend I knew and worked closely with in Somalia some years ago. I believe that the Lord needs you to come to ____________________ (and he named his border town)."

Ruth had already booked and purchased my plane tickets for the entire, tightly-scheduled trip. I responded to the man's e-mail, explaining that my itinerary included not only Vietnam and Thailand, but also Cambodia, Laos, and Myanmar. Then I explained further: "These are the last of the countries that I have already made plans to visit this year. I am expecting to be in your region late next year, so please be patient. I will be sure to get back in touch with you and I will gladly consider your invitation at that time."

After another stop to see the killing fields of Cambodia (where very few believers survived the Khmer Rouge reign of terror), I landed in Bangkok. From there, I went up and stayed for a time among the Karen people group living in the *Golden Triangle* region where Thailand's borders meet the borders of Laos. Then, I attempted to travel to what was once called Burma (now Myanmar). Several days later, I came back to Bangkok where I had another e-mail from same doctor.

This second e-mail was more insistent. "I really think that you should come now," the man wrote.

At that point, I responded with a slightly less gracious reply: "I am sorry, but I will *not* come your way until next year." At that point, I set out for yet another country on my itinerary. Just before arriving there, however, I received a phone call informing me that all eighteen pastors that I had lined up for interviews there had been arrested and were currently in jail. My primary contact in that country said, "This will not be a good time for you to visit us, unless you want to stay a lot longer than you had planned!" I certainly wanted to visit that country, but I had no interest in spending time in prison.

I wondered about this strange turn of events. Even more, I wondered if maybe it was some sort of a sign. I changed my plans immediately and returned to Bangkok. I am not sure if I was really surprised or not, but I received another e-mail from this same annoyingly persistent doctor.

This time I replied even more bluntly. I didn't want to sound rude, but I was confident in the plans that I had made. In effect, I said to him: "Please stop asking me to visit; I am not coming to your country at this time!" A few days later, I prepared to leave Bangkok for my next destination. After leaving Bangkok and before I reached my next stop, however, I received a phone call from an in-country contact. This phone call informed me that some of the pastors who were planning to talk with me had been in an automobile accident.

Several others were sick in the hospital, and several others were under tight surveillance.

"I am sorry," I was told, "but this is no longer a good time for you to visit. We will contact you to let you know when you might try again."

Once again, I returned to Bangkok. Arriving there, I was startled to find yet another e-mail from the European doctor.

Again, he insisted strongly: "I really believe God wants you to come here now."

Given the recent events and the apparent closed doors that I was facing, I was suddenly more open to his request. I broke down, swallowed my pride, and called the doctor. After introducing myself, I sheepishly admitted, "It suddenly looks like I really don't have anything else to do for the next couple of weeks. I guess I'll be coming your way after all."

I flew into the capital city of his country, then traveled on to a smaller city. From there, I took a smaller plane which landed on a short dirt runway outside a small border town. As soon as I exited the airplane, I spotted the man who was obviously the doctor. Standing beside him were five men in traditional Muslim dress who also seemed to be waiting at the remote desert airstrip for my plane to land.

As the doctor and I exchanged greetings, I asked him, "Who are your friends?"

"You don't know who they are?" he reacted in surprise.

"No, I didn't know even who you were until thirty seconds ago," I told him.

"Well, Dr. Ripken," he said, as he cast a furtive glance over his shoulder, "If you don't know these men—and if I don't know these men—then we have a serious security problem. They told me that they had come to meet you."

"So," he continued rather abruptly, "I'm going to have to leave you now. Here's my cell phone number. If everything turns out all right, call me, and I'll come back and get you."

Then he turned and walked away.

I was stunned, and it dawned on me that I was already praying. I felt that I was well-trained in being careful in the midst of danger, so there was no way that I was going to leave with these five men. As I dragged my bag toward the small terminal, I was already thinking about how quickly I could catch a flight out. The men followed me. They tugged on my clothes trying to get me to stop. I tried my best to ignore them. Finally, one of them said in broken English, "Sir, stop. Please stop. We are followers of Jesus."

I immediately stopped and turned to listen to what they had to say. The quick summary of their story rang true. Against my better judgment, but sensing the hand of God on our meeting, I went with my five unnamed new "friends" to a room that they had rented in the nearby town.

When we got there, we sat down together on the floor in an unfurnished apartment. They simply looked at me and smiled. They seemed perfectly content to wait. I had no idea what was expected of me. I shared briefly about myself, though my words were more guarded than usual. I talked a little about where I had been, how I had been traveling around the world, the research that I had done, and why I wanted to talk to believers in different parts of the world. I even speculated a little on why I might have ended up in this tiny corner of the world.

One of the men spoke English. He translated my words to the others. After he finished, all five of the men began to laugh.

I was confused and I wanted to know what they thought was so funny.

They shook their heads, smiled, and said to me, "You may think you know why you have come here. But we would like to tell you why you are really here."

They briefly sketched their own personal stories. They had each had dreams or visions that had raised spiritual questions and prompted a long search for answers. They had each miraculously found a copy of the Bible to study. After reading through the entire book several times, they had each, on their own, decided to follow Jesus. They had each been rejected and disowned by their families. Eventually they had to flee their country. They made their way across the border to this small border town. Somehow, they had found each other and they realized that they all shared the same newfound faith in Christ.

They didn't really know what to do next, but they instinctively started meeting in this tiny third-floor apartment. They met daily from midnight until 3:00 in the morning, hoping that no one would notice them. They read the word of God secretly and tried to provide spiritual support and encouragement for one another.

Two months earlier, they explained, they had started praying this prayer: "Oh God, we don't know how to do this! We grew up and were trained as Muslims. We know how to be Muslims in a Muslim environment. We even know how to be communists in a Muslim environment. But we do not know how to follow Jesus in a Muslim environment. Please, Lord, send us someone. Send us someone who knows about persecution, someone who knows what other believers are doing, someone who can encourage and teach us."

Chills were running up and down my spine as they explained what had happened when they had been together in this same rented *upper room* earlier that very day: "At 1:30 this morning, we were here praying when the Holy Spirit told us to go to the airport. The Holy Spirit told us that we were to go to the first white man who got off the plane. The Holy Spirit told us that He was sending this man to answer our questions."

"So," they said as they smiled at me again, "that is why you are here. Now you can do what God has called you here to do. Before you start teaching us, however, we have one other question for you: Where have you been and what have you been doing for these last two months?"

I shook my head in embarrassment. I confessed, "Well . . . I guess I have been being disobedient! I tried my best for weeks not to come here at all. Please forgive me!"

They did. And we had a great time of teaching and learning from each other over the next few days. I listened to each of their personal testimonies of faith and asked them specific questions about the details of how and when they encountered Jesus and became His followers.

One of the five men told me, "I dreamed about a blue book. I was driven, consumed really, by the message of the dream. 'Look for this book,' the dream said, 'read this Bible!' I began a secret search, but I could not find a book like that anywhere in my country. Then, one day, I walked into a Quranic book shop and saw this sea of green books lining the walls. I noticed a book of a different color on a shelf in the back of the store, so I walked back there and pulled out a thick blue volume to discover that it was a Bible. It was published in my own national language. I actually bought a Bible in the Islamic bookstore, took it home, and read it five times. That's how I came to know Jesus."

Another one told me, "I dreamed about finding Jesus, but I didn't even know how or where to look. Then one day I was walking through the market when a man I had never seen before came up to me in the crowd. He said, 'The Holy Spirit told me to give you this book.' He handed me a Bible and disappeared into the crowd. I never saw him again. But I read the Bible he gave me three times from cover to cover, and that's how I came to know and follow Jesus."

Each one of the five men told me a different variation of this same story. Each one of them had come across a Bible in some unusual, miraculous way. Each one had read the Gospel story of Jesus. Each one had decided to follow Him.

After hearing their stories, I felt drawn to open the book of Acts. With an entirely different point of view, I began to read the story of Philip and the Ethiopian eunuch. For the first time in my life, as I read that passage, I wondered: *How in the world did an Ethiopian, a eunuch, a man of color, and a foreigner get a copy of a scroll containing the book of Isaiah?*

In New Testament days, even partial copies of Scripture were handwritten on scrolls. They were very rare and very expensive. What's more, the Jews had strict rules and restrictions about who was even allowed to touch the Holy Scriptures and where the Scriptures could be opened and read.

By all accounts, this Ethiopian official would not have been allowed to touch a copy of Scripture, or open it and read it, or possess it. Yet, Philip finds this Ethiopian man in a chariot on a desert road in Gaza poring and puzzling over Isaiah 53. When I read the story on this night, the fact that this Ethiopian official was actually going home with a copy of a portion of the Jewish Bible suddenly seemed extraordinary and unlikely.

In fact, it was so extraordinary and unlikely that I blurted out a question: *Where did this man get a copy of Your Word?*

In reply, the Holy Spirit spoke to my heart: *I have been doing this for a long time. If you will take My Word out into the world, I will get it in the right hands.*

What a marvelous, miraculous, and mysterious partnership this is! We have no clear understanding of what sent that official of the Ethiopian queen on a spiritual pilgrimage to Israel. Something or someone (Someone?) did. How did that man miraculously get his hands on that part of the Word of God? And why was he on that empty stretch of desert road, at that very moment, reading that particular chapter of Isaiah?

I had to admit that I did not know the answers to any of those questions.

Yet, now, after being among believers in persecution, I was pretty sure that God must have had to work a number of small miracles for that encounter between the Ethiopian man and Philip to take place. In God's marvelous timing, this encounter happened in exactly the right place and at exactly the right time. Almost two thousand years later, the exact thing had happened when I walked off of a plane to meet five Muslim men who had miraculously found Jesus. I had never intended to be an answer to prayer that day, but evidently I was.

Reading from the book of Acts that evening was a completely new experience. Two thoughts stayed in my mind: *this is what God did then and this is what God does now.* Suddenly, my modern world didn't look all that different than the world of the Bible.

Much, much later, after years of gathering stories, I came to understand that the tales told by these five new friends were actually pretty commonplace. Time and again, in the years since, Muslim-background believers from many different countries and cultures have told me about being directed by dreams and visions. They have told me about finding Bibles through amazing circumstances. They have mentioned reading the Bible multiple times. In the reading, they have talked about feeling drawn to Jesus. They have told me of a personal decision to follow Him. Many of those pilgrimages to faith involved a Philip who miraculously showed up at exactly the right time, in the right place, with the right words that finally pointed the seeker directly to Jesus.

While I was in that part of the world, the European doctor helped arrange a number of other interviews. Some of those encounters took place in major cities in neighboring countries.

One man agreed to let me interview him if we could meet in a secure, non-public setting where I would not even be able to see his face or attempt to learn his name. I accepted his conditions. I had learned to let those in the greatest danger set the security parameters.

I followed his instructions and traveled to another city. Finding the specified apartment building, I climbed three sets of stairs, knocked on a door and walked into a small, unfurnished living room. I saw only the silhouette of a man. He stood in total shadow behind a large potted plant in the far corner. A bare light bulb hung from the ceiling between us; its glare in my face further obscured my vision.

Those were the ground rules.

I could not really see the man at all, but I could hear him perfectly. So I had no problem taking notes. He told me that I was permitted to record our interview. He insisted, however, that I not try to identify him, find out where he lived, or use his real name.

I listened to his story for about six hours. I quickly concluded that he was probably the toughest man I ever met in my life.

During an earlier invasion of his country, the man told me that he had led a squad of fifteen soldiers committed to repel foreign invaders. He calmly recounted his experience: "I took great joy in the name of Allah when I could sneak up behind an enemy soldier at night, silently cut his throat, and allow his blood to wash over my hands as an offering to Almighty God."

His descriptions were so graphic, yet so matter-of-fact, that at one point I almost unintentionally asked a question: "How many people have you killed?"

"I stopped counting when the number reached one hundred," he confessed. "Those were people that I killed personally, not in battle."

My mind boggled at that number. He went on to tell me that, after a time, he started to have a dream. It was a recurring dream that came to him over and over again. He dreamed of spots of blood on his hands. Night after night, he would have the same dream. Over time, the spots of blood grew larger. Eventually, he was dreaming that the blood was running down and dripping off his arms.

He realized, early on, that in his dreams he was imagining the blood of all those people he had killed. The dreams were so vivid and so disturbing that he dreaded falling asleep at night. "I really thought that I was going insane," he told me. "When I began to see the blood during my waking hours, I was even more upset. And no amount of washing or scrubbing with sand or pumice could get the blood off."

"I soon became convinced that I was going absolutely insane," he went on. "Then one night the dream changed. As I stood there helplessly watching the blood run down my arms, I also saw in my dream a man standing before me. He was a man clothed in white with a scarred head. He also had scarred hands, a scarred side, and scarred feet. The scarred man said. 'I am Jesus the Messiah and I can get the blood off—if you will just find me and believe in me.'"

The dream told him to find Jesus. He had no idea how to do that. Still, he began his search. It took him over a year to locate a copy of the Scripture. It took even longer for him to understand what he was reading. From time to time, he would find people who could answer some of his questions. And, finally, this man said that he had found Jesus. When he had invited Jesus into his heart, the man said, "I got the blood off. Jesus took that blood onto Himself."

Immediately, his dreams ended.

At that point, he didn't have anybody to disciple him. In his country, there was no church that he could attend, no Bible study that he might join. On his own, he kept reading and studying the Bible. And he did everything that the Holy Spirit told him to do.

Eventually he began to smuggle Bibles, Bible portions, other Christian materials and even the *Jesus* film over the mountains from another country into his own. He did that for two years. One day, he rounded a bend in one of the high mountain passes and found himself face-to-face on a narrow trail with the squad of fifteen men that he used to lead. They had been on the lookout for their old commander ever since he had deserted them and disappeared. It had even been reported that he was now a traitor to Islam.

Now they had found him. They threw him to the ground and began to beat him. It was their plan to beat him to death.

In that squad of Muslim militiamen, however, there was another new believer in Jesus Christ. No one knew about his faith. That man boldly spoke up to caution the others. He said, "Stop! Let's think about this! Maybe we're being foolish. If we kill our old commander here and now, we may never know who he is working with, who the traitors are on this side of the border, or on that side of the border."

"So let me take him down to the town at the bottom of the mountain," the man continued. "I can get him patched up and hold him prisoner. When he is well enough to talk again, we can interrogate him, torture him slowly if we have to, until he tells us what we need to know. We might learn something important if we are patient and do this right."

His suggestion was convincing. The other men thought that his plan sounded reasonable. They left their old commander with this secret, believing Good Samaritan. He loaded him on a donkey and smuggled him down and out of the mountains. He patched him up and saved his life by letting him resume the work that he had been doing.

As I listened to this incredible story, I assumed that this storyteller would never be more than a shadow and a voice for me. And I was fine with that.

But I had interviewed so many people that I could sometimes hear what people were not saying and what things they were uncomfortable talking about. At the end of almost six hours of listening to this man's life story, I expressed my respect and appreciation for his willingness to talk with me. I told him how inspired I was by his testimony and I praised God with him for all that the Lord had done in and through him. I told him that, because of his testimony, my life and faith would never be the same again.

At the same time, I probed just a bit into his story. I said, "You have told me that you are married, that you have sons, that you have led your wife and your children to Christ, and that you have even baptized them. What I'm wondering is this: Where do they fit into your ministry? You haven't talked about that. How do they help you? What is happening with your family?"

I was not expecting what happened next.

The man leapt out of the darkness and suddenly stood face to face with me. He clamped his scarred hands down tight on my shoulders, and his fierce dark eyes bored like lasers into mine. I instinctively thought of my earlier question about the number of men that he had killed.

For hours, I had listened to his inspiring story. But, now, I was terrified as he shook me and demanded to know: "How can God ask it? Tell me! How can God ask it?"

I think maybe that's when my heart started beating again. I realized that maybe he was angry at God, not me. My confusion cleared up even more as he went on to exclaim, "I have given Him everything! My body has been broken. I have been jailed. I have been starved. I have been beaten. I have been left for dead!" His words sounded a lot like the apostle Paul's recitation of all that he had suffered in the service of Christ.

"I have even been willing to die for Jesus," he pleaded. "But do you know what I fear? When I go to bed at night, what keeps me awake, and what actually terrifies me, is the thought that God might ask of my wife and my children what I have already willingly given Him."

"How can He ask it? Tell me! How could God ask that of my wife and children?"

I paused for a few moments and prayed that the Lord would guide my words as I responded: "Brother, my wife is safe in Kentucky," I said. "My two living sons are in school, doing well." I told him a little bit of Timothy's story; we had already talked together about my time in Somalia.

Finally I told him, "I personally cannot answer your question. But I would ask you another question that I have had to ask myself: 'Is Jesus worth it? Is He worth your life? Is He worth the lives of your wife and your children?'"

He was undoubtedly the toughest man I ever met. He began to sob. He wrapped his arms around me, buried his face in my shoulder and wept. When he finally stopped, he stepped back and wiped away his tears. He seemed angry at himself for this display of emotion.

Then he looked me in the eyes again, nodded, and declared, "**Jesus is worth it.** He is worth my life, my wife's life, and He is worth the lives of my children! I have got to get them involved in what God is doing with me!"

With that, the toughest man I ever met said good-bye. He turned and walked out of the room.*

*My encounter with this man was more than a dozen years ago now. The last I heard, he and his family were still doing for the Kingdom of God the work that he described to me. And he is still the toughest man I have ever met!

32

HeartSongs

Returning home, I marveled again that the interview stories sounded like stories right out of the New Testament. As I shared the stories with my family, with the college students, and with our Persecution Task Force, they reached that same conclusion on their own. That, in itself, was a wonderful affirmation. Sharing the stories, almost invariably, led to animated discussions about the implications and applications of what I had heard from these believers in persecution.

In particular, the story of "the toughest man I ever met" seemed to touch people deeply. By this point, I had reached another conclusion about him. I realized that he was willing to endure great suffering for his faith for two reasons. First, he understood the nature of persecution and the intent of his persecutors. Second, he knew the One for whom he was suffering. This man not only knew Jesus—he was also convinced that Jesus was worth whatever his faith might cost him. This had been true of so many believers that I had met around the world—and it was certainly true of this man that I had most recently interviewed. Those reflections led, time and time again, to long discussions about what our faith costs and how much we are willing to endure for Jesus' sake.

I shared repeatedly how God had used that persistent doctor to help me pay attention to a truly divine appointment. I confessed my embarrassment that it took four very direct e-mails to get my attention. I was uncomfortable that it had taken such effort to get me to the place where God obviously wanted me to be. Miraculously, I had encountered five Muslim background believers in a tiny corner of the world. If it had been up to me, I would have missed the entire experience. Those men had been praying that God would send someone to help them, encourage them, and teach them. It turned out that I was the answer to their prayer. But it grieved me that I actually fought against God's purposes. In our gatherings back at home, we talked about how we can recognize God's direction—and about how we can easily miss what He might be doing. We celebrated God's remarkable creativity in accomplishing His purposes, but we also humbly confessed how often we cannot—or do not—hear His guidance.

The time at home was rich and restful. It was a joy to share the stories. At the same time, I found myself growing impatient to resume my journey to hear and collect more stories that I could then bring home to share.

By this point, I felt confident that there would be many more stories to hear and many more lessons to draw from them. I would be returning to Southeast Asia to visit several countries that I had missed before. Specifically, I would be visiting Buddhist and Hindu cultures. Eventually, I would make my way to Bangladesh and Pakistan. Then I planned to move even deeper into the heart of Islam, first in Central

Asia, then in the Gulf and the Middle East, and finally back where this journey had begun for me in North and East Africa.

Over the years, we have met so many people with so many stories that it will take many other books to share much of what we have heard and seen. Originally, Ruth and I envisioned this task as a two-year journey. It has now become the passion of a lifetime. Fifteen years later, we are still learning how to identify and articulate the right questions to ask believers in persecution so that they can mentor us ever more effectively.

Clearly, only God's guidance made my encounter with the five believers in Southeast Asia possible. Only the Lord could have arranged that appointment. The five believers had been waiting and praying for weeks that someone would show up in their remote Central Asian border town. In retrospect, I could see how carefully the hand of God had been guiding the overall schedule for our project from the very beginning.

If we had started seeking answers in the Muslim world where we had first started wrestling with our questions—if we had done our pilgrimage backwards and gone from the world of Islam first and then to China and then to Russia—I believe that our journey could well have been a waste of time and resources. It might even have been a disaster. The fact that we started where we did and followed the general plan that we followed wasn't the result of our strategic wisdom (though we might have thought so at the time).

It was the clear activity of the Holy Spirit. God was not only arranging encounters with specific individuals; He was involved even in the schedule that we were putting together.

If we had gone to the world of Islam first, the relatively few number of Muslim-background believers who we could have accessed and safely interviewed might well have discouraged us even further. From a research standpoint, the sampling size might have been too small to draw any statistically valid conclusions or to begin identifying meaningful patterns and trends. With just a few interviews in that setting, it would have been almost impossible to learn any helpful, applicable lessons at all.

On the other hand, by starting in Russia and Eastern Europe, we were able to learn what had helped and/or hindered the survival and growth of the long-established Body of Christ under decades of persecution. Interviews were abundant in number. Almost immediately, I found myself talking to people—many people, in fact—who had thrived in a setting of persecution. My time in China was more of the same. The literal explosion of faith throughout China in the house-church movement gave us access to a wealth of believers who could speak about what had happened. Multitudes of people were eager to bear witness to a faith that had not only survived persecution, but had thrived *because* of it.

With that beginning, we were finally ready to step into the world of Islam. By that point, we had identified significant patterns and trends (positive *and* negative) to be watching for. We had also, in large measure, discarded our first set of research questions. Instead, we were now simply asking believers to tell us their stories. Listening for thousands of hours, we were becoming more adept at connecting the dots, seeing patterns, and extracting applicable lessons for ourselves and for believers all around the world.

Originally, we had hoped to develop western-styled discipleship materials for those living and working in the most oppressive environments on earth. Our end result, however, was something different. *Instead of developing a curriculum, we were being taught by believers in persecution how to follow Jesus, how to love Jesus, and how to walk with Him day by day.*

At one level, we already knew this. But we were introduced all over again to a relationship with Jesus that is precisely what can be found in the New Testament. It is also a relationship that, even today, can still change lives.

For many years a western faith-based organization had operated a medical clinic in one of the cities of a large Islamic country. Most of the local population appreciated having ready access to quality medical care. As a rule, the people essentially ignored the staff's religious affiliation and background. The religious beliefs of the medical staff weren't much of a concern; what mattered was the medical care.

However, a few radical Muslims were concerned with the religious beliefs. And the most militant and outspoken opponent of the medical ministry lived right across the street from the clinic's front entrance. He owned a shop in that same location, which was only a few doors down from a local mosque.

Every Friday this shop-keeper, whom we will call Mahmoud, would stand in front of his store and stir up the Muslim crowd streaming by on the street as they made their way to worship. Later, at the mosque, he would accuse the evil infidels at the clinic of preying on, poisoning, or over-charging good Muslims. He would curse and condemn some of the medical staff by name. He was an angry and hateful man whose anger spilled over as he spewed animosity at anyone affiliated with this medical clinic.

Later, Mahmoud contracted an incurable cancer. His superstitious Muslim community considered him contagious and quit frequenting his shop. Now he was not only sick and dying, but he was also unable to feed and provide for his wives and children. The staff of the hospital learned of his sad plight and many of them actually began to go to his shop on their way to and from work.

The clinic personnel purchased goods from the shop of their most vocal antagonist. They conversed with him and asked about his family. They regularly inquired about and expressed concern for his health. They always made a point of letting him know they were praying for him. Eventually, they began to treat his suffering—and even washed his body when the need arose. As these followers of Jesus loved their persecutor and enemy of so many years, Mahmoud's stony heart softened. Over time, his attitude changed to one of gratitude and friendship.

In his last days, he continued to accept the compassionate and professional medical care of the "evil infidels." He trusted his former enemies to help him die in peace, with dignity. Before he finally passed away at the age of fifty-seven, Mahmoud made the decision to become a follower of Jesus.

Mahmoud's youngest wife, Aisha, suddenly became a twenty-four-year-old widow with four children. She had watched how the clinic staff had loved and cared for her husband after he had cursed and railed against them for so many years. During Mahmoud's last days, she also became a follower of Jesus. After her husband's death, Aisha became an outspoken witness to her new faith and perhaps the most effective evangelist in that area.

Her Muslim family and friends couldn't silence her witness. The authorities eventually took notice. Even though her nation didn't have a history of imprisoning women, the police finally arrested her.

She was lectured and threatened with every imaginable punishment. Her captors threw her not into an actual jail cell, but down into the dank, dark, unfinished cellar of the police station. In that place, there was no light at all. The unfinished cellar had a dirt floor. Spiders, bugs and rats skittered around her in the darkness.

Terrified, and at the point of giving up, she told us that she intended to scream out to God that she couldn't take any more. But when she opened her mouth in protest and despair, a melody of praise rose out of her soul instead.

She sang.

Surprised and strengthened by the sound of her own voice, and overwhelmed by the renewed sense of God's presence beside and within her, she began to sing her praise and worship to Jesus even more loudly. As she sang, she noticed that, office by office, the police station above her head became strangely silent.

Later that night, the trap door was opened. The light spilled down into the darkness of the cellar. The Chief of Police himself reached down, pulled Aisha out, and told her, "I'm going to release you and let you go home."

"Please, no!" she protested. "You can't do that! It's after midnight. I can't be seen on the streets alone." He, of course, knew that is was against the law for a woman to be out alone at night. She wondered if maybe this was a trick to get her in more trouble.

"You don't understand," the Chief told her. "There's no need to worry. I am going to personally escort you to your home . . . on one condition."

Aisha immediately suspected the man's intentions. But it turns out that he had nothing sinister in mind.

The Chief of Police, one of the most powerful men in the city, looked at twenty-four-year-old Aisha and shook his head in bewilderment. "I don't understand," he admitted. "You are not afraid of anything!"

He sighed and he shook his head again. "My wife, my daughters, and all the women in my family are afraid of everything. But you are not afraid of anything. So now, I am going to take you safely to your home tonight. Three days from now, I am going to come to get you, and bring you to my house. I want you to come to my house so that you can tell everyone in my family why you are not afraid. And I want you to sing that song."

In truth, I am certain that Aisha was afraid. She, like so many believers living in persecution, simply refused to be controlled by her fear. By faith, she found a way to overcome her fear.

Because of the testimonies that I had already heard, I was able to instantly recognize and understand the significant role that music and the HeartSong played in building and bolstering this young Muslim woman's faith. It was very similar to what I had already observed and heard from believers like Dmitri and Tavian in their very different cultures.

And thinking back to the book of Acts, I recalled the story of Paul and Silas and their imprisonment almost two thousand years ago.

In prison, Paul and Silas sang.

It was clear that a vibrant faith like Aisha's could take root, survive, and thrive in hostile conditions. That much was certain. Recognizing factors in her faith journey that I had seen in so many other places was fascinating and life-giving. Though I had never seen the connections before, they were now unavoidable. Suffering believers in Russia—and in China—and in Eastern Europe—and in Southeast Asia—and in the world of Islam—and in Bible days—were telling the very same story, doing the very same things to survive, experiencing the presence of the very same God.

Back in 1992, on one of my darkest early days in Somalia, during my first or second trip into Mogadishu, I was walking down a bomb-cratered city street with my Somali guards. We were scouting the neighborhood around our compound, looking for needs in the neighborhood that we might be able to meet.

The trouble was that there were so many needs that it seemed to be a ridiculous search. The people I saw in that neighborhood had nothing but needs! Where would I even start to help when I encountered death and destruction at every corner and around every turn?

As I walked those streets, I felt the presence of evil like I had never known before. It was a palpable, tangible presence. It felt like a vice tightening around my heart, slowly, steadily squeezing out any hope of helping. All that was left was discouragement and despair.

Suddenly, piercing that spiritual darkness, a sound came. At first, the sound was confusing. Then, it was shocking. Finally, it was simply amazing. The sound was completely out of place in that setting, but it was as welcome as the sound of a waterfall in a desert.

Walking through what had to be at that time the worst place on earth, I heard what sounded like angels singing. For an instant, I thought that I was hallucinating. I stopped dead in my tracks and I tried to determine the source or direction of the sound. My guards stopped too. I could tell that they were also hearing the sound.

"This way!" I said and we set off in a different direction. The singing grew louder. At the next corner, I listened and we turned again. We grew closer and closer to the music. We finally stopped outside the gate of a small compound from which the singing seemed to originate.

I pounded loudly on the gate. A guard appeared and tried to send us away. I pressed—and negotiated. Finally, he allowed us to enter what turned out to be a small orphanage. There, a chorus of children was assembled and singing their hearts out under the rather animated direction of a young Somali woman. Her name was Sophia.

I had no way of knowing at that time, of course, that Sophia, Ruth and I would have many surprising encounters and share many adventures in faith, heartache, laughter and loss in three different countries over the next ten years.

When I first met her that day in the orphanage, she had already lost her job, her home, and her family to the violent chaos and destruction that had marked Somalia's long and brutal civil war. Even those who had told her about Jesus many years before had now fled the country. Physically, she was ragged, worn out, and thin beyond belief. She stood a few inches over five feet.

Evidently, though, there was enough strength left in this little shell of a woman to have gathered thirty orphans together in this shattered neighborhood of Mogadishu. It seemed to be only the sheer force of her will that had kept the orphans alive and waiting for help to show up. They were looking to her—and she was waiting for someone to be an answer to her prayers.

In that hard time, she sang. And she taught the children to sing as well.

As I walked up to her, she whispered, "You are a follower of Jesus, aren't you? I have prayed that you would come."

Even before she said that, I had known that Sophia was a believer. I had seen the love of God shining in her eyes and I had heard it in the children's songs. I asked her to tell me her story. To my surprise, I learned that this smiling, joyful woman had a typically tragic Somali story. Her husband had been killed during the civil war. And her two young daughters had disappeared months ago; she assumed that they too had died.

Her entire family was gone. She had lost everyone she loved. Still, here she was trying to make a difference in the lives of these orphans who had also lost their families. She was a beacon of light shining in this very dark place. Her HeartSongs witnessed to faith. At the very same time, her songs strengthened her faith. The songs instilled happiness and hope in the souls of the orphans. And her songs also wafted through the streets of Mogadishu that day and strengthened the resolve of one western relief worker who had been temporarily paralyzed by overwhelming despair.

I had been scouting for needs. I was trying to figure out a logical place to start. No matter what else we might do in Somalia, I immediately knew that we would help Sophia and her orphans. And we did.

That was just the first of many ways that our lives and personal stories would become intertwined. Several years later, I would *just happen* to learn, and would be able to give Sophia the joyous news, that her two daughters were actually still alive. They were living in a Somali refugee camp in Ethiopia.

But then, at a later time, I had to console Sophia when her in-laws broke her heart by legally preventing her from taking custody or ever seeing the girls again. They took that legal step because they refused to allow their grand-daughters to be raised by an *infidel* believer in Jesus.

We eventually celebrated Sophia's marriage to another Somali refugee believer in a neighboring country. Sometime after that, we were able to use our contacts to help save her life and that of her new baby by arranging an emergency flight to get her medical care in yet another country. This happened after doctors and nurses at her local maternity hospital threatened to let her and her baby die rather than treat a former Muslim.

What a wonder that all that interaction and involvement in this woman's life started with a song.

It is surely obvious by now, but I am sometimes a slow learner. I don't know why I would have needed yet another example to drive the point home. But whether I needed it or not, I once more was reminded of the impact and power to be found in the songs of faith.

I was visiting a different Islamic country in the Middle East, hearing the story of a follower of Jesus imprisoned for his faith. Though rotations of guards watched him around the clock, each day this man would do his daily devotions in his cell. One day two of his guards came to him in alarm and insisted that he stop his singing. They told him to stop singing "so that your songs won't convert us."

Evidently, those Muslim jailors recognized the power in HeartSongs a lot quicker than I did. And they didn't need hundreds of interviews to reach that conclusion.

When I finally connected enough of the dots, I came to understand the significance of music as a faith factor and recognize its presence and power already at work in the Islamic world. Only then did I begin to grasp what was for me a new, much bigger, life-changing lesson.

I have always believed that Jesus was serious about his final earthly instructions to His followers. I have always believed that He indeed wants us to reach the world with His message. I am convinced that He elicits our help in that great task. In fact, one of the reasons for my discouragement in Somalia was my growing doubt about whether God really was at work in places like that. And, then, there was the follow-up question that haunted me: If God is not in places like Somalia, what does He expect His followers to do there in His absence?

Gradually, as my pilgrimage through persecution progressed, I began to understand that God is not helpless without us. Even though He wants our help, values our help, and calls for our help in changing the world, our all-powerful God is not helpless—even without us.

I also came to understand that our all-knowing God is completely aware of all that is happening in His world—even in places where evil seems to be running rampant. Even in these dark places, our ever-present God is not somehow absent until we show up ready to help.

It is crucial to understand that God values our help. But it is even more crucial to remember that our all-powerful God is able to work with or without us, that our all-knowing God is not blind to the evil in His world, and that our ever-present God is there . . . whether we are or not.

Indeed, one of the most exciting and encouraging lessons that my journey was teaching me was that God is always present and always working even in the most hostile places on earth. I understood that He had been at work in Somalia long before Ruth and I ever showed up. Rather than thinking that we are all alone and that we have to start from scratch in wolf country, a much better and more effective strategy for carrying out the great commission, especially in our world's toughest and most discouraging places, would be to learn what God already has been doing and is doing there, join Him, and together figure out how we can build on that.

Once we find out what God is already doing to show Himself, all we have to do is point others to Him.

For me, that was a hope-renewing thought. And I was beginning to wonder if it was time for me to start to sing again.

33

What If He Is Alive?

Over the last decade and a half, Ruth and I have conducted, recorded, documented, and analyzed more than seven hundred personal, in-depth interviews with believers from seventy-two different countries where followers of Jesus have been persecuted for their faith and/or are being persecuted for their faith. The number of interviews is still increasing month by month.

Ruth and I have shared this journey from the beginning. Our life and work have long been part of a shared adventure that neither started nor ended in Somalia. Our pilgrimage to and through persecution has always been (and is now more than ever) a joint journey of discovery that has taken us to places and parts of the world that we never expected to see. It has also taken us to spiritual heights and depths that we never knew existed.

Ruth has experienced every trip that I have taken on this adventure—even when I traveled alone. She was always my first and fullest debriefer when I got home. She was my most valuable sounding board from the planning to the reporting of every trip. She also transcribed thousands of hours of taped interviews and helped me organize and analyze our findings.

More recently, Ruth has sat in and participated in many of our interviews. And she has done many interviews on her own in places and circumstances where custom and culture would have precluded my doing so. For example, she can talk privately with women in countries where Islamic law forbids them to be interviewed by me.

We are no longer meeting together with that great group of ninety college students (sixty of whom have since gone out themselves to spread the light and love of Jesus with lost people in some of the darkest places in this world). But we have developed an even bigger and much more extended family that we belong to—the worldwide family of God. I suppose that I always knew how immense that family was. Through the interviews, however, I have become acquainted with so many family members that I never knew I had.

Ruth and I often share the stories that we have heard and the things that we have learned to help the western church and many of its congregations grasp a new, and perhaps more biblical, perspective on suffering and persecution in our faith. We share often about how suffering and persecution relate to our faith. We desperately want our western brothers and sisters in Christ to realize that the greatest enemy of our faith today is not communism, Buddhism, Hinduism, Atheism, or even Islam. Our greatest enemy is **lostness**. Lostness is the terrible enemy that Jesus commissioned His followers to vanquish with the battle strategy that He spelled out for them in Matthew 28:18–20. He was addressing this same enemy when He plainly clarified His purpose in coming: "I have come to seek and to save those who are lost."

Our hope is that believers around the world will get close enough to the heart of God that the first images that come to mind when we hear the word "Muslim" are not Somali pirates or suicide bombers or violent jihadists or even terrorists. When we hear the word "Muslim," we need to see and think of each and every individual Muslim as a lost person who is loved by God. We need to see each Muslim as a person in need of God's grace and forgiveness. We need to see each Muslim as someone for whom Christ died.

Nothing is more gratifying for us than taking the examples, the stories, and the experiences of one group of believers in persecution and sharing their spiritual wisdom with another group of oppressed Jesus-followers in a different place. Imagine the impact of telling Muslim-background believers that the leaders of ten million Chinese believers are calling their people to rise early every day to pray for their brothers and sisters in Islamic countries who are ***really*** being persecuted for Jesus' sake! When we shared that incredible word with Muslim-background believers, they wept. They cried out to God, "Oh God, please let us live long enough to go to China to thank our brothers and sisters who did not forget us and who are praying for us every morning."

How many of us who strive to follow Jesus today have ever wished we could have witnessed firsthand the kind of spiritual adventures and the world-changing, resurrection-powered faith experienced by believers in the New Testament? I believe that we can—and we don't need a time machine to do it. We need only to look and listen to our brothers and sisters who are faithfully living for Christ today in our world's toughest places.

When Ruth and I first departed for Africa with our boys almost thirty years ago, I was a young, naïve Kentucky farm-boy who believed that God was sending us around the world on a great adventure to tell people who Jesus was and to explain what the Bible was all about. Today, I realize that God allowed us to go out into the world so ***we*** could find out who Jesus was from people who really knew Him and actually lived the Word of God.

I have learned so much more than I have taught.

I now know that when Ruth and I began this pilgrimage into persecution fifteen years ago, we were asking the wrong questions and seeking the wrong sort of answers. What we discovered—through God's grace and with the help of hundreds of faithful people—wasn't so much a strategy, a method, or a plan. Rather, it was a Person. *We found Jesus—and we found that Jesus is very much alive and well in the twenty-first century. Jesus is revealed in the lives and words and resurrection faith of believers in persecution.*

These believers don't just live *for Jesus,* they live *with Jesus* every day.

These believers have also taught me a whole new perspective on persecution. For decades now, many concerned western believers have sought to *rescue* their spiritual brothers and sisters around the world who suffer because they choose to follow Jesus. Yet our pilgrimage among house churches in persecution convinced us that God may actually want to use *them* to save *us* from the often debilitating, and sometimes spiritually-fatal, effects of our watered-down, powerless western faith.

Like most other Americans, I have suffered little or no persecution for my faith. Given my background, I had a hard time getting my mind around the reality of spiritual oppression. Early on, my questions reflected a lot of my own experience.

Most of all, I wanted to know *why.*

Why is there so much persecution directed toward followers of Jesus around the globe?

Why are believers in Jesus in other countries kicked out of their homes, disinherited, beaten, jailed, and even killed?

Why is a young woman who comes to Jesus out of Islam routinely married off to a Muslim man thirty years her senior in order to silence her witness and limit her influence?

Over and over again, I wanted to know *why*.

Often, when we consider those kinds of questions, we already think we know the answers. The answers might be, for example, "The people who live in those places are uneducated. The people who inflict this kind of pain on believers are simply ignorant. Ignorance fuels persecution."

Another answer might be: "Better government is the answer. If these people would just embrace western forms of democracy that would guarantee civil and human rights—then persecution would be against the law and it would stop."

Another answer might be: "If people were just more tolerant, we could all live together in peace. Greater tolerance would end persecution."

But none of these suggested answers even comes near the foundational cause of persecution as it relates to the Christian faith. After almost twenty years of walking through this world of persecution and talking to hundreds of believers who suffer for their faith, we can say without a shadow of a doubt that the primary cause of "religious persecution" in the world today is *people surrendering their hearts and lives to Jesus.*

Think about the implications of this truth . . .

For decades the western church has been taught to pray and work for an end to the persecution of fellow believers around the world. We enlist our congregations, our denominations, and even our governments to speak out and pressure oppressive regimes in hostile nations to end discrimination. Sometimes we even demand that the persecutors be punished.

We seem to forget that Jesus Himself promised that the world would reject and mistreat His faithful followers just as it rejected Him. Could it be that the only way that Almighty God could actually answer prayers asking Him to end the persecution of believers . . . would be to stop people from accepting Christ as their Lord and Savior? If people stopped accepting Christ as Lord and Savior . . . persecution would end immediately. That would be the only way to completely end persecution.

It sounds like a ridiculous question, but should we really be asking God for the end of persecution? By doing that, we might unknowingly be asking that people not come to faith in Christ!

Ruth and I have seldom encountered a mature believer living in persecution who asked us to pray that their persecution would cease. We have never heard that request. Rather, believers in persecution ask us to pray that "they would be faithful and obedient *through* their persecution and suffering."

That is a radically different prayer.

Why is it that millions of the global followers of Jesus who actively practice their faith live in environments where persecution is the norm? The first and most basic answer is that these people have given their lives to Jesus. The second answer is that they have determined in their hearts that they will not keep Jesus to themselves. Having found faith in Christ, they have such a passion for Jesus that they must share the Good News of His sacrificial love and forgiveness with their families, their friends, and their neighbors. By doing that, these believers are choosing to be persecuted.

What that means is that, for most believers, persecution is completely avoidable. If someone simply leaves Jesus alone, doesn't seek Him or follow Him, then persecution will simply not happen. Beyond that, even if someone becomes a follower of Jesus, persecution will likely not happen if the faith is kept private and personal. If a person is silent about their faith in Jesus, the chance of being persecuted is very small.

So if our goal is reducing persecution, that task is easily achieved. First, just leave Jesus alone. Second, if you do happen to find Him, just keep Him to yourself. Persecution stops immediately where there is no faith and where there is no witness.

The reason for persecution, then, is that people keep finding Jesus—and, then, they refuse to keep Him to themselves.

Believers in persecution taught us another important truth. The freedom to believe and witness has nothing to do with the government or political system. The freedom to believe and witness has nothing to do with the civil and political rights that might or might not be present.

This is one of the most important lessons that we learned from believers in persecution: They (and you and I) are just as free to share Jesus today in Islamic, Hindu, Buddhist, and communist countries as you and I are in America. It isn't a matter of political freedom. It is simply a matter of obedience. The price for obedience might be different in different places—but it is *always* possible to obey Christ's call to make disciples. Every believer—in every place—is *always* free to make that choice.

Jesus' last instruction to His disciples was to be witnesses to all peoples. He did not limit His mission to western, democratic, or "free" countries. It was a blanket commandment. It was not a suggestion, or a recommendation, or an option. It was a commandment for all of His followers—to share His message with all peoples.

True to Scripture, believers in persecution would remind us that we are all equally free and equally responsible to share Jesus in every corner of the globe. The question is never, "Am I free to do that?" Rather, the question is, "Will I be obedient?" Believers in the world of persecution have already decided their answer to that crucial question.

Perhaps some of us have not yet settled the matter. The question we must answer is whether or not we have the courage to bear the consequences of obediently exercising our freedom to be salt and light to all peoples, wherever they live. The consequences for our obedience may be suffering and persecution. Even then, we are free to obey. Time and again, believers in persecution have demonstrated the power of determined and courageous faith. Time and time again, they have obeyed. They have willingly accepted the consequences of their obedience. Even in the most repressive places, these believers have understood that they are utterly free to obey Jesus.

Many of us, however, do not live in repressive places. Our biggest fear in sharing our faith might be mild embarrassment or rejection. In fact, we might even wonder why we should care about believers in persecution in other places.

The answer to that question is simple; when we care about believers in persecution, we identify with them.

Not long ago, Ruth and I were part of a response team that ministered to workers in a Muslim country after three colleagues were martyred by a militant Islamic fundamentalist. Understandably, that was a grief-filled, emotion-laden, and spiritually-challenging time.

Even so, what many of us who were there remember most from those days is *joy.* Of course, there was profound grief—immense grief. But the joy was unmistakable. During that time, we sensed an unearthly, heavenly identification. These servants, in their deaths, had partnered with our Master and His cross. They had shouldered their own crosses for the sake of Jesus and for the sake of witness.

During our time of grieving, we learned an important spiritual lesson: before we can grasp the full meaning of the Resurrection, we first have to witness or experience crucifixion. If we spend our lives so afraid of suffering, so averse to sacrifice, that we avoid even the risk of persecution or crucifixion, then we might never discover the true wonder, joy and power of a resurrection faith. Ironically, avoiding suffering could be the very thing that prevents us from partnering deeply with the Risen Jesus.

All over the world we encountered committed followers of Jesus who trust even His toughest teachings. They understand that anyone who wishes to save his life must first be willing to lose it.

They are willing to take that risk because they believe that, ultimately, good *will* defeat evil. Love will finally overcome hate. And life will conquer death forever by the power of our resurrection faith. They know that the final chapter of the greatest story ever told has already been written. And they know that, in the end, and, for all eternity, God will have His way.

In the meantime, in the here and now, a real battle continues. This is the same spiritual battle that the apostle Paul talked about. First-century believers understood Paul when he described an epic struggle that was "not against flesh and blood, but against the rulers, against the authorities, against the powers of this dark world and against the spiritual forces of evil in the heavenly realms" (Eph. 6:12). Followers of Jesus in persecution today understand this battle well.

In fact, everyone in the world today who claims to be a follower of Jesus plays a part in this battle. Faithful believers who are paying a personal price in pain and persecution for the cause of Christ truly understand the crux and the cost of their faith. Their witness, their lives and their examples should inspire and instruct us. Their experience reveals what is at stake, and their experience also reveals much about evil and its power.

Believers who know what it means to suffer for their faith help us recognize and understand the Enemy's tactics and his ultimate goal. Satan at his worst, evil at its core, and persecution in its essence does not overtly seek to starve, beat, imprison, torture, or kill followers of Jesus. The strategy of Satan is simpler and more diabolical than that.

What is Satan's paramount intent? Quite simply, it is this: denying the world access to Jesus!

Satan's greatest desire is for the people of this planet to leave Jesus alone. Satan desires that we turn away from Jesus—or that we never find Him in the first place. If Satan cannot be successful at that, he desires to keep believers quiet, to diminish or silence our witness, and to stop us from bringing others to Christ.

It is that simple.

Once we understand the nature of this spiritual battle and the strategy of the Enemy, we see clearly the role that believers have been called to play. We also see the importance of our choices regarding witness and faithfulness and obedience.

At the beginning of every day, we choose. It is simply a matter of identification. Will we identify with believers in persecution—or will we identify with their persecutors?

We make that choice as we decide whether we will share Jesus with others or keep Him to ourselves.

We identify ourselves as believers by taking a stand with, and following the example of, those in persecution. Or we identify with their persecutors by not giving witness of Jesus to our family, our friends, and our enemies. Those who number themselves among the followers of Jesus—but don't witness for Him—are actually siding with the Taliban, the brutal regime that rules North Korea, the secret police in communist China, and the Somalis and Saudi Arabias of the world. Believers who do not share their faith aid and abet Satan's ultimate goal of denying others access to Jesus. Our silence makes us accomplices.

When Ruth and I speak and teach and share with western churches, we are often asked if we believe that persecution is coming to America.

My response is often rather pointed. I say, quite sincerely, "Why would Satan want to wake us up when he has already shut us up?"

Why would Satan bother with us when we are already accomplishing his goal? He will likely conclude that it is better to let us sleep.

Our problem is not simply a lack of concern. And our problem is not that we are unaware or disinterested. We know what is happening around the world. Certainly, in light of what we have encountered in this book, we know about sacrifices that are made for the faith. We know more about the health and the whereabouts of other members of the body of Christ today than at any other time in history.

It's not enough to feel grateful for the blessed circumstances in which we live. It's not even enough to do a better job remembering and praying for the suffering believers around the world. It's not even enough to identify with the other parts of Christ's Body around the world.

Ultimately, the problem is one of emphasis and focus. Instead of recognizing, thinking about, remembering, praying about, identifying with and focusing on the *suffering* of fellow believers around the world, we would do well to shift our focus. Quite simply, we would do well to ask ourselves whether or not we are being obedient to Jesus. He is asking us—He is expecting us—He is commanding us to share Him wherever we go. He is commanding us to do that wherever we are today.

It is simply a matter of obedience. If He is our Lord, then we will obey Him. If we do not obey Him, then He is not our Lord.

Perhaps the question should not be: "Why are others persecuted?" Perhaps the better question is: "Why are we not?"

I cannot forget the words of my friend, Stoyan. He understood both the spiritual battle being waged and the significance of the decisions to be made. He said: "I took great joy that I was suffering in my country so that you could be free to witness in your country." And then he raised his voice to say: "DON'T YOU EVER GIVE UP IN FREEDOM WHAT WE WOULD NEVER GIVE UP IN PERSECUTION—AND THAT IS OUR WITNESS TO THE POWER OF THE RESURRECTION OF JESUS CHRIST!"

Stoyan had made his own decision long ago. It was settled for him.

You and I make the decision each morning: will I exercise my freedom to witness for Jesus today or will I be silent?

34

It's All a Miracle . . . And the Journey Begins

I have already confessed that I began my life work naïvely believing that God was sending Ruth and me around the world on a great adventure to tell lost people about Jesus and to teach them how the Bible applied to their lives. I now realize that God allowed me to go out into the world so that I could find out who Jesus really was and how the Bible is to be applied to my life. He wanted me to learn that lesson from people who knew Him far better than I did, people who were already living out His teachings on a daily basis.

Many of the people who I have encountered on this journey have not only become my personal mentors and friends in faith, they have also become spiritual heroes whose life examples humble and inspire me. No other part of Christ's Body in any other country has humbled, inspired, and taught me more than the house-church believers I met in China.

The rural house-church movement was so sheltered and so isolated that some of their leaders asked me whether or not word of Jesus had gotten beyond China yet. They wondered if people in other countries knew and worshiped Him.

There was a little more to that exchange that I didn't share earlier.

I informed the Chinese believers that they had hundreds of millions of fellow believers around the world. I told them that there were believers in almost every country on earth. When they heard that, they broke into applause and they shouted in praise.

Then they asked about my country. I told them that in the United States there were tens of millions of committed Christians who gathered to worship in tens of thousands of congregations large and small, in every city, town and village across our land. Hearing that, the house-church leaders actually cheered and wept with joy in celebration of the grace that God had bestowed on their American brothers and sisters. Then they excitedly peppered me with other questions: How did people learn about Jesus in my country? Did we have Bibles in America? What was worship like? Where did the pastors get their training? The questions seemed to be endless.

I attempted to describe for them the practice of Christianity in the culture of my homeland. They marveled at what I was telling them.

For a while. . .

Then the celebratory mood slowly, subtly started to shift. I noticed first one person who was very quiet and then began to cry. These were not joyful tears. He seemed sad and even anguished. Then others reacted in the same way.

I feared that I had said something that was culturally offensive. I asked what was wrong.

A visibly distressed Chinese pastor explained, "We are just wondering: why is it that God loves you believers in America so much that He blesses you more than He does us? Why would God do so many amazing things for you?"

I was stunned, distraught, and horrified at the question.

I immediately reminded my new friends of the many miraculous stories that Chinese believers had shared with me of God's grace in their lives. They had already told me about His loving provision of strength and courage in prison. They had talked about His repeated protection from authorities. They had shared many inspiring stories of answered prayers. There was also the supernatural way that God had led them through dreams and visions. I cited the historically unprecedented explosion of faith through the house-church movement that had brought at least one hundred million Chinese to Christ despite fifty years of oppression under communism.

I reminded them too of the incredible stories of healing that I had heard from them. I told them how much I wished that I was able to see someone raised from the dead. I insisted to my new Chinese friends that all these things were undeniable and miraculous proof of God's presence and power. I said that these things were incontrovertible evidence of His amazing grace and His abundant love for China and its people.

My friends heard my words and my explanation. And, then, they became my teachers. This is what they said:

> "You see how we are meeting with you here in secret, Dr. Ripken. We have told you how our house churches move from farm to farm, house to house, often at night. Yet you tell us that pastors can preach the gospel publicly in your country and that believers in America are free to worship wherever and whenever they want."
>
> "You have watched our leaders rip apart a Bible and divide up the pages, so that every house-church pastor can take home at least a portion of Scripture to share with his people. Yet you tell us that you personally have seven different versions of the Bible on a shelf in your office. And that you also own many Christian books and regularly read Christian magazines and newspapers."

"None of us has ever owned our own hymnbook or chorus book to sing from. Yet you tell us that your churches have hymnbooks for everyone, that you can purchase them in bookstores or order them by the case from publishers. And you tell us that Christian music is on many radio and television stations."

"You have described how everyone in your country, even those who are not believers, celebrates the birth of Jesus with a national holiday. And you tell us that some churches actually re-enact the nativity scene to attract and entertain the public."

"We have explained how so many of our leaders have been arrested that prisons have become the place where our pastors gain their most important theological education. But you tell us that in America you have special training schools just for Christian students."

"Yes, you have heard us tell about praying for sick people and how many of them have been miraculously healed. Yet maybe only one in a thousand of those who are healed will give any credit to God or will ever find Jesus as a result. However, you tell us that believers in your country can actually choose to go to Christian doctors and even Christian hospitals if they wish."

"So tell us, Dr. Ripken, which of these things do you think are the greatest miracles?"

When they asked me that question, it was my turn to weep. In that moment, I began to realize how much I take for granted. I suddenly saw all the things that I have allowed to become *common,* things that would be considered miracles in the eyes of millions of believers in persecution.

The truth is, these things that we take for granted are all miracles!

Chinese house-church believers taught me that. Their remedial lessons gave me new eyes to see and appreciate the miraculous power of God still present and at work in our world today. In the course of my long journey, my Chinese brothers and sisters, and other believers in persecution from all over the world, gave me back my church, my worship, my Bible, my faith, and so much more.

Now. . .

I never celebrate the Lord's Supper without thinking of that last communion in Mogadishu with my four Somali friends who would soon be martyred. I never partake of the bread and the cup without an awareness that I am doing so not just for myself, but on behalf of brothers and sisters around the world who do not have, and may never again have, access to the body and blood of our Lord in a service of Holy Communion.

Every time I open a hymnbook I think of Tavian, that old singing saint, sitting in his prison cell writing and composing over six hundred praise and worship songs that are now sung every week in churches all over his country.

When I worship on Sunday mornings with American congregations and we stand to lift our voices and spirits together in congregational singing, I am reminded of one of the most hostile countries on earth. Believers in that country secretly meet in groups of three or four or five, at different times each week to share, worship, and "sing" their favorite praise songs by silently mouthing the words together to keep neighbors from turning them in to the secret police.

On occasions, when my heart is moved by some piece of special music—an offertory solo or an uplifting choir anthem—I think of Aisha's courageous voice rising from the dark dungeon beneath her city's police station or I think of that great choir of fifteen hundred inmates standing at attention, arms outstretched, facing east as they sang Dmitri's heart-song back to him.

When I reach for one of the Bibles on the bookshelf in my study and have to stop to decide which version might be best for the passage and purpose that I have in mind, I think of those Chinese house-church pastors, each one going home from the clandestine conference clutching a handful of torn-out pages. They will preach from those few pages until they receive another portion of Scripture.

I also think of that youth conference in Moscow fifty years ago where the young Russian believers recreated the entirety of the four Gospels by memory.

I think of the hundreds of believers who I have interviewed who could quickly cite and recite for me "their verse" or Bible passage that provided them the comfort and strength to survive and to keep their faith alive and vibrant through long years of suffering and persecution.

The Ripkens left Somalia beaten down, discouraged and defeated. After Tim died in Nairobi, we packed up and headed home to America with our tails between our legs. We had nothing but a handful of suitcases, a small shipping container filled with all of our earthly possessions, and a boatload of emotional hurt and spiritual questions to show for a decade and a half living and working overseas.

Looking back fifteen years later, I feel certain that if Ruth and I had just stayed in Kentucky—with our old college community, our friends and our family—we might have found healing and restored hope, eventually. We might have. I honestly suspect that it would have been a lesser hope and a healing without depth. It turned out very differently, though. The people we met on our long pilgrimage among believers in persecution have not only given us a new and greater understanding of *what* we were called *to do*. They have taught us *who* we are called *to be*.

And the examples that they have lived—and the stories that they have told—have not only restored our hope and healed our wounds, they have also transformed our world perspective, redirected our careers, resurrected our faith and changed our lives. Forever.

Samira is one of the strongest, most courageous Christian believers out of Islam that Ruth and I have ever known. Young, single, and well-educated, Samira gave her life to Jesus after a series of dreams and visions. Miraculously, she had found a Bible and she had started reading it on her own. She had been discussing her questions and faith issues with a conservative imam. Through that God-guided pilgrimage, Samira gave her heart to Jesus.

When I met Samira, she had already been forced to flee her home country. She was working for the United Nations as a women's advocate in refugee camps on the border between two central Asian countries. She first surprised me by walking into the interview room covered from head to-toe in the most conservative Sharia-chic fashion. I was in for an even bigger surprise when she closed the door behind her and immediately began to shed her traditional Muslim garb. She first removed the hijab that covered her head and face. Then she removed the dark, flowing burka that enveloped and covered the rest of her. Moments later, she sat down on the other side of the table from me, smiling warmly and looking the part of an attractive, modern, western young woman in the casual outfit—colorful-yet-modest blouse over a pair of American blue jeans. She had been wearing this clothing beneath the burka.

Her transformation had been so sudden, so complete, so stunning that the best way, maybe the only way, I can describe it is to say: it was like watching a beautiful butterfly emerge from a cocoon.

In proficient English, Samira explained that her current job for the United Nations was to represent women who had been raped by Taliban militia. The leaders of the militia wanted to kill Samira because of her faith in Christ and because of her attempts to hold them accountable in a United Nations court of law. She had personally led more than thirty women to Christ, baptized them, and was now discipling them. She had done all of this in an environment nearly devoid of male believers who might be able to lend her protection.

I listened in amazement as she shared the story of her own spiritual pilgrimage. The Lord was obviously using her in a powerful way.

By the time she and I met, Samira's superiors were already seeking to extradite Samira to the United States—*for her own protection*. I begged her to stay among her own people because I couldn't see how God could replace this young woman of faith in such a dark and difficult place.

However, the slow-grinding, irreversible gears of international diplomacy had already been set in motion. Samira was whisked out of Central Asia and flown immediately to the American Midwest where she began to make a new life.

When I arrived home from my trip, I told Ruth all about this remarkable young woman. We arranged to fly her from her new home to Kentucky for a visit.

She spent a week in our home. We took Samira to a moderate-sized church in central Kentucky for Sunday morning worship. It just so happened that there was a baptism service scheduled for that morning; an entire family—mother, father, and two children—were to be baptized.

As their baptism progressed—with this young lady believer from a Muslim background sitting in the pew between Ruth and me—I noticed Samira beginning to fidget, twisting, turning, and rocking backward and forward. It was as if she was having an anxiety attack. In a quiet whisper, I asked her if there was something wrong.

Samira tugged on the sleeve of my jacket. She whispered forcefully in my ear: "I cannot believe this! I cannot believe that I have lived long enough to see people being baptized in public. An entire family together! No one is shooting at them, no one is threatening them, no one will go to prison, no one will be tortured, and no one will be killed. And they are being openly and freely baptized *as a family*! I never dreamed that God could do such things! I never believed that I would live to see a miracle like this."

I couldn't help smiling as I turned my eyes back toward the baptismal at the front of the church. A few seconds later, I noticed Samira glancing around the congregation, looking confused and little troubled. When she caught my eye she leaned toward me. "Why aren't all the people standing?" she wanted to know.

"What do you mean?" I whispered back.

"Why aren't all these people standing and cheering and clapping at such a miracle from God? I think that I am going to burst with joy! I think that I am going to **shout**!"

I nearly laughed out loud: "Go ahead, Sister! If you want to shout, I'll shout with you!"

For a minute or so, she looked like she might. But she didn't. And neither did I.

Ruth and I, however, spent the rest of that service with tears running down our own faces as we divided our attention between the family being baptized and the rapturous countenance of our friend Samira, this Muslim-background believer from one of the toughest places on the planet who had called us to take notice of the miracle of the moment.

Indeed, it *is* all a miracle!

Fellow believers around the world in countries of persecution have themselves discovered and reminded me: *There is no one like Jesus! And nothing can match the power of our resurrection faith!*

Traveling the world on this long pilgrimage through persecution, Ruth and I have been privileged to sit at the feet of many faithful followers of Christ. We have sat at the feet of Samira, Tavian, Dmitri, Stoyan, Aisha, Pramana, old Pastor Chang, and so many more. We have listened to their amazing stories. It is as if our Bible has been blown open, and the characters have exploded out of its pages.

Now I find myself humbly asking God a very different question from the one I wanted to answer at the beginning of the journey.

My question now is this:

What do I do with this now, Lord? You seemed a lot tamer—and my faith felt a lot more comfortable—when I studied your ancient Scriptures and simply left you in the past. Allowing you, your resurrection power, your glory, and your Word into the present changes everything! It makes the good news of the gospel great news for the world today!

So what am I supposed to do about this resurrection faith? Where do you expect me to go from here?

For the Ripkens, the adventure continues . . .

Do you care to join us? Do you want to know where to start?

Begin by following the instruction that the voice of the Holy Spirit gave to Pramana in his midnight vision: "Find Jesus. Find the gospel."

As you do that, know what countless believers from every religious background in the world have reminded us: "There is no one like Jesus. No one else offers a faith like His!"

Don't fear the cost or worry about the risk. Remember what the toughest man I ever met told me: "Jesus is worth it!" He is worth it all!

Begin a spiritual journey of your own. Discover for yourself the incredible peace and power that you too can experience when you live by faith resurrected. It will change your life and it will turn your world upside down.

I know this all sounds crazy. But I assure you that it's not.

It's just . . .

THE INSANITY OF GOD

The story you have just read would not have been possible without the partnership and support of the following churches and organizations. I highly recommend them to you and encourage you to go to their websites to learn more about the incredible work they are doing.

Antioch Community Church (antiochcc.net)

The Church at Brook Hills (brookhills.org)

Christ Church, Bartlett, TN (ccbartlett.org)

Elam Ministries (elam.com)

God's Stories (godstories.com)

International Mission Board (imb.org)

Loving Muslims (lovingmuslims.com)

Open Doors International (opendoors.org)

Mennonite Central Committee (mcc.org)

Secret Church (radical.net/secretchurch)

Sojourn Community Church (sojournchurch.com)

continue the journey at...